PLANT AND SERVICE TOURS IN OPERATIONS MANAGEMENT

Fourth Edition

PLANT AND SERVICE TOURS
IN
OPERATIONS MANAGEMENT

Fourth Edition

ROGER W. SCHMENNER

International Institute for Management Development
Lausanne, Switzerland

Macmillan Publishing Company
New York

Maxwell Macmillan Canada
Toronto

Maxwell Macmillan International
New York   Oxford   Singapore   Sydney

Macmillan Publishing Company
866 Third Avenue, New York, New York 10022

Collier Macmillan Canada, Inc.
1200 Eglinton Avenue, E.
Suite 200
Don Mills, Ontario, M3C 3N1

Library of Congress Cataloging-in-Publication Data

Schmenner, Roger W.
    Plant and service tours in operations management / Roger W.
Schmenner.–4th ed.
      p.   cm.
    Includes bibliographical references and index.
    ISBN 0-02-406831-4
    1. Industrial tours. 2. Service industries–Management.
I. Title.
T49.5.S36 1994
658.5–dc20   93-19376
                                      CIP

Printing: 1 2 3 4 5 6 7 8   Year: 4 5 6 7 8 9 0 1 2 3

To the memory of
my mother,
Gwendolyn Jackson Schmenner

PREFACE

Many things in our lives help prepare us to be better students of business. We are all consumers. We all have to deal with financial matters and with other human beings. In addition, the business press writes on such matters all the time and in some depth. As students of business, then, we can readily bring these experiences and knowledge to bear in learning more about marketing, finance, accounting, and organizational behavior. Moreover, our past experiences with these business functions are likely to whet our appetites for their continued study.

For the study of production and operations management — the study of how businesses effectively deal with the management decisions surrounding the production and delivery of goods and services — the situation is different. In today's world, fewer and fewer of us have firsthand knowledge of factories or service operations. Manufacturing accounts for only about a fifth of the workforce even though regional scientists are quick to maintain its role as the "economic base" of most communities. The business press typically does not report on operations with the same intensity as it reports on other matters. Thus, while operations management remains a critical business discipline, it is less a part of our consciousness and of our everyday lives.

This book is designed to help remedy this deficiency. Each of the ten "tours" in this book introduces a particular kind of manufacturing or service process. All ten processes described are different in important respects; together they span the entire range of process choices and fall into two categories: manufacturing and service. The manufacturing tours describe the following types of processes:

- Job shop
- Batch flow process
- Worker-paced line flow process
- Machine-paced line flow process
- Continuous flow process
- Hybrid process (part batch and part continuous flow)
- Project

Included in the service tours are the following:

- Service factory
- Service shop
- Mass service
- Professional service

The models for each of these process types are drawn from actual operations as they were functioning in 1991. Naturally, I am greatly indebted to the cooperating companies for spending a great deal of time with me discussing their processes and walking me around them, and also for reviewing and correcting my written descriptions of their operations.

Each tour consists of the process description followed by a discussion of the salient features of the process. The sequence of the tours highlights the differences among the processes. For example, the description of a continuous flow process (Tour A) is followed immediately by a description of a job shop, which lies at the opposite extreme of the manufacturing process spectrum. By playing up these contrasts, the unique features of each process may be kept more clearly in mind.

The Tour Summary compares and contrasts all ten processes and, in so doing, pinpoints the key elements of management choice and concern in each. These tours are constant reminders of the diversity, complexity, and challenge of the operations decisions faced by managers everyday in hosts of industries.

The questions and situations for study at the end of each tour are designed to reinforce the concepts presented and discussed. I am grateful to Professors Thomas Callarman and Joseph Biggs, as well as to several of my former students, for contributing them.

R.W.S.

BRIEF CONTENTS

Tour A.   A Continuous Flow Process
           (International Paper—Androscoggin Mill)   1
Tour B.   A Job Shop (Norcen Industries)   29
Tour C.   A Batch Flow Process (Jos. A. Bank Clothiers)   57
Tour D.   A Machine-Paced Line Flow Process
           (General Motors—Oklahoma City)   89
Tour E.   A Hybrid (Batch/Continuous Flow)
           Process (Stroh Brewery—Winston-Salem)   115
Tour F.   A Worker-Paced Line Flow Process and a Service Factory
           (Burger King—Noblesville, IN)   139
Tour G.   A Service Shop (Ogle–Tucker Buick)   163
Tour H.   Mass Service (Thalhimer's—Cloverleaf Mall)   183
Tour I.   A Professional Service (Arthur Andersen—Charlotte)   209
Tour J.   A Project (Geupel DeMars—Indianapolis)   229
Tour Summary   A Comparison of Production and Service Processes   246

CONTENTS

INTRODUCTION xv

Tour A A CONTINUOUS FLOW
  PROCESS 1
International Paper Company
Androscoggin Mill
Jay, Maine

PART ONE PROCESS DESCRIPTION 2
A Brief and Simplified Description of
  Papermaking 2
Maintaining the Environment 7
The Design of the Androscoggin Mill 8
Loading the Factory 10
The Workforce 14
Controlling the Operation 16
Evaluating Mill Performance 17

PART TWO DISCUSSION 18
The Process Flow 18
Information in the Process 19
Capacity 20
Demands of the Process on the
  Workers 21
Demands of the Process on
  Management 21
Questions • Situations for Study 23

Tour B A JOB SHOP 29
Norcen Industries
Jersey Shore, Pennsylvania

PART ONE PROCESS DESCRIPTION 29
Products, Sales, and Order Handling 29
Plant and Personnel 32
The Workings of the Shop 36
Technological Advances and Other
  Trends 42
Quality Control 43
Recordkeeping 44

PART TWO DISCUSSION 45
The Process Flow 45
The Information Flow 46
Capacity in the Job Shop 46
The Role of Standards and Incentives 49
Questions • Situations for Study 50

Tour C A BATCH FLOW PROCESS 57
Jos. A. Bank Clothiers
Hampstead Manufacturing Operations
Hampstead, Maryland

PART ONE PROCESS DESCRIPTION 58
The Process Flow 58
The Workforce and the Piece-Rate
  System 61
Production and Quality Control 70
Loading the Factory 72
Technological Innovation 77

PART TWO DISCUSSION 78
The Process and Information Flows 78
Capacity in the Batch Flow Process 80
The Role of Standards and Incentives 81
Demands of the Process on Workforce
  and Management 81
Questions • Situations for Study 82

Tour D A MACHINE-PACED LINE
  FLOW PROCESS 89
General Motors Corporation
Chevrolet–Pontiac–Canada Group
Tarrytown, New York

PART ONE PROCESS DESCRIPTION 91
How a Car Was Assembled: A Simplified
  Description 91
Loading the Plant 94
Synchronous Manufacturing 96
Revising and Controlling the Operation 101

The Workforce and the Personnel
    Department   106
Supervision   107

PART TWO   DISCUSSION   109
The Flow of the Process and of
    Information   109
Capacity   109
Demands of the Process on the
    Workforce   110
Demands of the Process on
    Management   111
Questions

Tour E   A HYBRID (BATCH/
    CONTINUOUS FLOW) PROCESS   115
Stroh Brewery Company
Winston-Salem, North Carolina

PART ONE   PROCESS DESCRIPTION   115
The Brewing and Packaging of Beer   115
Loading the Plant   119
The Workforce   125
Control and Evaluation of the Operation   126

PART TWO   DISCUSSION   129
The Process Flow   129
The Information Flow   130
Capacity Measures   130
Standards and Incentives   130
Demands of the Process on the Workers   131
Demands of the Process on
    Management   132
Hybrid Processes   132
Questions • Situations for Study   132

Tour F   A WORKER-PACED LINE
    FLOW PROCESS AND A
    SERVICE FACTORY   139
Burger King Restaurant
Route 37
Noblesville, Indiana

PART ONE   PROCESS DESCRIPTION   140
Restaurant Operations   140
The "Line": Layout and Job Description   142
The Drive-Thru Operation   144
Peak Versus Nonpeak Operation   144
Coping with Bottlenecks   147
Purchasing and Materials Management   148
The Workforce   148
Quality   149
Management   150
Facilities and Technology   150

PART TWO   DISCUSSION   151
The Flow of the Process and of
    Information   151
Demands of the Process on the
    Workforce   152
Demands of the Process on
    Management   153
Questions • Situations for Study   154

Tour G   A SERVICE SHOP   163
Ogle–Tucker Buick
Auto Service and Repair
Indianapolis, Indiana

PART ONE   PROCESS DESCRIPTION   163
Writing the Service Order   163
Dispatching   164
Shop Operations and the Workforce   166
Quality Control   169
The Parts Department   171
Body Shop   173
How Workers Were Paid   175
The Duties of the Service Manager   175
Promotions and Specials   176

PART TWO   DISCUSSION   176
The Flow of the Process and of
    Information   176
Demands of the Process on the
    Workforce   177

Demands of the Process on
   Management   178
Questions • *Situation for Study*   179

Tour H   MASS SERVICE   183
Thalhimer's—Cloverleaf Mall Store
Richmond, Virginia

PART ONE   SERVICE PROCESS DESCRIPTION   183
Layout   183
Management and the Workforce   189
The Transaction—and Supporting It   193
Managing and Controlling the Inventory   195
Variations on the Standard Receipt of
   Material   198
Shipping Items Out of the Store   198
Evaluating the Store's Performance   200

PART TWO   DISCUSSION   203
The Flow of the Process and of
   Information   203
Demands of the Process on the
   Workforce   204
Demands of the Process on
   Management   204
Questions • *Situation for Study*   205

Tour I   A PROFESSIONAL SERVICE   209
Arthur Andersen & Company
Accounting and Auditing Services
Charlotte, North Carolina

PART ONE   PROCESS DESCRIPTION   209
Lines of Business   209
Auditing Attest Services   211
Managing the Practice   214
Personnel Policy   219

PART TWO   DISCUSSION   223
The Flow of the Process and of
   Information   223

Demands of the Process on the
   Workforce   224
The Pyramid   224
Demands of the Process on
   Management   226
Questions • *Situation for Study*   226

Tour J   A PROJECT   229
Geupel DeMars, Inc.
Indianapolis, Indiana

PART ONE   PROCESS DESCRIPTION   231
Project Organization and Timetable   231
The Manual and Its Control   234
Contractor Bidding   235
Dealing with Contractors on the Job   236
Field Supervision   236
Scheduling   236
Budgeting   242

PART TWO   DISCUSSION   243
The Flow of the Process and of
   Information   243
Features of the Process   244
Demands of the Process on
   Management and the Workforce   245
Planning and Control   245
Questions   245

Tour Summary   A COMPARISON
   OF PRODUCTION AND
   SERVICE PROCESSES   246

PART ONE   MANUFACTURING   246
Trends   246
The Process Spectrum   250

PART TWO   SERVICE OPERATIONS   250
Comparison of Services   250

Index   263

INTRODUCTION

The tours described in this book can be arrayed along two spectrums, one for manufacturing and one for service. Before plunging into the tours themselves, it is useful to spend just a bit of time reflecting on the general nature of these processes—what makes them similar and what makes them different.

THE SPECTRUM OF MANUFACTURING PROCESSES

The factory tours in this book describe a rich diversity of technologies and approaches to a variety of the issues faced by manufacturing managers. The summary chapter at the conclusion of the tours compares and contrasts the processes in considerable detail. Suffice it here, at the beginning, to present a much more "bare bones" discussion of five major types of manufacturing processes that one can engage in. They form a spectrum (see Figure 1-1).

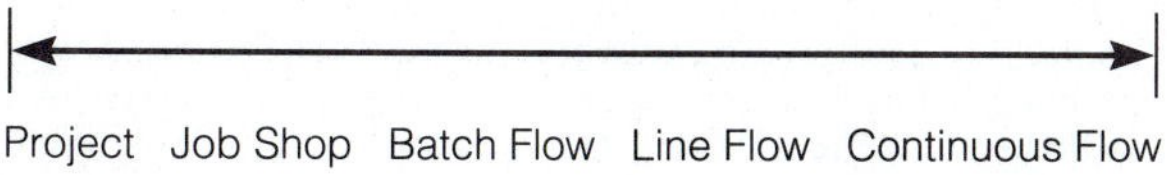

1. *The Project.* The project—building a skyscraper, bringing a new product out of the R&D labs, making a movie—is sometimes excluded from consideration as a manufacturing process because, by its nature, it exists only to do a particular, unique job. This is not to say, however, that one project may not look very similar to another. Many projects, be they large buildings, new products, or movies, require much the same

Project Job Shop Batch Flow Line Flow Continuous Flow

FIGURE 1-1. The Spectrum of Manufacturing Processes.

work to get them up and running. There are certain regularities present in a project, among them:

- Projects typically make heavy use of certain skills and capabilities at particular times and little or no use of those skills at other times.

- Projects can often usefully be seen as the coordination of part-time or subcontracted skills and capabilities (people, equipment, etc.). Skills and capabilities, of course, can be many and varied.

- The coordination of those skills and capabilities requires a lot of attention to planning and scheduling, and subsequently, attention to the control of that schedule and any rescheduling or expediting that may be required. Great attention must be given to which tasks must be accomplished before others (a precedence diagram) and what the expected durations for those tasks are.

- The quality of any project depends greatly on the skills and care of the members of the project team.

2. *The Continuous Flow Process.* At the other extreme of the process spectrum lies the continuous flow process. Many high volume consumer goods and commodities are made by continuous flow processes—oil refining, food processing, papermaking, lightbulb fabrication. The continuous flow process's most significant characteristic is how materials move through it—hardly ever stopping, moving constantly from one process operation to another. With a continuous flow process, one can estimate realistically how long it takes to transform raw

materials into a specific product. Work-in-process inventories exist at well-defined levels and are low relative to the value of output the continuous flow process generates. Capital investments and automation, on the other hand, are often higher than those of other processes, especially when contrasted with the workforce employed. Layouts are frequently product-specific, typically with a straight-line character to them, as the products in the making go from one operation to another.

Continuous flow processes can be very productive and very profitable, assuming normal sales levels. Only when sales levels plunge is the profitability of the continuous flow process in jeopardy.

3. *The Job Shop.* Lying next to the project in the process spectrum is the job shop. It is the most flexible process for creating a wide variety of products in significant quantities. (The project, almost by definition, does not produce in quantity.) Machine shops, tool and die shops, and many plastic molding operations are job shops, working to fulfill particular customer orders.

The job shop layout is often distinctly different from that of a continuous flow process; it groups similar equipment together, primarily because no single product generates enough sales volume to justify the creation of a product-specific array of equipment.[1] Often a job shop has a diverse array of equipment and capabilities to choose from.

The flow of material in a job shop can be complex and far from a straight line in character. Materials can be routed in many directions and can loop back to the same equipment later in the processing cycle. With each order (job) capable of such complexity, it is absolutely essential that information on how the order is to be routed through the factory, what is to be done to it at each step of the way, and how much time and effort is actually spent on it, follow the job. The job shop lives by its information flows. This information is vital because job shops typically bid for work. Without good information on costs, times (run times, set up times, labor content times), routings, and process steps, a job shop would be seriously disadvantaged.

4. *The Batch Flow Process.* One step toward the continuous flow process from the job shop is the batch flow process. The job shop and the batch flow process have a good deal in common. Their layouts are similar, with equipment grouped by function rather than by product.[2] The product is regarded as moving from department to department within the factory. A batch flow operation depends on information such as routings and process steps and tracks costs and times spent. However, batch flow processes typically have a set menu of products that they produce, frequently, in set quantities (lot sizes). The batch flow operation is thus somewhat more standardized than the job shop, particularly as it relates to routings and costs.

---

[1]Sometimes families of parts or products can be identified and exist in enough volume to justify the creation of a manufacturing cell (sometimes called "group technology") within the job shop. Such a manufacturing cell gathers various different pieces of equipment together in a product family-specific configuration.

[2]Here again, the innovation of the manufacturing cell is applicable. Defining manufacturing cells for the batch flow process rather than the job shop is likely to be much easier to do because the identification of a family of parts is likely to be easier.

While the job shop usually operates to fulfill an outside customer's order by an agreed upon due date and in whatever quantity is ordered, the batch flow operation usually produces product in established lot sizes that move into an inventory from which further production or final customer orders are filled. Batch flow processes are commonplace, especially when one considers all the times "fabrication" must be done. Examples of batch flow processes include much of the chemical industry, semiconductor fabrication, apparel, much of the steel industry, and huge chunks of the metal bending, metal forming, and metal machining industries.

6. *The Line Flow Process.* Between the batch flow and continuous flow processes, along the process spectrum, lies the line flow process. In reality it lies closer to the continuous flow process because it presents some substantive distinctions from the batch flow. The line flow process is most popularly exemplified by the moving assembly line that one finds in the auto industry, but it is also found in a host of other assembly industries such as consumer electronics and computers. In contrast to the batch flow process, the line flow process exhibits the following characteristics:

- A product-specific layout with different pieces of equipment placed in sequence ready to perform operations on the product. There are, of course, mixed model lines that can produce distinctly different models of the basic product, but the more diverse the products made, the less satisfactory the line becomes at producing them.
- The product moves readily from one operation to another so that there is little work in process inventory, nor is there a stock-

room in the product's path. This flow also means that there is a great need to examine the "balance" of the process so that the different tasks to be accomplished take roughly the same amount of time to perform and have the same capacities, not just over weeks of time, but over minutes of time.

- The paperwork needs of the line flow process are less demanding than the batch flow. Routings are not needed, and operations sheets can frequently be simplified, if not eliminated altogether. The need for tracking labor and machine inputs to particular products/parts also fades away.
- In contrast to the continuous flow operation, the line flow is somewhat more flexible and generally less automated and more labor intensive.

As one proceeds across the spectrum from project to continuous flow, one tends to move from a highly individualized, flexible process to one that is much more inflexible in the products it can make but, at the same time, much more productive and efficient in how it makes them.

Hybrid Processes

The five process types introduced above—project, job shop, batch flow, line flow, and continuous flow—are all "pure." Many factories are combinations of two (sometimes more) of these pure processes. Popular hybrids are the batch flow–line flow hybrid (auto engines, air conditioning, furniture) and the batch flow–continuous flow hybrid (breweries, many high-volume consumer products whose raw materials are made in batches, such as photographic film).

In these processes the first part of the flow of materials looks like a batch flow process (often, this part of the process is labelled "fabrication") while the latter part resembles a line or continuous flow process (and this part of the process is labelled "assembly" or "finishing"). Importantly, the two portions of the hybrid are separated by an inventory, typically termed a "decoupling" inventory. The batch flow process acts to fill up the inventory with parts or semi-finished product, which then is drawn down by the line or continuous flow process for assembly or completion.

The reason the hybrid process is divided into two parts is that the batch flow process is not normally as nimble as the line flow or continuous flow process. The batch flow may not be as nimble because significant chunks of time may be needed to set up the existing machines for a different component of the finished product. This need puts pressure on the batch flow process to allow for longer runs than would be needed to match precisely the product mix and quantities produced by the line or continuous flow process, which normally can change over to other products more quickly. If the batch flow process tried to match the line or continuous flow process precisely (say, hourly or daily), it would lose a lot of time to setup, and this downtime could rob the process of the capacity it needs to keep up with overall demand.[3] Thus, the batch flow process does not attempt a precise match of the line or continuous flow process's product mix and quantity but rather a quantity and product mix match over a much longer period of time, say weeks or months. The batch flow process then acts to replenish the decoupling inventory, while the line or continuous flow process acts to fill particular customer orders.

---

[3]Much of the push toward just-in-time (JIT) manufacturing can be interpreted as a remedy for this deficiency of batch flow processes. In essence, JIT tries to make the batch flow process operate with the efficiency of the line flow process.

DISTINGUISHING SERVICE OPERATIONS FROM MANUFACTURING

Six of the ten tours deal strictly with manufacturing operations. The other four, however, reveal significant distinctions between service and manufacturing. Some of the management challenges for service operations parallel those in manufacturing, but others are unique.

What is a service operation anyway? The answer to this question is surprisingly ambiguous. We may know service operations when we see them but have difficulty describing them in general. Perhaps the term can be better understood as what it isn't rather than what it is. Some have tried to define service employment as nonfarming and nonmanufacturing employment; others have also excluded government employment. This approach includes operations such as hotels, restaurants, repairs, amusements, health, education, real estate, wholesale and retail trade, transportation, and professional services like law, engineering, architecture, finance, and advertising. Although these selections may be intuitively clear, there are still some definitional problems. For example, what about public utilities? Some public utilities companies have service in their name (such as Public Service of New Hampshire), yet in many ways power generation is more manufacturing than service. And is a company like IBM a manufacturing company or a service company? As in the old story of the blind men and the elephant, the answer may depend on which part of the beast you are touching. Surely there are aspects of IBM that are strictly manufacturing, but there are other aspects that are service (examples are field repair and the sales force).

This ambiguity is growing. As technology advances, more and more labor will be driven out of manufactured products; that is, there will be less direct labor involved in manufacturing companies and more indirect labor—the kind of labor that is oriented to support services. Even now, some high technology companies have overhead rates that are six to ten times the direct labor component, mainly because of the substantial indirect labor in these companies. The traditional management focus on direct labor is becoming less and less relevant. Service operations management affects more than just service companies per se. Furthermore, the service sector will continue to grow. About two-thirds of the U.S. gross national product is now accounted for by services; the same fraction applies to the percentage of the workforce employed in service jobs. These fractions can only rise. Similar trends are observed in other developed countries.

Characteristics of Service Operations

Most services share certain characteristics to a greater or lesser extent. It is helpful to understand these characteristics and how they separate manufacturing from service.

1. The service provided is often something that the consumer cannot touch or feel. It may be associated with something physical (such as the food we eat, the airplane we fly in, the life insurance policy we hold), but what is valued about the service and may be the focus of management typically involves intangibles, such as ambiance, information, or peace of mind.

2. The service is often created and delivered on the spot, in many cases with significant involvement of the customer in the service process (consider salad bars in restaurants). Because the process is often more on display in service operations than in manufacturing, whether it functions well is critical.

The process cannot be saved by a quality control check at the end; it has to live with its defects. Therefore, training, process design, and employee relations are especially important to service industries.

3. Because of the visibility of the service process in many instances and the intangibility of many services, operations management and marketing are more interdependent than in manufacturing. Marketing and operations have to work together in service companies; they cannot afford to be antagonists.

4. Frequently, the consumption of a service is nearly simultaneous with its production. Services cannot be inventoried for use later on. This fact has some serious implications for capacity choice and capacity management in a service business. The site, size, and layout choices for service industries are critical. The wrong site, a size either too large or too small, or a poor layout can dramatically affect the performance of a service unit. This concern for capacity is heightened by the irregularities in the pattern of demand over time (whether a day, week, or season). Demand irregularities place a tremendous burden on a service operation to be flexible. They also force services to manage their demand via prices or the kinds of services offered.

5. Many service operations, although by no means all, require little in the way of capital investment, multiple locations, or proprietary technology. For these services, barriers to the entry of competing firms are rather low. Service companies are generally very sensitive to the real—or even potential—entry of others and must react quickly to the competition's actions and threats. Many service operations also possess rather low barriers to exit; that is, the assets of a service

organization can be sold easily (such as planes or trucks). Because firms can get in and out of the service business quickly, some service strategies can play for the "hit and run."

A SPECTRUM OF SERVICES

The characterization of services as service factories, service shops, mass service, and professional service can be useful as well for comparing service processes in much the same way that we compared processes across the manufacturing spectrum. Much as we have thought of manufacturing enterprises in terms of differ-

ent kinds of production processes, we can think of service operations in terms of distinct "processes." It is helpful to view these different service processes in terms of a matrix that contrasts the labor intensity of the process on the one hand with the degree of interaction with, and customization of, the service for the consumer on the other.[4] This matrix is shown in Figure 1-2. The quadrants of the matrix roughly define four reasonable distinct service processes.

_____

[4]See Roger W. Schmenner, "How Can Service Businesses Survive and Prosper?" _Sloan Management Review_, Spring 1986, pp. 21-32.

		Degree of Contact with, and Customization for, the Consumer		Challenges for Management
		Low	High	
Degree of Labor Intensity	Low	**The Service Factory** Airlines, trucking, hotels, resorts, and recreation	**The Service Shop** Hospitals, auto, and other repair services	Capital decisions, technological advances, managing demand to avoid peaks and to promote off-peaks, scheduling delivery of service
	High	**Mass Service** Retailing, wholesaling, schools	**Professional Service** Physicians, lawyers, accountants, architects	Hiring, training, methods development and control, employee welfare, scheduling workforces, control of often geographically spread locations, start-up of new units, managing growth
Challenges for Management		Marketing, making service "warm," attention to physical surroundings, managing fairly rigid hierarchy with need for standard operating procedures	Fighting cost increases, maintaining quality, reacting to customer intervention in process, managing advancement of people delivering service, managing flat hierarchy with loose subordinate-superior relationships, binding workers to the firm	

FIGURE 1-2   A matrix of service processes.

The Service Factory. Some service processes have relatively low labor intensity (and thus a greater fraction of service costs associated with the facility and its equipment) and also a low degree of customer interaction and customization. These enterprises can be characterized as service factories. Much of the transportation industry, hotels, and resorts, for example, are service factories as are "back-of-the-house" operations for banking and financial services companies. The Burger King Restaurant in Noblesville, Indiana (Tour F) is an example of a service factory.

The Service Shop. As the degree of interaction with—or customization for—the consumer increases, the service factory gives way to the service shop, much as a line flow operation gives way to a job shop operation when customization is required in manufacturing. Hospitals and repair services of all types are prime examples of service shops. Tour G of the Ogle–Tucker Buick auto repair operation is an example of a service shop.

Mass Service. Mass service processes have a high degree of labor intensity but a rather low degree of interaction with, or customization for, the consumer. Retail operations, retail banking, schools, and wholesaling are examples of mass services. The Thalhimers department store at the Cloverleaf Mall, characterized in Tour H, is an example of mass service.

Professional Service. If the degree of interaction increases and/or customization become the watchword, mass service gives way to the professional service provided by doctors, lawyers, consultants, architects, and the like. Arthur Andersen & Co.'s audit services in Charlotte (Tour I) provide an example of professional service.

With this review as a general background, we now turn to the specifics of the various tours.

A CONTINUOUS FLOW PROCESS
International Paper Company
Androscoggin Mill
Jay, Maine

The Androscoggin Mill, situated along the Androscoggin River in central Maine, was one of 28 domestic pulp and paper mills of the International Paper Company. It was one of the largest, built originally in 1965 with significant additions in 1968 and 1977. The plant occupied 478 acres of land, had 20 acres under roof, and represented a book value investment of nearly $400 million.

The mill, part of International Paper's Pulp and Coated Papers Group, produced three distinctly different kinds of paper: (1) forms bond, envelope, tablet, and offset paper for office or computer use; (2) publication gloss for magazine printing; and (3) specialty papers such as microwave popcorn and fast-food french fry grease-proof papers.

Androscoggin was a fully integrated mill; that is, it produced all the wood pulp it needed to make its paper. The mill was laid out to receive logs or chips of wood at one end and, about a mile farther down, to ship packaged "logs" of paper from the other end. (See Figure A1 for a layout of the mill; the production flow is from left to right.)

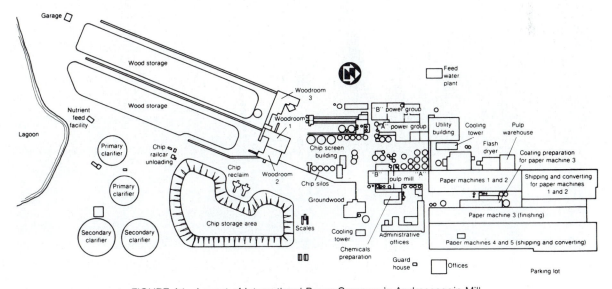

FIGURE A1   Layout of International Paper Company's Androscoggin Mill.

PART ONE

PROCESS DESCRIPTION

A Brief and Simplified Description of Papermaking

The paper we use today is created from individual wood fibers that are first suspended in water and then pressed and dried into sheets. The process of converting the wood to a suspension of wood fibers in water is known as pulpmaking, while the manufacture of the dried and pressed sheets of paper is formally termed papermaking. The process of making paper has undergone a steady evolution, and larger and more sophisticated equipment and better technology continue to improve it.

In the woodyard, wood being unloaded. (*Courtesy of International Paper*)

The Woodyard and Woodrooms

The process at Androscoggin began with receiving wood in the form of chips or of logs 4 or 8 feet in length. From 6 A.M. to 10 P.M. a steady stream of trucks and railroad cars were weighed and unloaded. About 40 percent of the deliveries were of wood cut from International Paper's own land (over 1 million acres in Maine), while the other 60 percent were supplied by independents who were paid by weight for their logs. The mill also received wood chips from lumber mills in the area. The chips and logs were stored in mammoth piles with separate piles for wood of different species (such as pine, spruce, hemlock).

When needed, logs were floated in flumes from the woodyard into one of the mill's three woodrooms. There, bark was rubbed off in long, ribbed debarking drums by tumbling the logs against one another. The logs then fell into a chipper; within seconds a large log was reduced to a pile of chips approximately 1 inch by 1 inch by 1/4 inch.

The chips were stored in silos. There were separate silos for softwoods (spruce, fir, hemlock, and pine) and hardwoods (maple, oak, beech, and birch). This separate and temporary storage of chips permitted the controlled mixing of chips into the precise recipe for the grade of paper being produced.

The wood chips were then sorted through large, flat vibrating screens. Oversized chips were rechipped, and ones that were too small were collected for burning in the power house. (The mill provided approximately 20 percent of all its own steam and electricity needs from burning waste. An additional 50 percent of total electricity needs was produced by harnessing the river for hydroelectric power.)

Once drawn from the silo into the digesters, there was no stopping the flow of chips into paper.

Pulpmaking

The pulp made at Androscoggin was of two types: Kraft pulp (produced chemically) and groundwood pulp (produced mechanically). Kraft pulp was far more important to the high-quality white papers produced at Androscoggin, accounting for 80 percent of all the pulp used. Kraft pulp makes strong paper. (Kraft is German for strength. A German invented the Kraft pulp process in 1884.) A paper's strength generally comes from the overlap and binding of long fibers of softwood; only chemically was it initially possible to separate long wood fibers for suspension in water. Hardwood fibers are generally smaller and thinner and help smooth the paper and make it less porous.

The groundwood pulping process was simpler and less expensive than the Kraft process. It took high quality spruce and fir logs and pressed them continuously against a revolving stone that broke apart the wood's fibers. The fibers, however, were smaller than those produced by the Kraft process and, although used to make newsprint, were useful at Androscoggin in providing "fill" for the coated publication gloss papers of machines 2 and 3, as will be described later.

The chemical Kraft process worked by dissolving the lignin that bonds wood fibers together. It did this in a tall pressure cooker, called a digester, by "cooking" the chips in a solution of caustic soda (NaOH) and sodium sulfide (Na_2S), which was termed the "white liquor." The temperature in this cooking process reached as high as 340°F, and the pressure was as great as 11 atmospheres. The two digesters at Androscoggin were continuous digesters; chips and liquor went into the top, were cooked together as they slowly settled down to the bottom, and were drawn off the bottom after about three hours. By this time, the white liquor had changed chemically to

A chip unloading station. (*Courtesy of International Paper*)

A groundwood log conveyor. (*Courtesy of International Paper*)

A debarking drum. (*Courtesy of International Paper*)

"black liquor"; the digested chips were then separated from this black liquor.

In what was known as the "cold blow" process, the hot, pressurized chips were gradually cooled and depressurized. A "cold liquor" (170°F) was introduced to the bottom of the digester and served both to cool and to transport the digested chips to a diffusion washer that washed and depressurized the chips. Because so much of the lignin bonding the fibers together had been removed, the wood fiber in the chips literally fell apart at this stage.

The black liquor from the digester entered a separate four-step recovery process. Over 95 percent of the black liquor could be reconstituted as white liquor, thereby saving on chemical costs and significantly lowering pollution. The four-step process involved (1) washing the black liquor from the cooked fiber to produce weak black liquor, (2) evaporating the weak black liquor to a thicker consistency, (3) combustion of this heavy black liquor with sodium sulfate (Na_2SO_4), and redissolving the smelt, yielding a "green liquor" (sodium carbonate + sodium sulfide), and (4) adding lime, which reacted with the green liquor to produce white liquor. The last step was known as causticization.

Meanwhile, the wood-fiber pulp was purged of impurities like bark and dirt by mechanical screening and by spinning the mixture in centrifugal cleaners. The pulp was then concentrated by removing water from it so that it could be stored and bleached more economically.

By this time, depending on the type of pulp being made, it had been between 3 1/2 and 5 hours since the chips had entered the pulp mill.

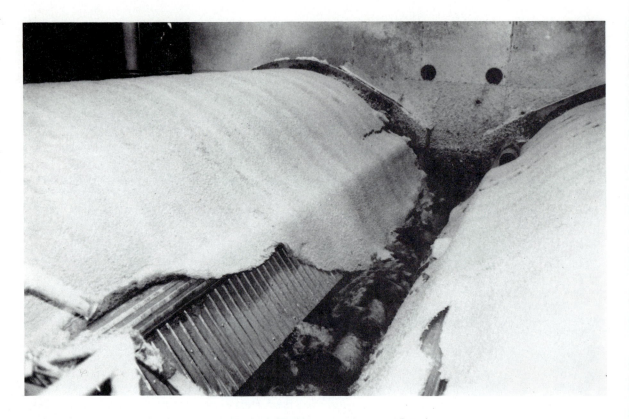

A pulp washer. (*Courtesy of International Paper*)

All the Kraft pulp was then bleached. Bleaching took between 5 and 6 hours. It consisted of a three-step process in which (1) a mix of chlorine (Cl_2) and chlorine dioxide (ClO_2) was introduced to the pulp and the pulp was washed; (2) a patented mix of sodium hydroxide (NaOH), liquid oxygen, and hydrogen peroxide (H_2O_2) was then added to the pulp and the pulp was again washed; and (3) chlorine dioxide (ClO_2) was introduced and the pulp washed a final time. The result was like fluffy cream of wheat. By this time the pulp was nearly ready to be made into paper.

From the bleachery, the stock of pulp was held for a short time in storage (a maximum of 16 hours) and then proceeded through a series of blending operations that permitted a string of additives (for example, filler clay, resins, brighteners, alum, dyes) to be mixed into the pulp according to the recipe for the paper grade being produced. Here, too, "broke" (paper wastes from the mill itself) was recycled into the pulp.[a] The pulp was then once again cleaned and blended into an even consistency before moving to the papermaking machine itself.

[a]It made a difference whether the broke was of coated or uncoated paper, and whether it was white or colored. White, uncoated paper could be recycled immediately. Colored, uncoated paper had to be rebleached. Coated papers, because of the clays in them, could not be reclaimed.

Continuous digesters at the pulp mill. These work like pressure cookers, dissolving the lignin bonds between wood fibers. (*Courtesy of International Paper Company*)

Papermaking

The paper machine was a simply awesome engineering creation, stretching hundreds of feet. At Androscoggin, there were five of varying size. The paper machine had a wet end and a dry end. The pulp entered the machine at the headbox, which released the heavily diluted pulp through a slit onto a moving belt of synthetic fabric. This belt was called the "wire" because originally it was made of bronze mesh.

As the wire with its deposit of pulp stock moved away from the headbox, water drained through it. Suction was also applied. Within 60 feet after the headbox slit, so much water had been removed that it could be said the wire carried paper, rather than a suspension of pulp in water. From the wire, huge woolen felts picked up the paper "web" and started it through a series of rollers and steam-heated drying drums, which pressed and evaporated even more water out of the web. If the paper was to be coated, the coating would be applied first to one side of the paper and then to the other and more drying done. If the paper was to be shiny, it would be pressed on smooth, shiny rollers called calenders. Drying and pressing having been done, the paper was essentially finished and was picked up from the machine on winders.

The speeds at which all this happened were incredible. The fastest machines (machines 2 and 3, devoted to publication gloss) produced over a mile of paper every 2 minutes. This great speed was made possible by continual improvements made by the machine's builders and by computerized process controls, which constantly adjusted the machine's settings based on the values registered by numerous electronic sensors scattered along the length of the machine.

Once on the winders, the "logs" of paper could be slit directly into widths the customers had ordered, or they could be slit into two logs of equal width and stored until needed. These stored logs, called "parent logs," were then placed on rewinders for successive slitting to customer order. Once cut to order, rolls were packaged, labeled, and then shipped.

MAINTAINING THE ENVIRONMENT

Being a relatively new mill, Androscoggin had environmental control equipment designed into it. Pulp and paper mills were large users of water. Androscoggin took water from the river, filtered it, and then used it in the process. Before being released back to the river, the water was treated in three stages to remove the effluent it had picked up.

1. A primary clarifier (two large cone-shaped basins) allowed particles to settle to the bottom. A slow-moving rake forced the settled sludge to the middle, where it was removed to be burned.

2. In a 37-acre lagoon the clarified effluent was aerated by a collection of churning fountains, and a special collection of microorganisms broke down the effluent over the course of 1 1/2 to 2 days.

3. A secondary clarifier (two more large basins) settled more solids (including dead bacteria from the lagoon) from the water.

The entire treatment process took 2–3 days.

Air pollution control was another area where great strides had been made since the early 1960s. Gas collection systems to collect and burn noncondensible gases from the digester and evaporators had largely eliminated the rotten egg smell that had been characteristic of paper mills. Scrubbers and precipitators on the stacks at Androscoggin had gone even further in removing sulphur and other particulates from the smoke and air at the mill.

THE DESIGN OF THE ANDROSCOGGIN MILL

Vertical Integration

The Androscoggin Mill was vertically integrated; that is, it combined pulpmaking and papermaking at the same site. Not all mills, especially not the older ones, were designed to combine both activities. Several advantages argued strongly in favor of vertical integration:

1. Integration removed the transportation costs of transporting pulp between a pulp mill and a paper mill. Vertical integration eliminated the double handling of pulp, a cost saving in any event. In addition, because the mill shipped all over the country and because it specialized in lightweight grades of paper, transportation costs for finished paper were not affected significantly by the mill's location; and so a location near the supply of pulp was highly desirable. Pulp drying and reslushing costs were also eliminated.

2. Integration provided for better quality control. Since the quality of the paper produced depended heavily on the quality of the pulp, vertical integration permitted hour-by-hour control over the quality of pulp entering each paper machine. Such control greatly reduced the chances for paper breaks on the machine and it also eliminated any quality problems caused by old pulp or other deficiencies.

3. The wood preparation and pulpmaking operations generated sawdust, bark, chemicals, and wood chips that could be burned as fuel for the whole plant, thus cutting down on plant-wide energy costs.

Although the Androscoggin Mill integrated pulpmaking and papermaking, the extent of the mill's vertical integration could have been even broader. For example, only about 40 percent of the wood used at the mill was cut from land owned by International Paper. The company could have integrated backward even more by raising that 40 percent figure. It chose not to do so, however, because the 40 percent figure, and modest variations around it, (1) permitted good forest management of International Paper's own land and (2) meant that the company could add directly to the area's economy by purchasing from independents. There were no substantial cost differences between independent and company tree harvesting. Only if independent loggers could not supply the mill's needs would the company have harvested more from its own land.

By the same token, the operations at Androscoggin could have been extended by forward integration, so that the plant converted more of its paper into end uses (for example, sheets of bond paper rather than rolls of it). The company chose not to do this as well. For one thing, adding converting facilities would have greatly increased Androscoggin's already large size and would have diluted management's attention from the mission of producing quality paper efficiently. Converting operations (and International Paper operated many of them) were also best located closer to markets, since the nature of conversion often placed the paper in bulkier and more awkward packages that were harder to ship and were often shipped in smaller quantities than Androscoggin's full truck and rail carloads. Splitting conversion from papermaking, at least for white papers, meant lower overall transport costs, whereas there were no real economies in the linking of the two operations.

Capacity

Over time, the size and capacity of individual paper machines had grown enormously. There were distinct advantages to this large scale of operation, since the largest and latest machines could produce more tons of paper per worker, thus reducing costs. At Androscoggin, for example, before 1981, machines 2 and 5 both manufactured carbonizing tissue. Machine 2, built in 1965, could produce paper 208 inches wide at a speed of 1750 feet per minute. Machine 5, in contrast, built in 1977, could produce paper 230 inches wide at a rate of 2000 feet per minute. In only 12 years, the capacity of the machine per unit of time had increased by over 26 percent. The capacity difference between

machines 1 and 4 was even more striking— 40 percent. The increases in machine size and speed enabled the newer mills to house fewer paper machines and employ fewer workers than older mills and yet produce more paper.

At its current size, the Androscoggin Mill was about as large as it was likely to grow. In 1980, the company rebuilt paper machine 2 and converted its production from carbonizing tissue to lightweight publication gloss. The project, which cost $71 million, included the addition of some groundwood pulping, supercalenders, and coating preparation processes. The output rates of its five paper machines (over 500,000 tons per year, up from approximately 410,000 tons per year before the conversion of machine 2), its two continuous digesters, its groundwood mill, and its three woodrooms were all reasonably well balanced. As it was, the pulp mill had been deliberately built larger so that another mill down the river and other International Paper mills could be supplied with pulp.

Location

The Androscoggin Mill's general location in central Maine was attributable largely to three factors:

1. The production of strong, good-quality white office papers demanded long wood fibers. This demand favored a Maine location because cold winter weather favors the production of longer fibers in both the softwood and hardwood trees that Maine and neighboring Quebec grow in abundance.

2. A paper mill uses so much water that it has to be located on either a lake or a river, and preferably a river because of environmental factors.

3. This part of central Maine enjoyed the availability of a good supply of labor.

Paper machine 5, built in 1977. (*Courtesy of International Paper Company*)

Technology

In pulpmaking and papermaking, keeping abreast of the latest changes in process equipment and technology is critical to a company's continued success. At International Paper the main responsibility for keeping up with technology rested with the corporate staff. The staff was also instrumental in the selection of major new equipment or process changes. The plant, however, did play an important role by providing managers (such as the plant engineer or the paper mill superintendent) who joined the corporate staff in studying any new capacity addition or process technology change. This team was responsible for developing the project's capital appropriation request and its supporting documents.

LOADING THE FACTORY

Production Planning

Orders for any of the white papers produced at Androscoggin would be taken by the company's central order department in Memphis, Tennessee. Orders, as they were received, were

Paper machine 4. (*Courtesy of International Paper Company*)

placed in the next available open time in the planned weekly production cycles. One week before the start of the next weekly cycle, the manager of operations control planned the production schedule for that cycle. This production schedule allocated the types and weights of paper to be produced at each mill by each machine for every day of the weekly cycle. These machine assignments and the orders they represented were then transmitted to each of the company's plants.

Each quarter a linear program was run to develop the optimum schedule. Marketing and customer constraints were factored into the quarterly plan by operations control. This plan was reviewed with product line managers and was used to establish weekly cycles.

The assignment of types and weights of paper to each paper machine was a sophisticated enterprise. Because the company's machines were all slightly different from one another, due primarily to their different vintages, their capabilities differed. That is, they were often relatively more successful and/or more cost efficient at making certain types and weights of paper than others. In assigning products to machines, therefore, the corporation took care to make the assignments in such a way that the company's total contribution to profits and overhead was maximized. This assigning

A paper machine coater. (*Courtesy of International Paper*)

A paper machine heated dryer "cans." (*Courtesy of International Paper*)

required not only information on the mix of papers demanded for the period and on machine capabilities, but on distribution and transportation costs as well. Thus for some grades, colors, or weights of paper, depending on the situation, Androscoggin might have filled an order that might otherwise have been filled by a mill much closer to the customer.

At present, Androscoggin's five paper machines were likely to be assigned the following "paper machine products":

- Machine 1 — various types of bond or offset paper in white or colors
- Machine 2 — coated publication gloss
- Machine 3 — coated publication gloss
- Machine 4 — various types of bond, ledger, envelope, and tablet paper (all white)
- Machine 5 — specialty grades

Since machine 4 was both larger and faster than machine 1, it was devoted to fewer different kinds of paper and thus to longer production runs than machine 1. In that way, the mill could produce more total paper than if machine 4 continually had to be interrupted and reset for different colors, grades, or weights. Better to interrupt machine 1 for such changes.

Demand for paper products was cyclical in nature. Volume requirements tracked the general economy very closely, although lagging it slightly both upward and downward. In good economic times, Androscoggin and other mills could be running flat out, with sales so strong that customers had to be put on allocation and orders monitored very closely. This situation was far different from some recessionary times when mills took any order and still had to cut back production.

While the company's central order department (operations control) decided what would be produced on what machine on which days, the mill still had its own considerable production planning problems. Customer orders not

only specified the type of paper but also the size (width) to be cut, the quantity (the diameter of the roll), and some other features. In planning for any specific run on a paper machine, the mill wanted to group together all those orders calling for the same diameter and in such a way that the entire width of the paper machine's output was accounted for. The mill did not like to leave any waste, since even an inch of paper unaccounted for could cost the company foregone revenue of several thousand dollars. The mill used a computer program to optimize paper machine trim.

The mill also wanted to schedule slitting the rolls to minimize additional handling. This goal meant slitting as much off the machine winder as possible; small widths, however, should be cut from the center portion to reduce the risk of distortion in slitting.

Two production planners scheduled orders on the mill's five machines. They had to remain flexible enough to allow at least some changes in customer orders as late as the Wednesday before the start of the next week's production. The mill also had to schedule trucks and railcars for order shipments.

Inventories and Purchasing

Most of the wood that Androscoggin Mill used was provided by contract for 10,000 to 100,000 cords per year. International Paper did not cut its own wood, but contracted that task out as well. The company's woodlands division was responsible for purchasing the mill's wood and managing the woodyard at economical inventory levels. In addition, the mill stood ready to purchase, by weight, the wood of small, independent loggers without prior commitments being made. The mill did, however, deliberately seek the building up of wood in inventory in the fall and winter so that the spring thaw and the mud it brought did not disrupt the mill as it disrupted logging. It was not uncommon

A paper machine take-up reel. (*Courtesy of International Paper*)

to have 30 days of production in pulp wood inventory. All the work-in-process inventories were small and temporary, used mainly to permit the mixing of different types of wood chips or pulp and to permit production to continue in case some portion of the process went down temporarily.

The extent of finished goods inventory varied. Comparatively few finished goods were held for the products of machines 2, 3, and 5. Some were kept to permit stray order fulfillment or order amendments, but most paper production was soon headed out the door, waiting only long enough for all items in the order to be gathered together. The parent log and finished goods inventories for machine 1 (bond and offset papers) were very much larger, typically about 15 days of production. Such a large inventory was required to meet customer needs on any of the 48 paper machine products that machine 1 was qualified to manufacture, while keeping to a minimum the number of machine setups over the course of a year.

At Androscoggin, all responsibilities for production planning, loading machines, product distribution to customers, and finished goods inventories rested with the planning, scheduling, and distribution department because it was felt that all of these items affected one another at the plant and should be controlled by the same authority.

THE WORKFORCE

The Androscoggin Mill employed about 1400 people, about 250 of whom were salaried. The 1100 or so hourly employees (paid according to the hours worked), were represented by three international unions. The United Paperworkers International Union (UPIU) represented the woodyard, woodroom, pulp mill, paper mill, maintenance, finishing, and shipping workers; the International Brotherhood of Firemen and Oilers represented the power house employees and plant electricians; and the Office and Professional Employees International Union represented many of the office and clerical workers at the mill. The agreements were specific to Androscoggin and had been negotiated by the plant's management.

Labor relations at the plant had been soured by an extended strike that lasted from June 1987 to October 1989. The UPIU, in an effort to reverse a series of concessions that it had granted other manufacturers, stood firm against the company's contract offer. The company, faced with increasing competition, felt obliged to reduce what it felt were costly concessions it had made in earlier contracts, specifically the pay of double time for Sunday and holiday work and the mandatory shutdown of the mill at Christmas. (Other companies had successfully altered these items in their new contracts with the UPIU.) The union finally accepted the company's offer, but not until all of the hourly employees then striking were replaced with other workers. Because of subsequent attrition, 250 of the 1100 who went out on strike were back working at the mill. A petition from the replacement workers to decertify the UPIU was, at the time of this tour's writing, under review by the National Labor Relations Board.

Work at the mill was defined as either day work or tour (shift) work. Most work was in fact tour work. At the suggestion of the workforce, the mill operated a modified 12-hour shift (see Figure A2). Workers worked 16 out of every 28 days. Every day, except Thursdays and Fridays, workers worked either 7 A.M. to 7 P.M., or 7 P.M. to 7 A.M. On Thursdays and Fridays, they worked more traditional 8-hour shifts. Workers worked no more than 5 days in a row and no more than 3 12-hour shifts in a row. This implied that workers worked 2 out of every 4 weekends, but got 3 days off for one weekend and 6 days off for the other weekend in every four.

Even though one crew or another was at the mill 24 hours a day, there were still some occasions that warranted overtime pay. Overtime

	Monday Tuesday Wednesday Thursday Friday Saturday Sunday	Monday Tuesday Wednesday Thursday Friday Saturday Sunday	Monday Tuesday Wednesday Thursday Friday Saturday Sunday	Monday Tuesday Wednesday Thursday Friday Saturday Sunday
7:00 A.M.— 3:00 P.M.	A A A A A D D	D D D D D C C	C C C C C B B	B B B B B A A
3:00 P.M.—11:00 P.M.	(1) D D D D C C C	(2) C C C C B B B	(3) B B B B A A A	(4) A A A A D D D
11:00 P.M.— 7:00 A.M.	C C B B B B B	B B A A A A A	A A D D D D D	D D C C C C C
OFF DAY	B B C C D A A	A A B B C D D	D D A A B C C	C C D D A B B

Notes:
1. Schedule repeats every 4 weeks.
2. Three out of every 4 weeks each shift works 5 days and is off 2.
3. One out of every 4 weeks each shift works 6 days and is off 1.
4. Average hours worked, 42.

FIGURE A2   Shift schedule for International Paper Company's Androscoggin Mill.

was paid on a daily basis past either 8 or 12 hours of the regular shift and after 40 hours a week of regular time.

All of the jobs in the mill were classified and assigned different rates of pay according to the hierarchy of knowledge and responsibilities required. When job openings came up, usually precipitated by a worker's transferring or terminating for one reason or another, workers in the next lower position were advanced according to seniority, assuming they demonstrated the abilities required of the new job. When a high-level job became vacant, a cascading of open positions was triggered, as workers moved up in the hierarchy. Transfers within the mill were permitted, in addition to promotions within the same department. Seniority governed transfers as well. For most hourly workers, the typical career path would entail transfers and promotions up to the highest paying jobs.

With the adoption of the latest contract, however, and its concept of more teamwork and more cross-training of the workforce, the number of specific classifications for the workforce had been significantly reduced (e.g., on a paper machine from 7 to 4 classifications, and in the technical department, from 9 to 2) and this shortened the lines of progression and at the same time broadened the content of jobs in the mill. This helped to keep work balanced across workers and fostered increased productivity.

Worker complaints were relatively few and, if not adjusted on the job, could be adjusted by a four-step grievance procedure involving successively higher levels of union and management officials. The fourth and final step was arbitration, which was seldom invoked— perhaps once a year.

Over the years, as papermaking equipment grew in size, speed, and sophistication (particularly with the advent of computerized process controls), papermaking became less and less an art and more and more a science. This change left its imprint on the workforce. Not only could a new paper mill be operated with fewer workers than an old one, but the requisite worker skills were less manual and more cerebral. The latest breed of papermakers were more highly educated, in general, and more analytical. As one would expect, some of the older workers were frightened by the automation and its demands on them.

Management had to be understanding of this, and considerable resources were expended on training. The adoption of a quality improvement process (QIP) that used teams of workers and managers to solve particular problems, many necessitating considerable data-gathering and mathematical and statistical analysis, had also required substantial training. Happily, the QIP had been a great and continuing success that had helped the plant to enjoy significant productivity gains that had stood it in good stead even as the economy turned downward. The mill, unlike many others, was not forced into shutdowns because of a lack of orders; its competitiveness had assured it of constant operation, and thus of a constant string of paychecks for its workers.

CONTROLLING THE OPERATION

The entire papermaking process at Androscoggin was designed to manufacture paper with as little downtime as possible. Equipment maintenance could generally be scheduled during the periodic changing of the paper machine's "clothing" (i.e., changing the worn wire and felt, accomplished every 2-3 months). Process control equipment and workforce skills were geared to react instantly to production disruptions, such as paper breaks, or to product changes in weight or color. The time it took to correct a disruption such as a paper break varied enormously (from, say, 3 minutes to an hour). But the average break time was in the 10- to 15-minute range. A color change normally took about 10 minutes, and a careful weight change could be done without any downtime.

Paper was continually being tested for quality, and the feedback to the workforce was swift so that any needed adjustments could be made. The workforce also kept their own process control charts that statistically tracked the process' ability to make quality paper and that signaled when changes to the process were called for.

In general, operations at the mill could be described as quiet and watchful. Because the elements of the process were so interdependent, skilled managers and workers were required in every phase of the mill's operations. Indeed, many of the mill's supervisors had been promoted out of the ranks and were thus intimately familiar with the mill's operations.

Changes in the process, routine capital acquisition and maintenance were the province of plant engineering. Plant engineering was constantly engaged in projects. Here is a sampling:

* A new, larger storage tank for broke (waste paper) for machine 4.
* A proposal to dry bark with exhaust gases.
* Installation of equipment to incinerate the sludge created as part of the effluent treatment process.
* Replacing a worn section of a debarking drum.

* Installing steam meters.
* Overseeing the repair of a roof.
* Laying out the specifications for a new gas scrubber.
* Replacing winders and supercalenders with state-of-the-art equipment.

EVALUATING MILL PERFORMANCE

The mill was evaluated as a cost center; it had no control or authority over prices, markets, or revenues. The mill operated to a budget. Given a sales forecast from the marketing function at headquarters, prices, and a product mix, the mill developed standard costs for producing the quantity of each paper product forecasted. The budget reflected these standard costs and the mill was held to the budget. However, if the product mix changed, the resulting cost changes were charged to marketing, not the mill. The mill was accountable only for those costs over which it had control.

While the efficient production of paper was an important goal, it was by no means the only aspect of mill operations that was evaluated. Others played an important role: employee safety; management and worker training; commitment to environmental controls (not only meeting present standards, but keeping the environmental control equipment balanced in capacity with the rest of mill operations and advancing in technology); expenditures for new capital appropriations and for maintenance; and industrial relations.

PART TWO

DISCUSSION

The International Paper Company is in no way responsible for the following views and presentation. They remain solely the responsibility of the author.

THE PROCESS FLOW

The process of making paper, while a frightfully complicated endeavor, follows a clear cut and rigid pattern. All of the paper that the Androscoggin Mill produces—however different in appearance, weight, and feel—proceeds through essentially the same production steps, from logs of wood in the woodyard to "logs" of

paper at the shipping dock. This kind of production process can be readily portrayed in a diagram like Figure A3, which is commonly called a process flow diagram.

The process flow diagram of Figure A3 is a fairly general one and could be made considerably more detailed. Whether more detail is desirable depends, naturally, on the use to which a process portrait like Figure A3 is put. Several points about the diagram ought to be noted:

1. Actual processing operations are usually distinguished from storage points in the process. In the diagram, processing operations are indicated by rectangles and inventories

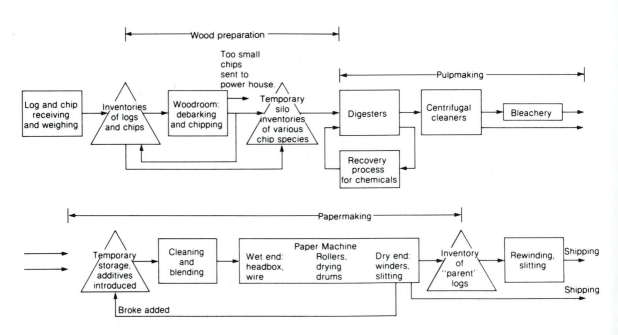

FIGURE A3   Process flow diagrams for International Paper Company's Androscoggin Mill.

by triangles. (Rectangles are used here because it is easier to fit the descriptions in them. However, typically in industrial engineering, circles are used to indicate processing operations and rectangles are used to indicate tests and inspections. See Figure 5-1 for the standard conventions.)

2. Several operations could be bypassed and are indicated by two arrows emanating from one operation and pointing to others. For example, all of the woodroom's output need not have gone directly to the silos but could have been placed in the woodyard for storage. The rewinders were superfluous for those orders that could be slit directly from the main winders.

3. The continuous nature of the process is evident by the very low level of inventories and by the designation of the silo chip and pulp additive inventories as temporary.

INFORMATION IN THE PROCESS

A production process is more than a series of operations performed on a collection of materials. What a process flow diagram can depict—the sequencing of process steps, the choice of equipment and technology, the capacity of process steps, the tasks required of the workforce—while critical, is only part of the story. Another part of the story involves the procedures that have been put in place to direct the process flow. We can usefully think of a companion to the process flow diagram—namely, an information flow diagram. Figure A4 provides an example of what might be placed in such a diagram. Note how the actions of different layers of managers and workers are distinguished in the diagram and how information is fed back up the channels of communication.

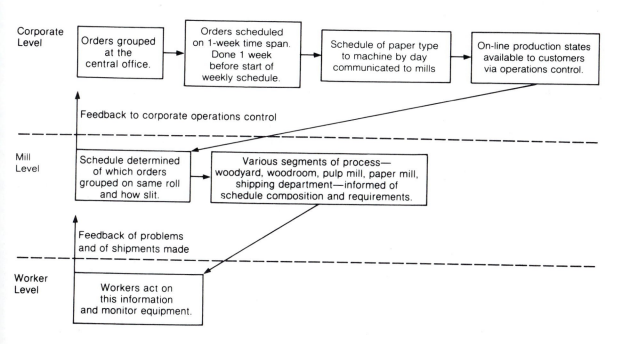

FIGURE A4   Information flow diagram for International Paper Company's Androscoggin Mill.

Most of the information flow in this continuous flow process is directed from the top down. Feedback is needed only to acknowledge receipt of information and to signal significant problems in the actual workings of the process. The process is designed with such care and the workforce so carefully trained that workers do not have to be in repeated touch with management to do their jobs well. The information needs of the process simply are not great, although the thought and effort standing behind that information (such as scheduling tasks of both the corporate office and the mill itself) are considerable and sophisticated.

CAPACITY

Capacity in this continuous flow process is fairly well defined and can be spoken of in physical terms—namely, tons of pulp and paper manufactured and cords of wood consumed. Likewise, there is a straightforward meaning to the term capacity utilization. In fact, all one needs to do is check to see whether the paper machines are running. If they are, capacity (all of it) is being used. Simply compiling the time the paper machines have run over some period of time and dividing that sum by the total available machine-hours gives a splendid indication of capacity utilization. Indeed, only when sales are insufficient or when the machine is broken or down temporarily for a setup or a change of "clothing" would we expect capacity utilization that was less than 100 percent.

Despite the relative ease with which we can talk of capacity and capacity utilization in this continuous flow process, on closer inspection of the concept a number of disquieting ambiguities surface. The ambiguities surface largely because the capacity of the mill is dependent on the number of factors. Among them:

1. *Product mix.* Some grades and weights of paper are more difficult to produce than others. Newer machines, of course, are apt to run at faster speeds than older machines, given the same kind of paper. But, given similar vintage paper machines, thin papers and high-quality finish papers have to run at slower speeds than others. Thus comparing the capacity of the Androscoggin Mill with that of other paper mills or with its own in other years can only be done with some understanding of the product mixes involved.

2. *Run lengths.* Every time a paper machine must be set up for a different grade, weight, or color of paper, capacity is lost. Although some changes are inherently more timeconsuming than others, every change implies at least a small reduction in theoretical capacity. The capacity of machine 1 was somewhat lower than that of machine 4 at least in part because machine 1 was scheduled to produce 48 different paper machine products in white and in colors, whereas machine 4 was devoted primarily to white.

3. *Maintenance.* A paper machine might also lose capacity because it was being repaired or because its "clothing" was being changed. The machines that could be kept running until only regularly scheduled maintenance interrupted production were those that lost the least capacity.

4. *Slitting schedule.* Slitting paper "logs" from the winders and rewinders was purposely scheduled so that as little waste as possible resulted. The more successful the schedule, the less waste there was.

For these reasons, the terms capacity and capacity utilization were not as unambiguous as might have been anticipated. Nevertheless, the process was extraordinarily well balanced and smooth running, and this made discussion of capacity and capacity utilization easy.

DEMANDS OF THE PROCESS ON THE WORKERS

Over the years, papermaking, like other continuous flow processes, has become a process where increasingly machinery "does it all." Pulpmakers and papermakers have been systematically removed from playing their traditional direct "hands-on" roles in the process. Instead, papermakers are more and more "indirect" labor-setters, monitors, and repairers of equipment that makes paper much faster and more reliably than any crew of traditional papermakers could using the older technology and their own skills. Where papermaking was "art," it is now "science." The former lengthy apprenticeships from sixth hand on a paper machine to machine tender are no longer justified by the need to learn the art. Despite the change to science, the level of skill required in the process remains high. The workforce may have been removed to gazing at control panels, adjusting knobs, and throwing switches, but the technical demands of the process are even higher in a modern, as compared to traditional, paper mill. Training is therefore an important consideration and an apprenticeship, while different from before, is still required. The lines of worker progression in the mill are clear (in fact, they were diagrammed for each department in the labor agreement), and workers are paid accordingly.

What comprises any job in the mill, while somewhat restricted, has been increasing steadily, however. The team concept, job rotations, and the collapsing of the traditional classifications into many fewer, had helped to broadened the definition of jobs at the mill. The new labor contract permitted those changes that encourage productivity and kept everyone well occupied.

Skilled workers are needed everywhere in the process, largely because the process is so interdependent. If one aspect of the process falls down (e.g., quality of the pulp), another aspect is likely to suffer (increased risk of a paper break).

DEMANDS OF THE PROCESS ON MANAGEMENT

The interdependence and capital intensity (a high ratio of plant and equipment value to labor payroll) of a continuous flow process like papermaking place tremendous demands on management, especially in the realms of coordination and of the choice and care of equipment. Furthermore, these demands are made not only of the mill's own management but of the corporation as a whole. Profitability in such processes largely rests on (1) assuring that the proper technology is selected, (2) balancing the capacities of all segments of the process so that as little capacity goes to waste as possible, (3) scheduling the use of that capacity as completely as possible, (4) keeping the equipment running up to speed and up to quality standards; and (5) an ever-continuing effort to improve in all areas of the operation. Let us review these points in turn.

Choice of Technology

The march of technological change is inexorable. While the output of continuous flow processes seldom changes by much, there can be upheavals in how that output is manufactured. The introduction of process control equipment to papermaking is a case in point. Management must be constantly aware of equipment advances across the industry, and savvy manufacturers engage in regular dialogues with equipment makers so that their own ideas and needs can be tried out in new equipment designs. The impact of technology is so fundamental that the corporate staffs of continuous flow process industries are usually charged with monitoring and selecting major new technology for all the plants of the company. Individual plants may have representatives on any plant and equipment choice studies, but corporate-level managers are apt to take the lead in the study and decision-making process. Many of the latest technological advances had involved changes spurred by pollution control issues or energy savings.

What is true for technology decisions is also true for decisions on how vertically integrated the process should be. This is generally also a corporate decision and one that is the province of corporate staff.

Balancing Capacities

The papermaking process, as we have seen, can be broken down into distinct segments (as in the process flow diagram); associated with each of these segments are machines and other equipment, often very large. Frequently, these machines and equipment are manufactured by different companies and do not come in just any size. It is management's responsibility to select the equipment for each process segment that represents both the suitable technology and size for the contemplated plant or plant expansion. One segment's capacity should be balanced, as well as possible, against that of other segments, so that as little extra capacity as possible has to be financed. After all, in an integrated, continuous flow process the capacity of the entire process is determined by the lowest capacity segment.

In reality, balancing process segment capacities is a difficult chore, and choices have to be made as to which process segments are to be assigned whatever excess capacity may exist. Often such a choice entails an investigation of equipment costs, with the relatively cheaper equipment being assigned any excess capacity.

In papermaking, for example, the big bucks get chewed up in financing paper machines and bleacheries. Woodrooms, digester, and rewinders are relatively less expensive. Thus, frequently, the spare capacity is to be found at the ends of the process (woodrooms, rewinders) rather than in the middle (bleacheries, paper machines). Having spare capacity at the rewinders increases the flexibility of the process as well to modifications of the product mix or order specifications. With excess capacity in place, unusual orders can be serviced without undue strain or delay.

The need for, and the expense of, maintaining a balance of capacities in a continuous flow process like the Androscoggin Mill are dramatically highlighted by the 1980 rebuilding of paper machine 2 and its conversion from carbonizing tissue to publication gloss. That conversion speeded up the flow of paper from about 20 miles per hour to nearly 35 miles per hour and raised the mill's net yearly tonnage by about 100,000 tons. To accommodate a change of that magnitude meant altering the pulpmaking capabilities of the mill as well as its papermaking capabilities. When process segments are tightly coupled, capacity changes echo throughout the entire process.

Scheduling

Large, high-speed continuous flow processes are geared to high-volume production of standard items. Typically, they are low-cost processes, but they often sacrifice the ability to respond quickly to changing customer specifications without introducing a lot of waste and thus destroying their low-cost character. In order, then, to satisfy customer orders at low cost, continuous flow processes must schedule their capacity well in advance, offering their customers longer lead times than may be common in other types of processes or else filling orders out of in-process or finished goods inventories.

At International Paper, as we saw, the broad "paper machine products" scheduling proceeded one week in advance for production and the schedule devised was of a 1-week period. The customer orders that were produced in each run, however, were set at the plant level only 2 days in advance of the production cycle. As many customer orders as could be slit right off the machine winder were scheduled, to eliminate rehandling and converting of paper logs. More exotic orders for special colors, grades, or weights from machine 1 were often filled out of finished goods inventory to avoid having to schedule special production runs. Scheduling at International Paper, as these observations indicate, was a sophisticated enterprise.

The idea, of course, behind such sophisticated scheduling is to keep the process flowing as continuously as possible. Generally, the process could be more responsive to customer orders, but to do so would necessarily mean interrupting production to set up equipment. Capacity would be reduced and costs increased. By stretching out deliveries or by keeping finished goods inventories, the continuous flow process can keep its costs down.

Equipment Maintenance

Most continuous flow process plants are evaluated as cost centers. As with the Androscoggin Mill, such plants are not given authority over revenues (no sales forces are tied to them), and so the plant is judged by how well it can adhere to a budget. The plant has an incentive then to keep its equipment well maintained; if it does not, it risks assuming costs that can be very high (equipment breakdowns force high repair costs and expensive makeup work.) Given such an evaluation scheme, most managers would opt to spend all of their budget for maintenance to avoid the chance, however slim, of suffering a huge cost increase and an instantly bad reputation for plant management.

QUESTIONS

1. The changeover of machine 2 from carbonizing tissue to publication gloss involved changes in other parts of the process. Why was this so? Speculate in as much detail as possible about the kinds of changes that would have had to occur as a consequence of such a paper machine changeover.

2. Much of the "higher-level" production planning for Androscoggin Mill occurs in International Paper's Memphis and New York headquarters, whereas "lower-level" production planning occurs at the mill itself. Why is there this division of responsibilities? What would happen if Memphis or New York handled all the production planning or if Androscoggin did it all?

3. If you were a production planner at the Androscoggin Mill, what might you be most likely to consider important? Why? How would these priorities affect your production plans?

4. Why did the Androscoggin Mill choose vertical integration for its design? What would be some of the advantages and disadvantages of increased forward integration for the mill?

5. How is the workforce organized at the mill? What are some of the operational implications of this workforce composition?

6. As a manager, which aspects of a continuous flow process appeal to you? Which aspects might not?

BEACON GLASS WORKS

Beacon Glass Works, located in Marysville, West Virginia, manufactures hollow glass tubing for use in catalytic converters. Beacon is a large division of one of the leading glass manufacturers, and was founded when the Environmental Protection Agency strongly urged the development of antipollution devices for trucks and automobiles. The hollow glass tubing manufactured at Beacon comes in around 30 different size combinations. The lengths are from 6 to 12 inches, and the inside diameter ranges from 1/32 to 1/16 inch.

These tubes are produced by extrusion. The molten glass is first forced through a die that determines the inside diameter of the tube. The tube then is cooled and cut to the proper length. After the cut edges have been finished so that they are smooth, the product is sent to a holding area where it waits to be packaged. Once the tubing is packaged, it is again stored, this time awaiting shipment to Beacon's customers, the four major domestic motor vehicle manufacturers.

The extrusion process is basically a make-to-stock operation driven by production scheduling. Based upon anticipated stock shortages, Jose Torrez, the production manager, schedules the next week's production, and the necessary dies are readied. Each die is used until about one month's demand has been produced. Then, the dies are changed and another product with a different inside diameter is run. Actually, since several lengths have the same inside diameter, several products can be extruded with one extrusion run.

Once the product cools to the proper cutting temperature, the cutting area cuts the proper lengths, again based upon the stock needs determined by the production manager. The product is then stored in a holding area waiting to be packaged. Packaging is usually done to customer order, as different customers want different quantities and want them packaged differently.

Sometimes, however, Jose will schedule the packaging department based on what he believes will be the customer orders, so that he can use the packaging machinery efficiently. This scheduling sometimes results in excess inventory for one customer while another customer's order is backordered because of a stockout.

Jose is concerned that his process scheduling is not as good as it could be and thinks that possibly the first step he should take is to diagram the production flow and the information flow for the process.

1. Diagram the production flow.
2. Diagram the information flow.
3. Discuss possible problem areas for Beacon's production process.

SITUATION FOR STUDY A-2

SUNMEADOW DAIRY

Sunmeadow Dairy produced and distributed a variety of products including whole milk, skim milk, 2 percent milk, ice milk, fruit drinks, buttermilk, eggnog, chocolate milk, and many different mixes used to produce ice cream. The production of milk, however, was 90 percent of the operation.

From 8 A.M. until 5 P.M., raw milk (unpasteurized milk direct from the farm) arrived by refrigerated tanker truck at or below 42°F. The raw milk was pumped from the tanker (capacity 5500 gallons) to one of three refrigerated storage silos (capacity 70,000 gallons total) adjacent to the receiving area. During this transfer, the milk flowed through a plate heat exchanger to lower its temperature to 37°F. From these silos, the milk was pumped to the second floor as needed for production and was stored in four of six storage tanks. The empty tanks were used for mixing and diluting the raw milk, which was 3.5 to 4.0 percent butterfat.

Because whole milk contains 3 to 5 percent butterfat (depending on its source) and some skim milk products contain as little as 0.5 percent butterfat, a certain percentage of butterfat had to be removed from the raw milk. A separator was employed to remove the excess butterfat. (A separator is a centrifuge in which raw milk is spun at high speed, forcing the separation of the butterfat from the heavier milk and allowing the isolation of the two fractions.) One by-product of this process contained 40 percent butterfat and was pumped off (at a rate of 1000 to 1500 gallons per day) into nearby holding tanks and shipped to a butter factory once a week. The other by-product was 0.5 percent milk; it was pumped into an empty tank and mixed with 3.5 percent raw milk to obtain the desired butterfat level for the product being packaged next in the plant. This mixing was called "standardizing" the product. From an information chart on obtaining the percentage of butterfat needed for each product, the separator operator determined the exact quantity of each input (3.5 percent milk and 0.5 percent milk) to be mixed in the empty tank.

From the holding tanks the standardized product was pumped into one of two pasteurizers (capacity 1500 and 4000 gallons per hour). (Pasteurization is the process of heating raw milk to 161°F for 16 seconds to kill harmful bacteria.) The pasteurized milk was pumped into one of two homogenizers, which blew the milk through a very small opening to break up the fat globules and create a uniform, or homogenous, mixture. The pasteurized, homogenized milk was directed into any one of seven pasteurizing holding tanks to await packaging on the first floor. Because packaging might start as early as 5:30 A.M. pasteurization usually began at midnight-to build a buffer inventory in the holding tanks for the first and second products to be run that day.

Milk could be pumped into one of five packaging processes:

1. The filler filled plastic gallons and half-gallons at a rate of 70 per minute. The plastic containers were made in the blow-molding department and arrived at this machine by overhead conveyor. This conveyor continued through the completely automated processes of filling, capping, and storing the filled containers in metal cases for shipment. These metal cases were stacked six high and sent to the cooler for order filling.

2. The H-75 machine produced paper half-gallons (capacity 75 units per minute) and automatically filled, sealed, and stacked them. Manual attention was needed only to take the wax cardboard containers from the adjacent stockroom and load them into the feed mechanism. Each carton was automatically unfolded, heat-sealed at the bottom, and filled with the product being produced in this run; the excess foam and overfill were drawn off the top, and the carton was heat-sealed. The cartons were then automatically stacked into metal cases and put on the conveyor for the short trip to the cooler.

3. The Q80-110 machine operated the same way as the H-75 but was for half-pints, pints, and quarts (capacity 80 quarts, 110 pints, and 110 half-pints per minute).

4. The NEP 210 machine (capacity 210 half-pints per minute) also operated the same way as the H-75. The unique feature of this process was that it produced only for schools.

5. Using the bag and box filler was a totally manual process for filling 5-gallon plastic bags inside boxes. These were shipped to local schools and hospitals for use in self-service milk dispensers.

While each process was running, there was at least one operator with each machine at all times. The high volume of production demanded constant attention and minor adjustments, especially to keep the product from becoming caught in the moving parts. Once packaged, the product was carried by conveyor from the packaging areas to the 38°F cooler, where it was stored according to how soon it would be used to fill orders on the daily trucks. The cooler operated on a first-in, first-out (FIFO) basis; rotating the product this way kept the buffer stock as fresh as possible. The product was moved to the loading areas on the same conveyor that circulated through the packaging and cooler.

Orders to the dairy were called in by the branches and other customers, usually 2 or 3 days in advance. The salesclerks wrote the orders on computer-generated, preaddressed order sheets for each account. Special phone orders and adjustments could be made until shipment, because of the buffer inventory in the cooler.

Local orders were written by the drivers of the route trucks while visiting each customer on their daily schedule. The day before shipment, the cooler supervisor scheduled and consolidated all orders for filling based on the usual arrival times of the incoming trucks. Two order copies stayed in the sales office, two copies were sent with the order, and one stayed with the cooler supervisor. After delivery, the signed order copy was compared with the original order and all necessary information was entered into the computer. This update triggered the daily report on actual production, cooler inventory, actual units loaded on all trucks by product line, and total amount needed for the next day's production. The plant manager received this printout early the following morning. Two 10-hour shifts were needed to accommodate each day's scheduled production. The same order of production was run each day (such as 2 percent milk first and chocolate last). To accommodate the trucks that started arriving at 4 A.M., the buffer inventory in the cooler at the start of the day for the last two products run might be as high as 60 percent of total production.

The quality control supervisor was responsible for product quality throughout the plant. Quality control was a major factor in the production of milk. As the tankers arrived from the farms, three quality checks were done to make certain the raw milk was within the acceptable range of temperature, bacteria count, and acidity. Except during pasteurization, milk was maintained at 38°F throughout the plant. In addition to the standardization checks for butterfat content, two tests were done after pasteurization to check the bacteria count and type of bacteria still in the milk. Raw milk arrived with a bacteria count of 10,000 to 20,000 per milliliter and was shipped out at about 500 per milliliter. Each worker was acutely aware of the importance of quality control, and all machinery and equipment were thoroughly washed at least once a day to ensure cleanliness. Most of the equipment — including tankers, silos, and storage tanks — was stainless steel to facilitate cleaning and reduce the chances of contamination.

1. Diagram the process and information flows.
2. What do you see as the challenges that the management of the dairy faced?
3. Recently the dairy lost a large contract for supplying milk to a chain of grocery stores. How do you think the loss of sales will affect the operations of the dairy? Be as specific as you can.

A JOB SHOP
Norcen Industries
Jersey Shore, Pennsylvania

It had been years since Joe Gehret finally gave in to his desire to control his own company and resigned his position as general foreman in the machine shop of the Litton Industries plant in Williamsport, Pennsylvania. In July 1967, Joe and a partner (who had since left the firm) began Norcen Industries by selling stock and taking over an old garage in Jersey Shore, about 15 miles west of Williamsport. They initially intended for Norcen to be a plastics distributor and fabricator, but it soon became apparent that both their experience and the demands of industry in north central Pennsylvania dictated a change of course. Norcen quickly became mainly a metal-working machine shop, and the machine shop accounted for almost 90 percent of gross revenues.

The company had experienced reasonably steady growth. In 1981, Norcen moved into a new, 21,000-square-foot building on the outskirts of town. Sales in 1991 had grown to over $2 million and employment to 40.

PART ONE

PROCESS DESCRIPTION

PRODUCTS, SALES, AND ORDER HANDLING

As a general machine shop, Norcen was capable of producing a seemingly endless succession of metal and plastic parts that a host of companies typically assembled into machines and other products. Norcen specialized in close tolerance work for the electronics and aerospace industries. Almost all of Norcen's customers were manufacturers, but 95 percent of this business Norcen had to win by submitting low bids. The purchasing departments of Norcen's customer firms generally requested Norcen and at least two other machine shops to "quote" the work they wanted done. The request always specified (1) the number of pieces desired, which varied enormously, from 5

Joe Gehret beside a recently purchased lathe. (*Courtesy of Norcen Industries*)

pieces to over 1000, although most lots were less than 250, (2) the nature of the material required and whether it was supplied by the customer, (3) the design of the piece (a blueprint would be sent), and (4) the date by which the order had to be received. During peak years, Norcen bid on as many as 250 such requests each week, knowing that on a long-run average its quote would be accepted about 15 percent of the time. (In the past this figure had sometimes been as high as 40 percent.)

Joe Gehret was responsible for deciding all metalworking quotes. Naturally, it was easier for him to quote jobs that Norcen had done before. Not only did he know the hourly charge-out rate (currently, $31.20 per hour for general machining and $40–50 per hour for electronic discharge machining (EDM)), which would cover both direct labor and overhead ex-

penses, but he had a past record of what the piece had actually cost Norcen to make on all previous occasions. (See Figure B1 and the discussion on record keeping below.) In addition, Norcen would already have a blueprint of the piece and a "process sheet" (Figure B2), which would outline the steps the shop had previously taken to manufacture it and the time standards for each of those steps. Deciding quotes for pieces Norcen had not previously made was more difficult. In such cases, Joe had to ponder the blueprint and develop, at least in his mind, a rough-cut process sheet.

Sometimes the request for the quote included a process sheet developed by the company itself, and this was a great aid. Other factors such as delivery dates (rush orders, being more trouble, commanded higher margins), and the prevailing load in the shop (the more

The table below is a record card for item "Transformer" (Company & Item 53147), Sheet #3, "Material Furnished".

VARIANCE	PRICE UNIT	PRICE TOTAL	HOURS	COST MATERIAL	COST LABOR	COST SERVICE	TOTAL	VOL.	COMP DATE 84	INVOICE	JOB 84	DATE 84	P.O. NUMBER
9 20	607 20					13 41	46	2/14	12107	17503	1/4	53368
9 20	708 40					53 87	77	1/16	11813			
9 20	579 60					747 93	63	1/12	11788			
9 20	322 00					263 14	35	3/19	12419			
9 20	956 80					37 00	104	3/28	12525			
9 20	883 25	136.9				60 13	96	4/16	12709	84		
8 90	453 90					483 36	51	4/12	13333	17582	4/8	55590
8 90	685 30						77	6/20	13416			
9 10	1 91 10						21	8/8	13846			
9 10	172 90					719 76	19	8/6	13833			
9 10	464 10						51	8/7	13834			
9 10	336 70					214 57	37	8/15	13911			
9 10	873 60					222 20	96	8/23	14009			
9 10	455 00					23 75	50	9/27	14360			
9 10	176 40 / 182 40	218.1				59 23	126	10/23	14492			
10 24	1382 40					622 72	135	1/25	15529		10/25	60938
10 00	1180 00	88.5	made on 18980			1217 79	118	2/8	15668		1/14	61673
12 24	722 16	26				255 89	59	10/2	18004	20414	9/16	65630

Notes:

1. This record card is for a so-called "transformer" (not what we would ordinarily term a transformer) for a company whose name has been withheld. This part is distinguished at Norcen by its part number, 53147, which also corresponds to a blueprint and a process sheet (see Figure B2).

2. The material to work on is furnished by the customer company.

3. This is a part that Norcen has machined for years. This record card is sheet #3. On this sheet, we can see at the top of the columns that the first order was placed on January 4, 1984, under purchase order (P.O.) number 53368. That job was assigned job number 17503 and consisted of 6 separate shipments of varying shipment dates (such as 2/14, 1/16) and corresponding and separate invoices to the customer (such as 121074, 11813). The shipment quantities varied as well (for example, 66 units, 77 units, 63 units). The total for the entire order is 441 pieces.

   The latest order (#65630), dated 9/10 and shipped 10/2, involved just 59 pieces. It carried job number 20414 and was billed on invoice 18004.

4. The quoted price for the first order on the card (job number 17503) was $9.20 per piece. The total billing for the first invoice (#12107) was $607.20. The total billing for the entire order was the sum of the six relevant invoices, $4,057.20.

5. A total of 136.9 hours of labor were spent fulfilling the first order. The total labor cost of the job was $1,175.44 (the sum of the cost total column).

   For the latest job, a total of 26 hours of labor was expended at a cost of $259.89. The total billing was $722.16 for the 59 pieces shipped, quoted at a price of $12.24 each.

6. Norcen Industries made its charge-out rate in the latest completed job. The labor hours of 26 times the prevailing charge-out rate of $24 per hour equals $624, which is below the actual revenue for the job of $722.16.

7. Two special notations are worth explaining: (1) The latest entry for P.O. number 55590 is a charge of $182.40 for an extra setup. The customer company had not provided the material on time, requiring Norcen Industries to incur an additional, unscheduled setup. Norcen charged the customer for that setup.

   (2) P.O. numbers 60938 and 61673, involving job numbers 18980 and 19206, were able to be run with a single setup. This was advantageous to the shop (denoted by the notation "made on 18980") and resulted in a lower quote for P.O. number 61673.

FIGURE B1   A sample record card for a particular item manufactured at Norcen Industries.

FIXTURES & TOOLS	MACH	SPEED	FEED	No	DESCRIPTION	No OF PIECES PER HR	PER PC	SET UP
					MATERIAL DESCRIPTION: OFHC Cu			
					COMPANY: Some company			
					PART NAME: Transformer			
					PART No: 512864			
					LINEAL INCHES / AREA (SQ IN) / DIMENSIONS / COMPUTATION-MTL REQD / PREPARED BY / PG OF / REV			
Arbor collet				10	Rough face to turn O D to size (972 974) on Arbor			
				20	Face waterfall drag down off of open end			
				30	Face off other end to 400 long			
				40	Deburr			
Collet template				50	Dress radius & grind radius in part holding length to size (381)			
				60	Deburr			
				70	Inspect			

Notes:

1. A collet holds the workpiece. An arbor is another device to hold the workpiece.

2. A template was used to help guide the grinding.

3. The waterfall was excess metal, a humpline bulge, that had to be machined off the part.

4. Various dimensions were given in steps 10, 30, and 50. They were also available on the blueprint of the part.

5. In the material description, OFHC Cu means oxygen-free copper, which is a very pure copper.

FIGURE B2   A sample process sheet used at Norcen Industries.

slack in the shop, the lower the margin) also influenced the quote.

The acceptance of a Norcen quote typically came by phone and was confirmed later by letter. Upon notification of acceptance, Joe's wife, Lillian, who was responsible for all bookkeeping, wrote up two copies of a job sheet (Figures B3 and B4). One copy was kept in a record book, and the other was attached to a blueprint and placed in a special tray. Joe was then responsible for looking over each job sheet to see whether any materials not provided by the customer needed to be ordered and whether any tooling needed to be done. Job sheets that awaited materials or tooling were kept in a sep-

arate tray. When enough materials were on hand to complete the order, the job sheet and blueprint were placed in a special drawer. This action released the order to the shop.

PLANT AND PERSONNEL

The machine shop operated on two shifts: 6:50 A.M. to 3:20 P.M. and 3:30 P.M. to midnight, with a half-hour break for lunch or dinner and two 10-minute break periods. The day shift consisted of 24 hourly workers, and the evening shift currently ran with only 9 workers. [This shift operated primarily the company's direct

ORDER No. _60938_____   JOB _18980_

PART No. _53147_____   LOT SIZE _____

MATERIAL _Furnished_____   245_____

DELIVERY _2/10_____

Checked By	Date	Name	Operation	Qty.	Hrs.	Acc. Hrs.
	1/14	RPM	255			
DM	1-16	J.L.	Lathe		8.0	8.0
	1-17	JL	LATHE		8.0	16.0
	1-18	JL	"		8.0	24.0
	1-19	JL	"		5.0	29.0
	1-21	JL	"		2.5	31.5
	1-21	Doyle	Deburr		3.9	35.4
	1-22	Doyle	Deburr-Buff		4.2	39.6
DM	1-22	DM.	Set up & Gr.		2.0	41.6
	1-22	O.R.	Gr.		0.7	42.3
JJ	1-23	OR	Gr.		8.0	50.3
DM	1-24	O.R.	Gr		8.0	58.3
JJ	1-25	JJ	Deburr		2.0	60.3
	1-25	Doyle	Wipe-Buff		1.5	61.8
	1/25	JJ	DeBuff Insp		1.5	63.3
	135 PCS		To Ship	1/25	JJ	
	1-25	OR	Gr.		8.0	71.3
JJ	1-26	OR	Gr.		2.5	73.8
DM	1-28	OR	Gr.		4.0	77.8
	1-29	OR	Gr.		4.5	82.3
	2-7	Doyle	CLEAN Deburr-Buff		5.2	87.5
	2-8	JJ	INSP		1.0	88.5
	118 Pcs		To Ship	2/8	JJ	

Notes:

1. This job sheet accompanied job number 18980 around the shop from the initial receipt of materials from the customer (255 pieces on 1/14) until shipments on 1/25 and 2/8 of 135 and 118 pieces, respectively.

2. The lot size on this job changed. It was increased to 245 (253 were actually shipped) when P.O. number 61673 came along, and the shop was able to do both jobs with a single setup.

3. Dates worked, worker initials, operation done, time spent, and total time to date on the order are filled in by each worker after he or she completes working on the job. Periodically, others have checked the order's work (RTM and JJ).

4. The accumulated labor hours are 88.5. This figure is also displayed on the record card.

FIGURE B3   A sample of the job sheet used at Norcen Industries.

ORDER No. __60938__   JOB __18980__

PART No. __53147__   LOT SIZE __245__

MATERIAL _____

DELIVERY __2/10__   __10.24__

Checked By	Date	Name	Operation	Qty.	Hrs.	Acc. Hrs.
	1/13	SL.	246	50		29
	1/20	GJ	33	25	3.5	32.5
		SL.	21	25	2.5	35
		OR	231	20	27.2	62.2
		DM	19	00	2	64.2
		DD	71	52	9.6	73.8
			622	72		
		chgd	155.29			
	1/27	OR.	72.25		8.5	82.3
	2/3	DD	40.04		5.2	87.5
		GJ	9.50		1	88.5
			121.79			
		chgd.	156.68			

Notes:

1. This job sheet was compiled by Lillian Gehret after job 18980 was completed. The information for the job sheet was derived from (a) the job sheet (Figure B3) that follows the job around the shop, (b) worker time cards (Figure B5), and (c) information on worker hourly rates.

2. The top portion of this job sheet contains the same information as Figure B3 and includes as well the quoted price on the job ($10.24 per piece).

3. Worker times are gathered by the week, with the weeks being dated from their start on a Sunday (1/13, 1/20). Workers' hours spent on this job in each week are listed in the Hrs. column. The cumulative hours for the job as a whole are totaled in the Acc. Hrs. column. In the center columns are listed the worker pay for the week due to the job. By dividing this pay by the hours, one can see that workers have different hourly wages. GJ has an hourly wage of $9.50 ($33.25/3.5).

4. The total wage bills for the job are $622.72, charged to invoice 15529, and $121.79, charged to invoice 15668. Recall that job 18980 combined two purchase orders and ran them on the same setup.

FIGURE B4   A sample showing Lillian Gehret's office copy of a job sheet.

numerical control (DNC) lathes and mills and was also used to expedite rush jobs.] Norcen's hourly wages (the highest paid by any of the machine shops in the area) started at $8.50 per hour for unskilled workers and went to $12.75 per hour for the most demanding work. This pay was augmented in two ways:

1. Overtime pay at time and a half
2. A bonus plan, payable at Christmas and in the summer

The size of each bonus depended on the fortunes of the company over the previous 6 months. Currently, bonuses averaged about $1500 per employee, greater by far than the dividends paid to the company's shareholders. In leaner years, of course, this bonus was much lower. The size of the bonus for each worker, like the number of vacation days, depended on seniority. The workers recognized this system as an incentive for continued good work. In the words of a lathe and drill press operator: "The better we are to the company, the better the company is to us."

A rough layout of the plant, showing the general groupings of machines, is included as Figure B5. An inventory of the most important

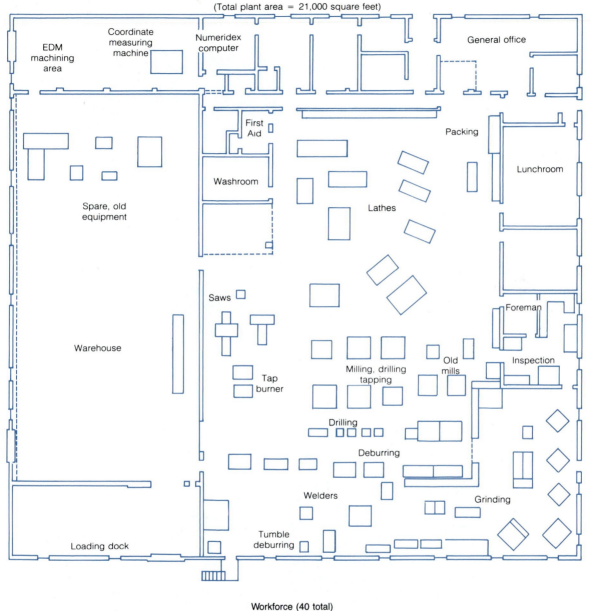

(Total plant area = 21,000 square feet)

Workforce (40 total)

1 general manager	26 machine operators
1 production manager	1 full-time inspector
1 QC manager/project engineer	1 inspector/operator
2 foremen	1 maintenance man
1 bookkeeper	1 shipper/receiver
1 computer programmer	2 utility people (clean-up, etc.)
	1 manager of the plastics business

FIGURE B5   Plant layout and workforce at Norcen Industries.

machines in the shop, along with their weekly average hours in use, is provided in Table B1.

The Workings of the Shop

Although Joe Gehret spent a good deal of time on the shop floor, responsibility for shop operations rested with Rob Thomas, the production manager, and Dan Steinbacher, the shop foreman. Their duties were varied, but the first concern for the smooth running of the shop was to see that all workers were assigned tasks and that they understood these tasks well, both their nature and their time standards. Moreover, Rob and Dan knew that it was important to the success of the company that tasks be assigned in a way that saved Norcen money. Cost reductions from such

The shop as seen from a balcony. (*Courtesy of Norcen Industries*)

The shop as seen from a balcony. (*Courtesy of Norcen Industries*)

TABLE B1   Inventory of Major Machines at Norcen Industries

Machine and Number Owned		Percent of Scheduled Time Machine Is Run
1	Hardinge HXL	100
1	Hardinge Conquest superprecision lathe	100
5	Hardinge CHNC II lathes	100
2	Large slant bed lathes	100
3	Hurco machining centers	100
2	Matsuura machining centers	100
1	Fadal machining center	100
1	Kitamura Mycenter machining center	100
2	Mitsubishi traveling wire EDM machines	75
1	Sodick die-sinker EDM machine	30
1	Blanchard-type grinder	40
1	Do-All automatic cut-off saw	40
1	Sheffield coordinate measuring machine	50
2	J&L 20" optical comparators with power feed & digital read-out	75
2	O.D., I.D. universal grinders	50
1	Super-precision universal tool & cutter grinder	30
1	Heat treat facility (size limitations, muffled main furnace, nitrogen induction)	75
1	Special roll grinding unit	50
1	110 ton Cincinnati hydraulic punch press	30
1	20 ton Perkins crank press	70
	+ surface grinders, manual mills, old lathes used for very small runs or for tool and die work or in support of the highly used machines (i.e., for creating fixtures, tooling)	25

scheduling and advance planning could come about in several ways:

1. Before an operator could machine any of the myriad jobs Norcen was capable of performing, the necessary machine had to be set up. The setup varied from about a half-hour for simple jobs to 4 hours for the most complex. An average setup was about 1.5 hours. Since, once set up, the machine could produce any number of pieces with only minor adjustments, it made sense to run full lots whenever possible. In this way, setup costs were spread over all the units in the order.

2. Frequently, especially with automatic equipment, the running time of the machine per piece produced was long enough so that, by staggering operations, a single operator could attend two different machines at the same time. That is, while one piece was being machined, the operator could be working at another machine, typically inserting new material or removing a finished piece. To exploit these possibilities,

A Hurco machining center down for a changeover after machining some white plastic parts. (*Courtesy of Norcen Industries*)

Rob and Dan had grouped similar kinds of machines together on the shop floor. It was to Norcen's advantage for Dan to identify and to match together those jobs that permitted this kind of labor savings.

3. As might be expected, some operators could perform certain machining tasks relatively better than others and thus held a comparative advantage over other workers in the shop for some jobs. It was worth it for the foremen to keep these special capabilities in mind in his assignment of jobs.

4. Cost reductions could also occur through improvements in the process sheets that were kept in special binders. Often, changes in the sequence of drilling, cutting, milling, grinding, tapping, threading, deburring, and so on, could have profound effects on the total time Norcen had to allocate to a particular job. Rob and Dan had to be alert for possible improvements they could make in the process.

5. The probability of successfully reducing costs was naturally greater for more complex operations and for repeat business. Furthermore, cost reductions could lie in more than process sequence changes. To cite an example, Norcen machined a part composed of a thin molybdenum strip bonded to steel. The customer's initial process specifications called for cutting two semicircles into the part using a lathe, but Joe Gehret recognized this technique as a high-risk, low-yield way to machine this part. By changing the process to use a specially adapted grinder, Norcen was able to machine the part successfully with much higher yields than would otherwise have been the case. Such dramatic success was not to be found often, but its significance was great enough to demand a good deal of the foremens' thoughts.

Even more important to the foremen than assigning tasks in money-saving ways was seeing to it that the delivery schedule was met. Norcen could not miss deliveries and still expect to receive repeat orders. The foremen were constantly aware of the promised delivery dates, and they attached high priorities to imminent deliveries due. The scheduling of jobs was further influenced by Norcen's cash flow

A Hurco machining center. (*Courtesy of Norcen Industries*)

The Hardinge Conquest superprecision lathe. (*Courtesy of Norcen Industries*)

needs. Other things being equal, and particularly at the end of the month, small jobs were given preference so that billing could proceed at once.

The foremen dealt also with worker morale, training, and development, with materials handling, and with quality control. But job scheduling was the most demanding on the foremen's energies. They tried to stay one day ahead of the workers, so that they knew precisely which job would go next to every machine, who would work that job, and when they would start on it. As Joe Gehret put it: "Scheduling is the most difficult function we have around here. It's the easiest thing in the world to say no to a customer, that we can't fit

his job into the shop. But after a few noes, you may not have a customer."

During the recession period of 1990–91, scheduling was even more difficult than usual. The drop in orders then meant that the foremen had fewer chances to group compatible orders together to avoid bottlenecks or to create labor-saving opportunities. In busier times, the foremen could choose among the many orders in the shop, spreading out demand for particular pieces of equipment and taking advantage of the economies possible.

Frequently, planned schedules had to be interrupted because of customer desires for expedited delivery, because materials were received late from the customer, or because of the breakdown of the machine or its tooling. In these cases quick, remedial action had to be taken. Often, this remedial action took the form of adding a new job or rerouting an existing job through the shop. Norcen had enough equipment on hand, typically, to permit a new or rerouted job to be set up on an unused machine. Joe Gehret purchased new machines for the shop with this kind of compatibility in mind. Not all jobs, of course, could be rerouted through the shop if things went awry, but it was possible with a sizable number, especially those that were not too complex. Some jobs could even be machined in an alternative sequence (e.g., milling could be done first rather than third), and this helped when remedial action was necessary. In general, the foremen preferred to have lathe work performed first, then milling, and only then grinding; but they were willing to abandon this sequence if necessary.

Some aspects of just-in-time manufacturing had repercussions for machine shops such as Norcen. Customers were now placing orders that required multiple, time-phased deliveries of smaller-than-usual lots. Even though many of Norcen's new machines were capable of running small lots economically, this trend did serve to complicate scheduling.

The Sheffield coordinate measuring machine.
(*Courtesy of Norcen Industries*)

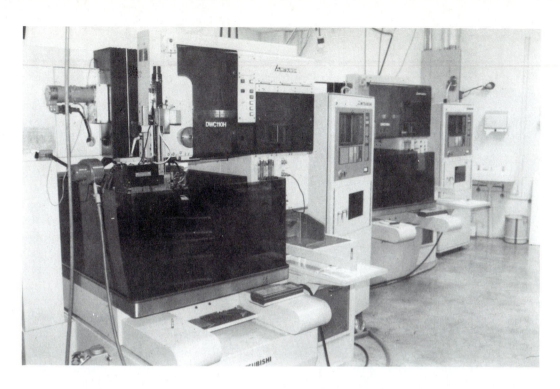

The Mitsubishi traveling wire EDM machines. (*Courtesy of Norcen Industries*)

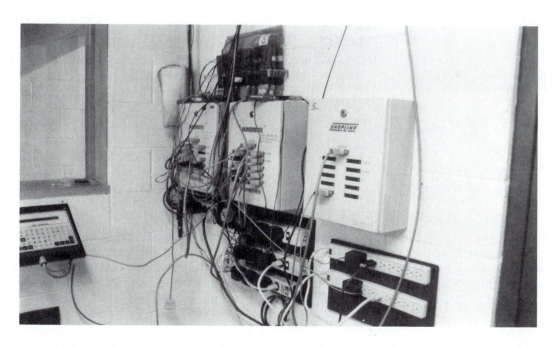

The control box for the fiber optic cables of Norcen's CAD/CAM network. (*Courtesy of Norcen Industries*)

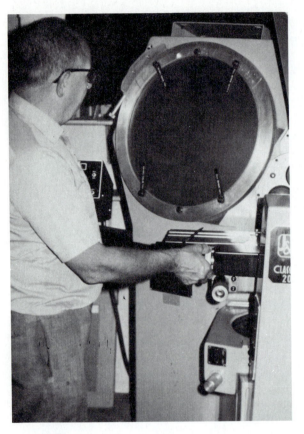

Joe Gehret with some inspection equipment.
(*Courtesy of Norcen Industries*)

TECHNOLOGICAL ADVANCES AND OTHER TRENDS

Over the years, technological advances, especially in computers, have been revolutionizing the machine tool industry. The old fully manual lathes, mills, grinders, and other tools had been supplanted by a succession of newer tools:

1. The first set of newer tools were NC (numerically controlled) machines that could repeat operations exactly by reading punched paper tapes. The paper tapes had to be specially pre-pared and thus were typically suitable for only high-volume, repetitive jobs. Naturally, in job shops like Norcen with many low-volume, one-of-a-kind jobs, NC machines could find only limited use.

2. The next generation of equipment, the computer numerically controlled (CNC) machines, found more of a home in job shops like Norcen Industries. Much of this machinery was programmable, enabling operators to enter, at the computer console, the depths, speeds, and feed rates of cuts to be made along X-, Y-, or Z-axes. In addition, they could operate from tapes (paper or magnetic). These newer machine tools were more versatile, more accurate, and faster than previous ones. Their automatic features easily permitted an operator to run more than one machine at a time, although this doubling up was often less feasible for machine shops running small parts (Norcen) than for shops machining large parts.

3. The latest generation of equipment, the direct numerical control (DNC) machines, could be run directly by a computer, eliminating the need for the preparation of tapes or the case-by-case programming of the CNC machine. All of Norcen Industries' were now DNC controlled. These machines made use of Norcen's CAD/CAM equipment and a fiber-optic cable network that linked the computer to the machines it controlled. Parts could now be designed using CAD computer software (Norcen used CADKey). The design could then be translated by CAM software (Norcen used IGES translation and the Anvil 1000 MD CAM program) into the precise settings for each machine's operation, and then downloaded to that machine via the cable network. Norcen kept a library of its past jobs, so that any repeat job could be pulled from the library and the machine set in exactly the way it was done before, without any extra work.

All of Norcen's lathe operators programmed their own jobs as did some of the machining center operators. The computer programmer and the foremen helped to troubleshoot particularly difficult jobs.

Norcen Industries was continually buying new, trading in old, and upgrading existing equipment. Joe Gehret remarked that the introduction of new technology meant that Norcen could produce some parts for costs that were less now, in current dollars, than those same parts cost in 1967, when the company was started.

Doing more and more machining were some of the latest machines to be added to the shop: three electrical discharge (EDM) machines. These machines used wire electrodes of various, and often small, diameters to machine parts of any conductive material, such as metal. The conductive material would be charged positively and the wire electrodes negatively and the material would be "burned off" by the travelling wire. EDM machines produced no burrs (thus, no need for grinding) as they machined parts, and they were capable of very precise machining, even in previously hard-to-work corners of the material. This equipment was kept in its own air-conditioned "clean room."

Norcen did not have any flexible machining centers (FMS) that one could sometimes find in larger fabrication areas nor did it operate any machining cells. FMSs linked several machines together and used sophisticated conveyors to move pieces from one machine to another. FMSs did not make sense for a job shop like Norcen because the tooling needed was too great and expensive, and jobs could be moved around more efficiently by the existing workforce. Similarly, machining cells were not employed because the continually changing nature of the product mix in the shop precluded the creation of product families with similar routings for those machining cells.

Nevertheless, the advent of the new technology permitted the shop's management to devise a number of cost-saving procedures. For example,

1. With carbide cutting tools and with EDM machining, Norcen could now harden metals by heat treating and could then machine them afterward. Previously, parts were machined, heat treated, and then re-machined (e.g., ground).

2. The new machines had multiple tool holders so that more facets of the job could be done while the part was held in position.

3. Parts could now be held in programmable indexers which could automatically rotate the part so that different sides could be machined without operator intervention.

4. Some machines had multiple vices on them so that 2 or 3 pieces could be set up at once.

5. Some of the lathes had automatic bar-feeds.

The movement for just-in-time (JIT) manufacturing and concern for quality and inventory levels were affecting operations at Norcen Industries. Customers were less lenient about scrap, no longer providing an extra 10 percent of material as a matter of course to cover potential scrap. Customers were also requiring multiple deliveries of their orders, forcing Norcen either to hold the inventory or to set up the job more than once. Concern for rapid delivery had also recently led the company to purchase a 110-ton punch press so that it could make its own blanks quickly for many of its parts. The press had also permitted the development of some press work for outside customers.

QUALITY CONTROL

Quality at Norcen was pursued by following what the quality control manager termed "the

Norcen way." Typically, these steps were followed in working on a job:

1. The foreman wrote the process sheet.
2. The foreman would then discuss the process sheet with the assigned operator and make any changes.
3. Each operator was responsible for his own setup.
4. The first piece would be checked, first by the operator, usually with the shop's coordinate measuring machine, and then by an inspector.
5. The job would be run in lots of 5 (usually) and each 5th piece would be inspected. If it did not pass inspection, all the previous 4 pieces would be checked 100 percent, and the next 5 pieces would be inspected 100 percent as well.
6. Quality was the joint responsibility of the operator and of quality control.
7. All finished jobs would be sampled by QC for final inspection.

The QC manager noted that the keys to quality were following the proper steps for the job and performing some steps with such tight tolerances that subsequent work, which relied on the previous machining, all fell within acceptable limits.

Recordkeeping

When an operator completed his assigned task on any job, he completed the job sheet (Figure B3) attached to the blueprint. On this sheet he filled in his name, the date, the operation he performed, the quantity he completed, and the length of time it took him to complete the task, including setup time. In

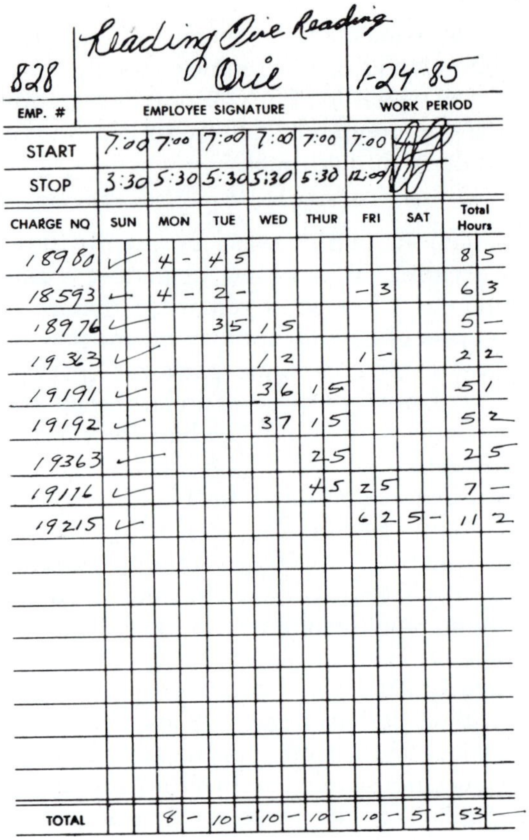

EMP. #: 828 | EMPLOYEE SIGNATURE: Reading Orie Reading / Orie | WORK PERIOD: 1-24-85

START	7:00	7:00	7:00	7:00	7:00	7:00		
STOP	3:30	5:30	5:30	5:30	5:30	12:00		
CHARGE NO	SUN	MON	TUE	WED	THUR	FRI	SAT	Total Hours
18980	✓	4 -	4 5					8 5
18593	✓	4 -	2 -			- 3		6 3
18976	✓		3 5	1 5				5 —
19363	✓			1 2		1 -		2 2
19191	✓			3 6	1 5			5 1
19192	✓			3 7	1 5			5 2
19363	✓				2 5			2 5
19116	✓				4 5	2 5		7 —
19215	✓					6 2	5 -	11 2
TOTAL		8 -	10 -	10 -	10 -	10 -	5 -	53 —

Notes:

1. This is Orie Reading's time card for the week beginning January 24, 1985. This was a busy time at Norcen, and Orie worked 53 total hours during the week, including two hours of overtime from Tuesday through Friday and five hours on Saturday.
2. During the week, Reading worked on nine different jobs. He worked on the job we are most interested in, #18980, on Monday and Tuesday, for 4 and 4.5 hours, respectively. On Monday he also worked 4 hours on job 18593, and on Tuesday, he worked on job 18976 as well.
3. By totaling the hours by each worker on each job as recorded on these time cards, Lillian Gehret has another, independent estimate of the hours worked on any job. These estimates can be compared with the hours totaled on the job sheets.

FIGURE B6 A sample of an operator's time card used at Norcen Industries.

addition, at the end of the day, each operator completed a time card (Figure B6), listing the time spent on each job during the day.

In this way, Lillian Gehret had two records of the time each operator spent on each of the jobs done in the shop. Knowing the times and the wages of each operator involved in any job permitted Lillian to calculate the labor cost of that job. She made this calculation weekly and took care to see that any discrepancies in the two time records were resolved. Usually, the daily time cards were more accurate than the job sheets.

Knowing this information, at the close of every job Lillian would complete the record card (Figure B1), which Joe relied on for making quotes on repeat business. As a rule of thumb for calculating the profitability of a job, Lillian multiplied total labor-hours by the relevant charge-out rate ($24 to 30 per hour) and com-pared that total with the total price Norcen had quoted. She alerted Joe to any major deviations in that comparison, either positive or negative. Subsequent bids could be based accordingly.

In the summer of 1991, Norcen Industries committed to the purchase of an IBM A/S 400 minicomputer so that it could run some job shop-specific job control software. This software would automate much of the bookkeeping work now done by hand. Job histories would be kept on the computer, by customer and by part number so that quoting would become easier. It would handle order entry of jobs; billing and shipping; financial tasks such as payables, receivables, and the general ledger; inventories; and job tracking in the shop itself. Information for tracking jobs would come from the daily information now kept by hand. There were plans eventually to use bar-coding to collect the shop information.

PART TWO

DISCUSSION

Norcen Industries is in no way responsible for the following views and presentation. They remain solely the responsibility of the author.

The Process Flow

Compared with the continuous flow process at International Paper's Androscoggin Mill, the job shop process at Norcen Industries is strikingly loose and ill-defined. A process flow diagram becomes difficult to draw in any precise or meaningful way. For example, we might sketch a process flow diagram such as in Figure B7. Although many of the parts made at Norcen Industries would have passed through exactly this sequence of operations, many more would have required a different set of operations and a different order. Some of the differences might be minor, but there are a host of parts for which the differences are major. At best, Figure B7's flow diagram can be termed a dominant flow or, perhaps, a preferred, simplified flow. For the most part, the job shop process exhibits great product flux and flexibility. Work-in-process can be routed anywhere within the shop so that even

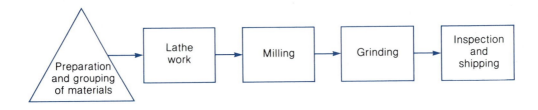

FIGURE B7   A dominant, or preferred, process flow diagram for Norcen Industries.

extraordinary machining requirements can be met.

THE INFORMATION FLOW

What is not flexible but is almost totally rigid in the job shop is the flow of information through it. In stark contrast to the diversity of paths a machined part can take through the shop, information flows in a prescribed way (see Figure B8). Record keeping is done in the same manner for every order; the responsibilities of the workers, bookkeeper, and managers toward information in the process never vary. Everyone has fixed information tasks to perform: quoting, job sheet and blueprint preparation, release to the shop, filling out of job sheets and time cards, labor cost calculations, updating of quote record cards, and signaling of any variances.

The reason for all this rigidity, of course, is that the job shop lives and dies by its ability to process information. Significantly, too, the information flows in the job shop are as much from worker to management (job sheets, time cards, process suggestions, machine breakdowns) as from management to worker (job and machine assignments, schedules, quality control checks, troubleshooting, training). With-

out suitable records, there would be no clear or readily available means of routing an order through the shop or of specifying exactly what should be done to satisfy it. Without suitable records, the job shop's managers would have little idea how to bid for various jobs. Without suitable records, advances in productivity would be more sporadic and less well retained for future use. Without suitable records, managers would not be able to load the shop effectively. Information and the responsibility of everyone in a job shop to maintain its accuracy and smooth flow constitute the glue by which this type of process is held together.

CAPACITY IN THE JOB SHOP

In the job shop at Norcen Industries, capacity is as ambiguous as the process flow's pattern. No single measure of capacity makes complete sense. While a paper mill can measure its capacity rather straightforwardly in tons per day or some similar measure, a machine shop like Norcen Industries cannot readily do the same thing. The large and constantly changing mix of products in the typical job shop ensures that a simple count of units produced is a meaningless way to gauge what the shop's effective capacity really is. We must avoid that simple

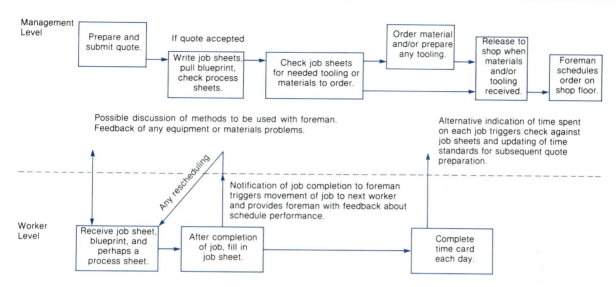

FIGURE B8   An information flow diagram for Norcen Industries.

measure in favor of one that transcends the product mix problem. The easiest remedy is to measure capacity in dollar terms, but that still leaves us with a variety of options. Dollars of typical output per unit of time? Dollars of output per worker? Dollars of output per machine? Dollars of output per dollar of machine value (at cost? at replacement cost?)? All of these measures grab a piece of what we mean intuitively when we say capacity, and yet no one of them fully describes the concept. Only over the long term, when we can feel comfortable that the mix of products has been representative, can we point at differences in shop output over time or output per worker or output per machine as valid measures of high or low capacity. In the short run, no capacity measure is clearly appropriate. Any measure of the shop's capacity is dependent on a host of factors, such as:

1. *Lot sizes.* The larger the lots ordered, the fewer setups in any one day and the greater the number of pieces produced, other things being equal.

2. *Complexity of the pieces worked on.* The more complex the piece, the more likely it will require a large succession of operations and thus the more likely its manufacture will demand a succession of time-consuming setups and difficult scheduling decisions. Of course, this factor is relatively more important in accounting for differences in the number of units manufactured than it is in accounting for differences in dollar value measures of capacity.

3. *Mix of jobs already on the shop floor.* The number and nature of orders already released to the shop floor affect the capacity of the shop in at least two ways: shifting bottlenecks and worker–machine interference.

    Many of the orders in the shop may require the services of particular machines. We can expect, then, that some orders may back up while awaiting a particular machine or operation. Further, we can expect to see such bottlenecks occurring from time to time all over the shop. That is, we can expect to see work-in-process inventories building up in different places and at different times in the shop. A smooth-running, well-scheduled job shop will have a low number of such "shifting bottlenecks," but given the diversity of output and run lengths within a job shop process, they are absolutely unavoidable.

In a typical job shop, there will be many machines that require the constant attention of a worker when they are in operation. Increasingly, however, automatic equipment is entering the shop with its ability to perform without the constant "hands-on" attention of the workforce. This advance is not without a challenge of its own. While automatic equipment frees up worker time, only the (sometimes fortuitous) scheduling of two or more jobs to the same worker actually leads to greater worker productivity apart from any speed advances built into the automatic equipment itself. If the scheduling cannot mesh two or more jobs together, the machine can be said to "interfere" with the worker, and capacity in the shop drops relative to the situation where the worker can easily operate two or more pieces of equipment at once. For this reason, Joe Gehret and his managers positioned machinery within the shop to maximize the possibilities for reducing worker-machine interference.

4. *Ability to schedule work well.* As Joe Gehret himself put it, "Scheduling is the most difficult function we have around here." The matching of workers to machines and of workers and machines to jobs often separates a profitable job shop from an unprofitable one. Good scheduling lessens shifting bottlenecks and worker–machine interference. Poor scheduling introduces more work-in-process inventory to the shop than is necessary. In particular, if too many rush orders are permitted in the shop, their scheduling will become difficult, often necessitating the interruption of runs on machines already set up.

As was noted in the process description, in recessionary times management has many fewer jobs from which to choose to keep all the shop's machining centers busy and to avoid bottlenecks. In better economic times, management can search through the released orders for jobs that can help smooth the flow of work through the shop.

5. *Process improvements.* Any advances in the methods employed in producing a part at Norcen Industries permitted the shop to increase its capacity and thus its profitability. With so many orders passing through the shop, there are many opportunities for improving the process: resequencing of operations, different use of machines, quicker setups, special jigs or fixtures for increasing speed and/or accuracy, possible redesign of the piece ordered. Because any of these improvements takes time to work through, it is likely that only the higher volume, repeat business will benefit from such attention.

6. *Number of machines and their condition.* It is obvious that, even without expanding the workforce, the addition of equipment to the shop is likely to increase capacity detectably. For one thing, rush orders will be less likely to necessitate the dismantling of existing machine setups before completion of the run. Having more machines also increases the probability of finding favorable combinations of orders to lessen worker–machine interference. Fewer bottlenecks, too, are likely to occur with the addition of more equipment. It is evident as well that machines in good condition are less likely to break down and thus demand attention both for themselves and for the rescheduling of operations through the shop.

Technological advances, notably the evolution from manual to NC machines to CNC machines and then to DNC machines, have greatly influenced the shop's capacity. Setups are often easier with the more advanced machine tools; more time can be spent actually cutting metal. Moreover, the newer tools permit fancier machining (such as curved shapes) to be done with greater accuracy, higher speed, and less scrap. And given that the machining was accomplished via tape or computer instruction, the new equipment does not tie up workers as long as the older equipment did.

7. *Quantity and quality of labor input.* Another obvious set of factors affecting the capacity of a job shop is drawn from the labor force itself. Overtime and second shift work is a standard way to augment capacity with the same stock of plant and equipment. Employing inexperienced workers and having to train them is a drain on capacity, however.

Obvious in identification but subtle in design and application is an incentive system for the workers. At Norcen Industries, the bonus plan that was dependent on company profits was viewed by the workers as a fair and reasonable spur for continued good work. But it is not the only payment system that could be installed; different systems might have different effects on worker effort and thus on capacity.

Increasing the capacity of a job shop in the way outlined here, at little or no cost, is important to the shop because that is how it makes its money. Of course, the shop must be flexible enough to bid on a tremendous variety of jobs, but the shop's ability to earn any profit, once granted the business, is linked fundamentally to its capacity and its knowledge of that capacity. As we have discussed, these two items are influenced by a number of factors, many of which require the accurate processing of information around the shop.

THE ROLE OF STANDARDS AND INCENTIVES

Time standards for all of the operations to be performed at Norcen Industries are an integral feature of its cost estimation and bidding responsibilities. Some of the standards are developed internally, mostly through past experience doing the same thing; but others are supplied by the customer when bids are solicited, having been worked out for or by the customer.

The standards are a useful guide for both workers and managers. For the workers, the standards (written on the job sheet) provide continual feedback on how well they are doing the job. For managers, the standards provide information on how long certain jobs should take and thus how they might be scheduled. The standards also provide management with a yardstick for worker performance that is useful not only for making advancement/layoff decisions but also for determining which tasks each worker does relatively better.

Other than by furnishing feedback for each worker, the time standards are not tied formally to any incentive system. Incentives for good work and/or for speedy work are provided either through knowledge that such work often contributes to better company profits (although such work is not the only determinant of profits, by far) or by the prodding and cajoling of the foreman. In job shops like Norcen Industries, the foreman carries much of the responsibility for pacing work through the shop and for ensuring that the quality is satisfactory.

QUESTIONS

1. Write up a hypothetical job sheet for an order and briefly explain each column entry. How do the functions of the job sheet and the record card differ?

2. Can you make any generalizations about cost reductions from the example of Norcen Industries? Do these generalizations apply to any other process with which you are already familiar?

3. Why might scheduling be "the most difficult function" in a job shop?

4. "The job shop lives and dies by its ability to process information." Discuss this comment and compare the information flow in the job shop with that in another type of process.

5. Discuss three of the factors that influence a job shop's capacity. What might be "the perfect set of circumstances" in a shop foreman's eyes?

6. As a worker, which would you prefer: the calm predictability of the continuous flow process or the frequently frantic unpredictability of the job shop? As a manager, which would you prefer? How might your attitude affect the setting of standards and incentives in each process?

7. Norcen's foreman places particular emphasis on meeting customer due dates. Due dates thus significantly affect the scheduling that is done. Suppose, however, that due dates were not as important to you as the foreman. What other factors could take precedence? How could they serve as the basis for scheduling jobs through the shop? Under what circumstances might different factors take precedence in establishing scheduling rules?

8. Suppose that you were forced to justify to upper management the purchase of new technology, such as a CNC machine, for an existing job shop. Where would you look for the benefits of such an addition to the shop? How would you measure the extent of those benefits?

9. What advantages do you see to a layout such as that used at Norcen Industries? What disadvantages do you see?

SITUATION FOR STUDY B-1

OWENS, INC.

Fred and Ralph own and operate a small machine and metal fabrication shop. Most of their business involves small orders from local industry. These orders are usually ones that the larger customer firms farm out because they do not have the excess capacity. In other words, Fred and Ralph provide "slack" capacity to the larger firms. Figure B9 shows the plant layout.

Fred and Ralph feel that if they can once get an order in their shop, they can learn how to make the part and then underbid on future orders. Moreover, they think they can make most parts more cheaply than the customer can in house.

They are currently considering bidding on part 273. Figure B10 is an engineering sketch of this part. For the first order the customer will supply a coil of 1 5/8 cold-rolled steel (CRS), but Fred and Ralph are investigating to see whether other processes might use other sizes of raw material more efficiently. The proposed order is for 500 pieces, with possible future orders of 500 per month. The proposed bid must be submitted in 2 weeks, the bid

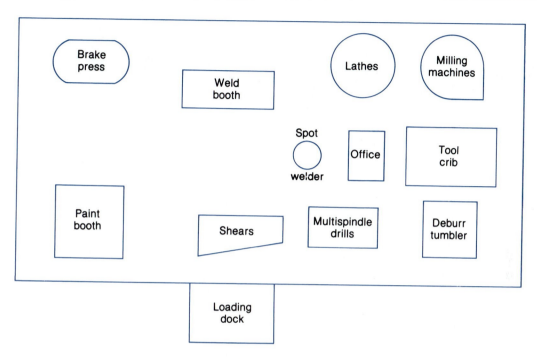

FIGURE B9   Plant layout for Owens, Inc.

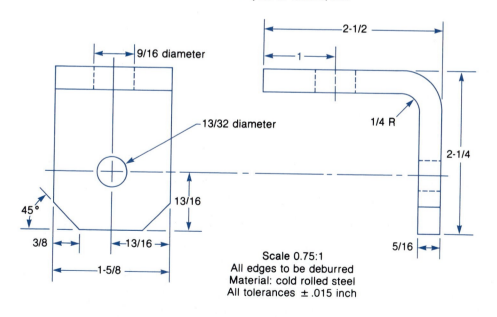

Scale 0.75:1
All edges to be deburred
Material: cold rolled steel
All tolerances ± .015 inch

FIGURE B10   Engineering sketch for part 273, a bracket.

Table B2 Process sheet for part 273 (Owens, Inc.)

OPERATION SEQUENCE	MACHINE	OPERATION	SETUP TIME (minutes)	OPERATION TIME PER UNIT (minutes)
1	Shear 3	Shear to length	5	0.030
2	Shear 3	Shear 45° corners	8	0.050
3	Multispindle drill press 1	Drill both holes and deburr	15	3.000
4	Brake press	Bend 90°	10	0.025
5	Tumbler	Deburr	5	a
6		Pack in boxes		30.000

a The deburr operation can be left unattended, so the only labor required is to load and unload.

award determined within 1 week, and the 500 units delivered 1 month after that.

Fred has generated the estimates shown in Table B2. The cost estimates used for bids are $10.55 per hour for labor and $18.50 per hour for machines—or $29.05 per hour for one worker/one machine operations. Any time "sold" at this rate makes Owens a margin of 25 percent with which to cover indirect costs such as administrative costs.

1. If you were Fred and Ralph, what other aspects of the shop, the market, and the future would you consider regarding the bid for part 273?

2. Analyze the current proposal and then generate a bid to the customer and a rough shop schedule.

SITUATION FOR STUDY B-2

STREETER DIE & STAMPING COMPANY

Streeter Tool & Die Company was founded in 1956 by entrepreneur Jack Streeter. For 20 years the small firm flourished, furnishing tools, dies, jigs, and fixtures to metal stamping firms. In 1976 the firm became Streeter Die & Stamping Company (SDS) and began a move toward a new business. Today SDS has two plants in Toledo, Ohio, furnishing metal stampings and assemblies primarily to the major U.S. automakers. In the most recent year, General Motors (GM) accounted for 85 percent of SDS's sales.

The main plant (plant 1) had 14 presses, ranging in power from 20 to 1000 tons, that stamped out metal parts from raw steel. Production was usually based on firm customer orders, but occasionally some forecasting of future orders was done in an attempt to get longer, more efficient production runs.

The secondary plant (plant 2), representing a type of forward vertical integration for SDS, was more labor intensive than plant 1. Plant 2 specialized in the assembly and welding of parts stamped at plant 1. Extra space at plant 2 was used as a finished goods warehouse for any parts made at plant 1 or 2 that would not be shipped within 1 week.

The orders that SDS normally produced were contracts that SDS had won by submitting quotes to the customer. In the case of GM contracts, it was known at SDS that price was not always the deciding factor; SDS's record for quality and timeliness played an important role in winning many of these contracts.

Raw materials arriving at SDS, almost all of them coils weighing 1 to 5 tons, were stored in a warehouse adjacent to plant 1. When the steel was needed in the shop, a forklift picked it up and brought it to the press where it was to be used. From this point, the steel could go through many different combinations of presses and operations, depending on the specific part being made.

In general, the first operation involved running the steel through an automatic press. Steel coils were hoisted onto a reel and fed into the press automatically. The stamped parts fell off the press into bins, which the press operators occasionally checked to see whether the parts were being stamped properly. When the order had been completed, the remaining part of the steel coil was removed from the reel and stored against the shop wall. For several parts this operation was the only one necessary; a random sample of these parts was inspected by quality control and, if the parts were good, they were taken to the loading dock and prepared for shipping.

After passing a quality inspection, bins of more complex parts were moved to nonautomatic presses for the rest of their stamping operations, such as piercing, drawing, and forming. These operations were much slower, because the parts had to be placed manually into the dies by the press operators. These operations completed some parts. Other parts were sent to a vendor for sandblasting, painting, heat treating, and/or deburring before being shipped to the customer; still others were sent to plant 2, where several component parts were welded and/or assembled into the finished product.

The finished goods inventory at SDS was relatively small. Parts that were to be shipped within one week were stacked along the walls of the loading docks at both plants so that forklift drivers could easily spot which parts must be loaded onto a certain truck.

Smooth operations at SDS were extremely dependent on a coordinated, accurate information flow. The information flow followed a cycle that began and ended with engineering submitting a quote for a contract. If information was not accurate at one point in the cycle, the results could have a domino effect on the various departments at SDS. To help improve information flow, all departments at SDS used an IBM System 34 computer extensively.

After analyzing customers' blueprints and past SDS results on similar parts, engineering quoted prices per piece for lot sizes ranging from 100 to 600,000 pieces per year. Reflecting the fixed costs of initial tooling, the price per piece decreased as the lot size increased. After winning a contract, SDS had 6 to 8 months before its first shipment was due on a new part and 3 to 4 months on a carryover part.

During the 6 to 8 months before the first due date, engineering was responsible for getting the shop ready for production. This included ordering the tooling from a vendor, drawing up process sheets for each subassembly, determining what presses could or should be used to stamp each part, assigning part numbers to new parts, and entering all pertinent data about each part into the computer. Engineering also sent a copy of the contract and process sheets to production planning so that they had a record or parts that had to be scheduled in the near future.

Production planning needed no further information until 13 weeks before the first shipment due date. The data systems manager had designed a computer program that received information directly from GM's computer each Monday morning and printed out a list of SDS's week-by-week requirements over the next 13 weeks; the first 2 weeks were required by contract to be firm. When new parts showed up on the list, production planning had to (1) check with engineering to see how the tooling was progressing, (2) order materials, and (3) schedule a sample run. No full production runs could be shipped to GM or other top customers until samples had been approved.

The Monday morning printout listed other important information for each part, such as the number of pieces on hand, the week in which the number on hand would be insufficient to cover cumulative requirements, and the amount of components and raw materials on hand for each part. The production scheduler used this report to determine which parts would have to be made 2 weeks into the future. The scheduler filled out a small card for each operation that must be performed and posted the card on a schedule board that enabled him to schedule work on each press for the present week and the next 2 weeks.

While the scheduler was busy loading the presses, a production planning assistant used another copy of this report to determine raw material requirements over the entire 13 weeks. Any materials that SDS would not have enough of to meet these requirements were written on a material requisition, which was delivered to the purchasing agent for further action.

Each morning, after surveying the progress on the shop floor, analyzing the previous day's production summary, and updating the schedule board, the scheduler brought to the shop foreman (1) a schedule of parts to be stamped in each press, (2) routing cards for each part, and (3) process sheets with pictures of each operation. Press operators used counters on the presses to count the number of pieces stamped each shift, each day, and each production run. When the total count for the run reached the

number on the routing card, the operator signed the routing card, wrote on his activity card his shift count and his hours spent on the part, and signaled the foreman for a new job. At the end of each shift, the foreman gathered all the activity cards and summarized the data into the daily production summary. In addition to the scheduler's use of this summary, the inventory control specialist combined this information with shipping and receiving data to update inventories on the computer files daily. Keying in this inventory data and some additional cost data also updated financial and job cost data, thus completing the information flow cycle and ensuring that accounting and engineering had access to the information necessary for preparing monthly financial statements and accurate quotes on parts contracts.

A somewhat separate line of information flowed between the shipping department and the billing clerks. Each day shipping filled out a list of the parts, with quantities, that it had shipped. This list was delivered to the billing clerks who, at the end of each day, wired these shipments into the customers' computers. With this method, the customers' procurement agents knew exactly from day to day which parts were in transit, and both SDS and its customers had a common reference date if questions arose about a particular shipment.

Often, the information flow was less formal when customers' procurement agents called and asked for early delivery or when SDS was behind schedule on a part. Information flow became a matter of someone from production planning personally expediting these orders through the shop and arranging special rush transportation.

1. To the extent that you can, diagram the process and information flows.

2. Sales at Streeter Die & Stamping recently increased and bottlenecks emerged in the

operation, although the exact cause of the bottlenecks was not immediately obvious. How would you determine where any bottlenecks were? Be specific.

3. How would you control the levels of inventory? How would you monitor and, perhaps, change the status of jobs in the company? What things could the computer do?

A BATCH FLOW PROCESS
Jos. A. Bank Clothiers
Hampstead Manufacturing Operations
Hampstead, Maryland

Jos. A. Bank Clothiers was a maker of high-quality, traditionally styled men's and women's clothes—primarily suits, sport coats, slacks, and skirts. It sold these clothes along with shirts, ties, and other accessories through 40 retail stores[a] and an extensive mail-order business. Compared with retailers of similar clothes, the company used lower price mark-ups and had a lower overhead. These features, combined with manufacturing efficiencies, permitted Jos. A. Bank to market its high-quality clothes at prices significantly lower than those of its competitors. In early July 1981, Quaker Oats purchased Jos. A. Bank Clothiers from the Bank family, who had owned and operated the company since its founding in 1902. Quaker Oats, in turn, sold the company in late 1986 to a group of investors in a leveraged buyout.

The company employed 625 people in manufacturing, 34 of whom were salaried managers. There were three manufacturing plants in Maryland—one in Baltimore and the other two in rural Hampstead. The Hampstead plants did all of the company's cutting, and produced men's coats and all the women's clothes. The Baltimore plant, situated on North Avenue, produced men's coats and all the pants. All warehousing and distribution were accomplished in Hampstead.

The Hampstead plants were located within a few miles of each other. The larger of the two, a former Black and Decker manufacturing site that was acquired in November 1986, housed both the distribution center and the cutting room. As a result of its acquisition, an older, multistory operation in downtown Baltimore was closed and the work and workforce relocated to either the North Avenue or Hampstead facilities.

---

[a]Two stores were in the Baltimore area (on Light Street in downtown Baltimore and in Towson, north of the city). Other stores were located in Atlanta, Birmingham, Boston (2), Buffalo, Charlotte, Chicago (4), Cincinnati, Cleveland, Columbus, Dallas, Denver, Detroit (2), Houston (2), Indianapolis, Los Angeles, Louisville, Memphis, Minneapolis, Nashville, Philadelphia (2), Pittsburgh, Raleigh, Richmond, Rochester, St. Louis, Stamford, Summit (NJ), Washington, D.C. (3), and Winston-Salem.

PART ONE

PROCESS DESCRIPTION

THE PROCESS FLOW

The making of a high-quality sportcoat or suit coat was a complex endeavor, encompassing 140 to 150 distinct operations (see Figure C1). The coat was an assembly of various parts, including sleeves, backs, fronts, facings, collars, and pockets. Each of these parts, in turn, combined the basic fabric for the coat itself (known as piece goods) with 40 to 50 trim items. These trim items included linings, fusings (the firm material fused by heat to various parts of the piece goods to help them retain their shape and resist wear), pocketing, stays, tape, thread, and buttons. The assembly of pants and skirts was less complex.

The Cutting Room

The assembly of a suit or coat began when a bolt of fabric (the piece goods) was withdrawn from raw materials inventory and examined. Any flaws were marked so that they could be trimmed out during the cutting process. The examined fabric was then carefully laid on long cutting room tables. This task was known as "spreading" the cloth; depending on the particular order, the number of layers spread ranged from 1 to 110. Once spread, a paper pattern known as a marker was placed over the layers of fabric.[b] The coat, vest, pants, and/or skirt pattern pieces were carefully arranged on it so that as little fabric as possible was wasted. This

[b]Only occasionally would a pattern have to be chalked on fabric by hand.

arrangement was generated by one of two special computer-based marker-making instruments (AM-5s, made by Gerber Garment Technologies) and was printed out, ready to be used. The AM-5 could easily adjust sizes and arrange the pieces in the most efficient pattern. For example, certain suit sizes (such as 40 regulars and 41 regulars or 39 regulars and 43 regulars) might be combined efficiently on the marker pattern. The markers were stapled to the layers of fabric and the fabric was cut using either electric cutters or manual shears, depending on the number of layers and the outline of the pattern.

The pieces that composed the same coat and/or pants were cut from the same layer in the spread fabric. After being cut, they were matched together and assembled (this assembly was termed "fitting") into various groups of materials—one group, for example, for the pants, one group for the coat. These matched and assembled cutouts of fabric were then stapled with special identifying numbers by the Soabar marking and ticketing machine (see Figure C2). These numbers were critical in ensuring that material cut for the same suit would stay together throughout the process. After being tagged, the pieces destined for a coat, pants, skirt, or vest were subdivided and assembled, or "fitted", into special bundles with an average of 12 units in each bundle. Bundle sizes ranged from 1 to 22. Bundles were fitted for various segments of the coat, such as sleeves, fronts, backs, collars, facing, and linings. (Flaps and welts (pockets), being movable items, were fitted in the coat shop itself).

continued on p. 61

```
                    MODEL MASTER LISTING                        RPT-PAY032
```

MODEL—S361BCSSHC PLN

OPER	DESCRIPTION	WRKCTR	PRICE	S-A-M	SINGLE	SUB-FLAG
SUB ASSEMBLY 00023—SLEEVE						
27	JN 1ST SLEEVE	00401	.1029	.8542	.1132	
76	FUSE CUFF	00401	.1073	.0000	.1181	
77	MAKE CUFF	00401	.1292	.0000	.1422	
75	JN ELBW SEAM	00401	.2704	.0000	.2974	
128	UNPRE FIR SLE	00401	.0865	.7835	.0909	
129	UNPRE SEC SLE	00401	.0898	.9624	.0940	
SUB ASSEMBLY TOTAL			.7861	2.6001	.8558	
SUB ASSEMBLY 01017—SLEEVE—LINING						
226	MK SLEEVE LIN	00402	.1533	1.0259	.1685	
273	MK BTN SHANK	00402	.0360	.3190	.0376	N
277	FEL CUF1TURN	00402	.1585	.9938	.1744	
281	SEW 3BUT1TURN	00402	.1525	1.5159	.1679	Y
376	TK LN1TURN	00402	.1253	1.0853	.1315	
427	MATCH SLEEVE	00402	.0465	.4607	.0488	
SUB ASSEMBLY TOTAL			.6721	5.4006	.7287	
SUB ASSEMBLY 04058—BACK						
744	MK BK FUL LIN	00405	.5091	3.9938	.5601	
777	FUSE BK TAPE	00405	.0463	.3321	.0510	
822	PR BK FUL LIN	00405	.0986	.2128	.1036	
834	TK VT SM FL	00405	.0880	.5365	.0924	
836	FIT BK FUL LN	00405	.1351	.8169	.1419	
902	MATCH BACK	00406	.0475	.4285	.0498	
SUB ASSEMBLY TOTAL			.9246	6.3206	.9988	
SUB ASSEMBLY 05001—CANVAS						
954	CUT GORES	00406	.0522	.3187	.0547	
SUB ASSEMBLY TOTAL			.0522	.3187	.0547	
SUB ASSEMBLY 06043—FACING—LINING						
1031	JOIN LINING	00407	.1986	1.4979	.2185	
1215	PREPARE PKT 2	00407	.0622	.5304	.0683	
1055	REECE IBP	00407	.1389	1.1577	.1527	
1080	FIN 2IBP WFS	00407	.2378	1.9717	.2615	
1085	BANK LBL IBP	00407	.0626	.4668	.0657	
1088	SW XTRA LABEL	00407	.0675	.4622	.0708	Y
1111	SEW CR LB IBP	00000	.0478	.3576	.0501	N
1155	PRESS FACING	00407	.1260	.9002	.1385	
1202	PAIR IN FACING	00407	.0475	.4285	.0498	
SUB ASSEMBLY TOTAL			.9889	7.7730	1.0759	
SUB ASSEMBLY 08036—FLAP						

Notes:

1. This portion of a Model Master Listing details the specific operations to perform, in sequence, for various subassemblies for the coat of suit model 361, a plain fabric Kent Model. These subassemblies include the sleeve, sleeve lining, back, canvas (fusing), facing-lining, and so on. The entire listing contains 13 different subassemblies.

2. Each line consists of an operation number, a description of the operation, the workcenter number where it is performed, the piece rate price for a standard bundle, the standard allowed minutes (not applicable to the Hampstead coat shop), and the piece rate price for a single unit. The Sub-flag column denotes exceptions to the standard that are made for selected coats.

FIGURE C1   Model master listing extract for a man's coat.

The Gerber AM-5 marker making machines. (*Courtesy of Jos. A. Banks Mfg. Co.*)

Spreading cloth in the cutting room. (*Courtesy of Jos. A. Banks Mfg. Co.*)

FIGURE C2 A sample Soabar ticket used by Jos. A. Bank to identify cut fabric.

Each bundle (batch) of materials to be processed in the coat shop would have the same operations performed on each of the pieces in the bundle. For the most part, workers in the shop did the same things to successive bundles of materials. A record of what was to be done to each bundle and how many items were in each traveled with the bundle.

The Coat Shop

Most operations in the coat shop consisted of sewing pieces of the fabric together and/or attaching various trim items to the fabric. The bundles representing parts of the coat were worked on separately in various areas of the coat shop. Periodically, some were brought together to make larger subassemblies before these were joined in the assembly that was the coat itself. At two key places in the shop and at several minor locations, these parts were matched before being sewn into a major subassembly. These matching stations served to control the process, ensuring that all pieces in each bundle were accounted for and that only those pieces of fabric that had been cut together would be assembled into a coat. Once the coat was fully assembled—linings in, welts and flaps sewn, facings fabricated and assembled to fronts, and sleeves assembled to the rest of the coat—it was ready for finishing. In finishing, basting (temporary stitches) was removed, various parts of the coat were pressed, and the coat was thoroughly inspected. Finish pressing for

all coats was accomplished at the central pressing facility at the North Avenue factory. There, each part of the coat was pressed with specific equipment designed to finish it in an impeccable manner. Once inspected, the coat was transported to the matching warehouse in Hampstead. At the matching warehouse, pants and coats for the same suit were placed together and taken to the adjacent distribution center. Orders were filled from the distribution center.

The Skirt Shop

Skirts underwent similar, although simpler processing (see Figure C3). Much as with coats, the cut piece goods for a skirt had been fitted into bundles of from 1 to 20. The cloth was then serged to prevent fraying. The processing that followed could differ from one model to another, but in general, these steps were followed. Cloth for any pleating was sent outside to a vendor with special equipment for putting pleats into skirts. Once returned, the pleats were stitched down. Pockets and zippers were sewn in and any vents were constructed. Then sides were seamed, linings attached, and the waistband was sewn in. The seams were underpressed and the waistband was top stitched. The skirt was then ready to be hemmed. Button holes were cut, buttons sewn on, and finish pressing was accomplished. Inspection concluded the process and the completed skirts were then sent on to the matching warehouse. The skirt shop had a capacity of 225 skirts per day.

THE WORKFORCE AND THE PIECE-RATE SYSTEM

Except for some nonunion clerical workers, all the workers in the Hampstead manufacturing facilities were members of the Amalgamated

```
                    MODEL MASTER LISTING                    RPT-PAY032
```

MODEL-K12XBKS5HS PLN

OPER	DESCRIPTION	WRKCTR	PRICE	S-A-M	SINGLE	SUB-FLAG
SUB ASSEMBLY 21014-WAISTBAND	-					
9000	FIT PNL W/BND	00601	.1974	1.4885	.1974	
SUB ASSEMBLY TOTAL			.1974	1.4885	.1974	
SUB ASSEMBLY 22133-ASSEMBLY	-					
9025	FUSE W/B	00602	.0608	.3435	.0608	
9027	PIPING WB	00602	.0540	.0000	.0540	
9052	SRG PNLS SHRD	00602	.2054	1.5368	.2054	
9100	CUT ZIPPER	00602	.0286	.1618	.0286	
9285	MK FRNT PLTS	00602	.0803	.0000	.0803	
9425	MK BACK GORES	00602	.0671	.8748	.0671	
9474	JN 1CNTR BKSM	00602	.0897	.8465	.0897	
9510	SET ZIPP&FAC	00602	.1899	.8207	.1899	
9526	OV/LK 3SEAMS	00602	.1196	1.5476	.1196	
9531	JOIN SIDESM 2	00602	.1676	1.5808	.1676	
9549	OVERLOCK PKT.	00602	.0827	.8925	.0827	
9554	ATT TP PKT WB	00602	.3143	.0000	.3143	
9577	SW BND BTM VT	00602	.1405	1.1191	.1405	
9604	HEM BOTTOM LN	00602	.1114	1.0178	.1114	
9614	MK VENT ZIPPER	00602	.0814	.8082	.0814	
9615	MAKE VENT LNG	00602	.0814	.8082	.0814	
9620	MK FRTVT CRNS	00602	.1233	1.0854	.1233	
9625	PRS VENT	00602	.0594	.6093	.0594	
9647	ATT LNG WST	00602	.2720	2.1815	.2720	
9700	SEW WAISTBAND	00602	.1758	2.0291	.1758	
9741	SEW 2 LABELS	00602	.0463	.4044	.0463	
9745	MK EXT & CRNR	00602	.1483	.8302	.1483	
9777	T/ST W/B	00602	.1143	1.4745	.1143	
9786	LOCK ZIPPER	00602	.0848	.6536	.0848	
9803	PRS OPN S/S 6	00602	.1131	.0000	.1131	
9810	HEM BOTTOM	00602	.1269	1.2973	.1269	
9811	TACK VENT BTM	00602	.0381	.0000	.0381	
9911	BARTACK ZIPP	00602	.0339	.0000	.0339	
9951	MARK&MK 1 BH	00602	.0473	.3651	.0473	
9961	SEW 1 BUTTON	00602	.0486	.5051	.0486	
9975	OFFPRS.TOPPLT	00602	.1938	1.4340	.1938	
9982	OFPRS BDYW/VT	00602	.2098	1.9258	.2098	
9990	CLEN,EXAM HNG	00602	.2581	2.5879	.2581	
SUB ASSEMBLY TOTAL			3.9685	29.7415	3.9685	
MODEL TOTAL			4.1659	31.2300	4.1659	

Notes:

1. This portion of a Model Listing details the specific operations to perform, in sequence, for the two subassemblies, waist band, and assembly making up skirt K12XBKS5HS, a plain fabric model.

2. Like the Model Master Listing for the coat, each line indicates operation number, operation description, workcenter number, standard bundle piecerate price, standard allowed minutes, single unit piecerate price, and the sub-flag (exceptions) indication.

FIGURE C3   Model master listing for a woman's skirt.

Some hand cutting of cloth. (*Courtesy of Jos. A. Banks Mfg. Co.*)

A roll of cloth on the inspection equipment. (*Courtesy of Jos. A. Banks Mfg. Co.*)

The Soabar ticketing machine. (*Courtesy of Jos. A. Banks Mfg. Co.*)

Clothing and Textile Workers Union. These workers were paid an incentive wage, although the type of incentive differed across departments. Workers in the coat and skirt shops were paid piece rates. These piece rates were the prices in dollars per piece that the company paid for each piece of sewing, pressing, matching, or inspection.

When workers finished their assigned tasks, they detached the appropriate cardboard coupon from the perforated sheet of coupons (Figure C4) that traveled with the job. On the coupon was an operation number that was uniquely identified with the piece rate for performing the indicated job. By accumulating these coupons and turning them in at the end

of the day, workers were paid for exactly what they had done. There was no minimum payment and no maximum payment. In actuality, the wage payment averages in the coat and skirt shops ran about 110 percent of the established standard, with a range for experienced workers from 80 percent of the standard to 160 percent. The coupons that workers turned in were read by a laser wand so that payroll and work-in-process were tracked automatically.

This piece rate system was modified somewhat for the cutting room workers. Before about 1978, workers in the cutting room were paid by the hour. At that time, however, it was felt that the output of the cutting room could be increased if it, too, were put on some incen-

FIGURE C4   Coupons.

Notes:

1. This is a portion of a page of coupons that had been placed onto a sheet of paper as a record of what a piecerate worker (B. Fuhrman) had done during the day. Whenever she completed a bundle, she detached the relevant coupon. The payroll department then wands the top row with a laser scanning wand and creates this record page.

2. The top row is used for payroll purposes only and indicates the shop number, bundle number, and operator number.

3. The middle row provides a description of the operation and, where appropriate, indicates what trim items are to be used.

4. The bottom indicates the bundle number, the cut number (same as shop number), the operation number, and the quantity in the bundle.

5. The Coupons Entered—50 and Count Entered—130 are merely check codes for the payroll office.

tive plan. A consulting firm was brought in, and standards were set for all operations in the cutting room—spreading the fabric, cutting the patterns, and other tasks. The standards set were called "standard allowed minutes" (S-A-M) for doing particular jobs. All the jobs in the cutting room were studied and rates were set. Thus, workers in the cutting room were paid for the standard allowed minutes that they acquired rather than for the pieces of work that

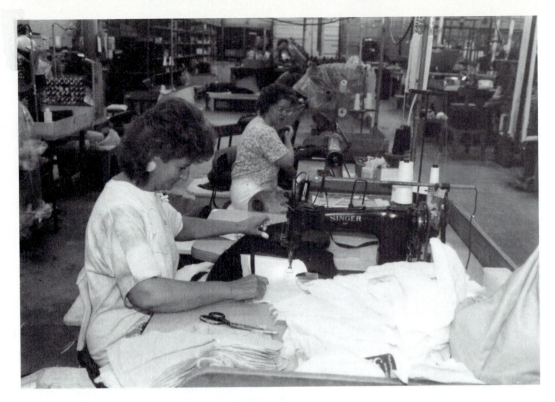

Seamstresses in the shop. Note the bundle in the foreground.
(*Courtesy of Jos. A. Banks Mfg. Co.*)

A seamstress in the dress shop.
(*Courtesy of Jos. A. Banks Mfg. Co.*)

The major matching station.
(*Courtesy of Jos. A. Banks Mfg. Co.*)

they were able to finish. However, a pay floor was established; workers who did not accumulate 8 hours of standard allowed minutes during the day earned a set base rate. Workers who accumulated more than 8 hours of standard allowed minutes were paid for those minutes. In fact, the average in the cutting room ran between 120 and 125 percent of the established standards, with the range being between 100 and 160 percent for experienced workers. Workers were paid by filing incentive declarations that documented start and stop times for various operations. There were no coupons to detach as in the coat or skirt shop. This incentive system did, in fact, increase the productivity of the cutting room dramatically.

There were times when workers were not paid piece rates but were paid the average of their work. This occurred whenever a worker was taken off his or her standard job to do something else. For example, if a worker was asked to fill in for an absent colleague, that worker was taken off the piece-rate system. Similarly, if a worker was asked to work on something new or something special, piece rates were removed.

Once a piece rate had been established, it could not be changed without some change in model, materials, methods, or machinery. There were literally thousands of piece rates that could apply in the shop, and typically less than 10 percent of them were changed each year. Some had remained unchanged for years. Many changes were, in fact, triggered by a worker's retirement. (Turnover was only 2 to 3 percent a year.)

Management recognized that the piece-rate system caused some wage inequities in the factory, but there seemed to be no clear solutions. It was known, for example, that some piece rates were tight whereas others were loose; but if no changes were contemplated to those jobs, management could not remedy those inequities easily without union consent. Spotting such inequities was not always simple. Variations in performance across operators doing the same job could range from 90 percent of the standard to 150 percent. Given such variations, it was often hard to say that a particular piece rate was loose when for at least some workers it might be considered tight.

Setting New Piece Rates

Establishing new piece rates was the responsibility of the factory's industrial engineer, who spent about 60 percent of his time determining piece rates and the rest of his time calculating the factory's unit costs and following up on special projects (such as studying new equipment purchases). The first step the industrial engineer took in setting a new piece rate in the coat or skirt shop was to meet with the foreman in charge to discuss the procedure that the foreman thought was required to do a good-quality job. An operator was then brought in and informed of the new task. He or she was given some time to become familiar with the work. After that time the industrial engineer observed the operator for about an hour and a half, informing the operator that this study would result in the establishment of the piece rate.

During this observation period, the industrial engineer used an electronic time study board—a clipboard to which was attached a special digital readout stopwatch that kept track of various times. By pressing a lever the engineer could indicate the beginning of one element of the job (jobs were composed of 2 to 30 elements) or the end of another. The time study board would then freeze the duration measured so that the engineer could write it down while at the same time accumulating the time of the next element of the job. In this way the industrial engineer isolated particular movements and tasks. The engineer could also evaluate whether the operator was working as

Pressing a coat. (*Courtesy of Jos. A. Banks Mfg. Co.*)

efficiently as possible and just where improvements could be made.

Setting piece rates was complicated by an agreement the company had with the union. That agreement specified that workers would be given the opportunity to maintain the same average wage no matter where they worked in the shop. Abiding by this agreement meant that new piece rates for established workers in the company had to be constructed specifically for those workers. As could be expected, new jobs with new piece rates were generally assigned to new workers, since that was one means by which costs could be kept under control.

This company–union agreement made setting piece rates in the coat and skirt shops somewhat more difficult than setting rates in the cutting room. To comply with the agreement in the cutting room, all that needed to be changed was the base pay of the operator. The standard allowed minutes for a task remained the same. However, for average wages in the coat and skirt shops to be maintained, some juggling of the piece rates normally assigned to a worker had to be done. The old piece-rate system was not as "clean" as the newer standard allowed minutes system. (In fact, the North Avenue factory and the Hampstead distribution center had adopted the standard allowed minute system from the start.)

Once the piece rate was established, the industrial engineer informed the worker of it.

The union was also notified. Often this was all that was needed, although many times some negotiation with the union ensued. Sometimes a restudy of the job was done to dispel any disagreements. Some restudies lasted as long as 8 hours. When a piece rate was first changed, it was deemed "unapproved," but usually after a month the union and management would agree that the piece rate was fair. Then the rate was formally approved until it had to be changed because of changes in model, materials, methods, or machinery. The company wanted to set rates that could be beat if the workers worked hard—but not so tight that the workers felt they were not earning a fair incentive wage. In 9 out of 10 cases there was little problem in establishing a piece rate, although company and union both had to compromise their initial positions to some degree.

The Nature of the Workforce

Most of the workforce had had years of experience in the apparel industry. The union was a great help in recommending skilled workers to the company. Thus, there was little problem in educating new workers to tasks. They already knew fairly well what was required of them; with a little training and help from supervision, these workers were able to meet Jos. A. Bank's high quality standards.

For the most part, once a new operator was assigned a job, it was likely that he or she stayed at that job until retirement. Almost all of the workers spent many years at the same level in the company; only about 10 percent attempted to elevate their grade. Advancement was possible, and workers could request transfers to higher-rate jobs through a formal job posting system for vacancies.

The company's relations with the union were good. It helped that the company was growing in an industry that, for the most part, had suffered severe employment declines. In the last 20 years there had been only one strike, and it was resolved very quickly. Worker complaints were few—only two or three informal complaints each week, and these were usually resolved quickly. In general, complaints related to earnings, such as:

- A piece rate was set too low.
- Bundles were not large enough. With bundles of less than 12, the operator suffered some inefficiencies, so a high number of low-count bundles sometimes sparked complaints.
- Too many plaids were put through the factory in a week. Plaids required a great deal of pattern matching and slowed up work in the factory considerably.
- Changes to a new model should require a new piece rate.

As many as 90 percent of these complaints were resolved by the factory's first-line supervision. There was, however, a formal grievance procedure, which involved supervision at the first level, the plant manager at the second level, the vice-president of manufacturing at the third level, and then arbitration at the fourth level. There had been only two arbitration proceedings in the last 15 years. Most of the complaints taken to higher levels of the grievance procedure related to firings, which typically occurred for absenteeism or poor quality of work. For the most part, union involvement could save a worker from the first threat of firing; but if the worker did not improve, management could fire the worker without union intercession. The only instant and uncontested dismissals were for theft, gross insubordination, or fighting in the factory.

Dismissal, of course, was the most radical form of discipline that the company used. Other levels of discipline were usually used before a dismissal. The most minor form of discipline was a verbal warning, and in most cases two or three verbal warnings were given before a written warning was issued. This written warning would give the reason for the warning, suggest a way for the worker to correct matters, state what the next step would be if the worker did not improve, and indicate at what future time the worker would be reviewed again. If the worker did not improve, there might be another written warning, and after that would come suspension from work. Some suspensions carried definite starting and ending dates, while others were of indefinite duration. Only if these measures did not resolve matters would the worker be dismissed.

Worker pay depended on the task and the shop. Average hourly wages in the Hampstead coat shop averaged $8.34; in the cutting room, $8.25; in the skirt shop $8.05; and in the distribution center, $7.21.

In addition to these wages, Bank paid about 41 percent of base salary in benefits. These included medical and disability insurance, life insurance, a pension plan, an eye care plan, a prescription plan, and holiday and vacation pay. All of these plans were administered through the union.

It was the responsibility of the factory's industrial engineer to monitor costs and piece rates once they were set. Foremen also helped monitor tasks, since they had to sign off on all worker summary sheets and were required to calculate the percentage efficiencies for each worker. Thus, the workers who were consistently making well above average on their piece rates were known. If their high pay was a surprise, their jobs and/or quality were sometimes studied to make sure that they were not taking shortcuts.

PRODUCTION AND QUALITY CONTROL

Jos. A. Bank's quality standards were rigid. Not only did the company not tolerate sloppy work

in the factory, but it also wanted to make sure that a 40 regular one year exactly matched a 40 regular in every other year.

Quality control started at the beginning of the process. Numerous areas of the factory had their quality checked by the appropriate foremen on every coat or skirt processed. The chief final inspection area, however, was in pressing, after the coat or pair of pants was fully assembled.

The foremen, who supervised between 30 and 35 people each, were responsible chiefly for checking quality and for instilling in the workers an appreciation of what quality is and a desire to flag quality problems themselves. It was the foreman's task as well to approach workers with any rework. Workers were responsible for the quality of their own work, and any rework on their portion of a coat or pants was done without pay. It was to the worker's advantage to do things right the first time, every time. The chief role of first-level supervision at Bank was to check and maintain quality. Nothing else took so much time and care.

The control of production, as opposed to quality, was chiefly the responsibility of the production managers to whom the first-level supervisors reported. These production managers were as well known to the workforce as the foremen. It was as if factory supervision had been split in two, with the foreman responsible largely for quality and the production manager responsible largely for materials and production control.

The factory could produce 550 coats per day, of which about 25 were usually special orders, single coats that were processed separately. The rest were standard orders batched together into the standard bundles. It generally took 5 to 6 weeks for a coat to travel through the process, from the laying out of fabric in the cutting room to the transport of the finished coat to the distribution center. The primary concern of production control was to make sure that all the parts for a coat moved smoothly through the factory and arrived at the various matching stations at about the same time so that they could be joined with specific other parts for further processing. Naturally, some parts took more labor than other parts to complete. For example, backs might be sewn in 5 minutes, while fronts might take an hour. To ensure a steady flow of goods through the factory, the workforce on fronts was 12 times larger than the one on backs. If parts were not ready, production had to shift to another lot, and operations were not as smooth as they could be.

Matching

Two critical matching stations helped control the flow of parts through the process and uncover any shortages. The first matching station, located about a quarter of the way through the process, was where backs were matched with fronts. The other key matching station was where sleeves were matched with the front and back subassembly; this occurred when the coat was about 75 percent complete. Matching was accomplished by looking at the tickets that had been attached to the materials near the start of the process. As we saw in Figure C2, the ticket numbers supplied various information: the model processed, the cloth lot to which it belonged, the size of the coat being fabricated, and the shade (a number for the bolt of cloth, which was the same for all pieces belonging to the same coat). The matching stations collated pieces by using these numbers.

If there were quality problems or if particular parts could not be located, fabric sometimes had to be recut. Naturally, Jos. A. Bank wanted any recuts to be from the same bolt of cloth that the original had come from; thus, lot numbers and shade numbers, as well as shop numbers, were recorded for any item that had to be recut. One day was allotted to do a recut and to rework the materials so that they could rejoin their bundle in the standard flow of work through the shop. Production control did not want to break apart any bundles of material except for super-rush jobs, which occurred about once a week. For all other jobs the bundles were kept the same.

Formal records were kept showing which lots were started in the shop through the fitting operation, and where the bundles were in the shop. Using the laser wand on the worker coupons provided the information needed to keep this tracking up to date.

Because of rework needed or production problems that might be encountered, the capacities of the upstream operations tended to be slightly higher than the capacities of the downstream operations. To avoid the accumulation of work-in-process inventory, the factory wanted to make sure that it could easily recoup any extra time spent in the early stages of the process. Some models were more difficult to make than others—for example, game coats with gusseted bi-swing backs and bellows pockets. When and how many of these coats to make at one time had to be carefully evaluated. This concern for extra capacity in the early stages of the process was particularly evident when plaids were done. As mentioned previously, plaids were the most difficult fabrics to work with because of pattern alignment for pockets, collars, back seams, and so on. This pattern alignment led to a 10 to 15 percent drop in production and a good bit more rework. (Rework in plain fabrics amounted to only 2 or 3 percent of any production lot, but in plaids the rework figure generally climbed to between 5 and 8 percent.) With this in mind, the target for the easy control of work through the factory was to have 60 percent of the work in plain fabrics, 20 percent in stripes, and the remaining 20 percent in plaids. This grouping was the ideal; sometimes, of course, the percentage of stripes or plaids would have to be increased to meet demand.

Supervision

As noted earlier, the first-level supervisor's prime responsibility was quality. Another of his or her tasks was to deal with absences. The first 15 minutes of the morning were spent determining whether everyone was there (absences averaged only 5 percent) and finding replacements for those absent. A number of the workers were cross-trained to fill in on other tasks; when such a switch occurred, they were paid their average earnings rather than the piece rates for these jobs. (There were also some specified utility workers who were paid their choice of a flat rate or a piece rate for the job.) The workers who were put on absentee work generally came from those who were ahead of the pace of the factory as a whole and could thus afford to take time off from their jobs.

The flow of information to the worker from the foreman generally concerned rework or methods. The flow of information from worker to foreman could be for a variety of problems: machine malfunctions, damaged goods, poor quality upstream. The production manager handled all grievances about piece work and about change in the operation. Sharing the complaint load was another advantage to the split of supervision between the foreman and the production manager. The foreman would, however, handle gripes about the size of the bundles for particular workers.

LOADING THE FACTORY

The specific planning for, say, the next year's spring fashions began in March. From March through June, the merchandising division reviewed planned sales for both retail stores and the catalog. As a result, manufacturing received a production "layout" for spring deliveries. From the layout, purchase orders for goods were sent on to manufacturing, authorizing production.

Orders for particular bolts of cloth (piece goods) were then placed with various mills. Jos. A. Bank had long had dealings with many mills and knew exactly which mills it wanted to produce particular fabrics. For many piece goods, about 10 percent extra was purchased so as to give the company some flexibility if demand exceeded the forecast. Since Jos. A. Bank fashions changed in only subtle ways from year to year, any surplus material could probably be used the following year; being caught with more fabric than required was not nearly as much a problem as being caught with too little. On those rare occasions when there was not enough fabric for a particular model, the merchandising division sometimes was able to reorder fabric from the mills. The fabric ordered for the next year's spring fashions arrived during the summer, any necessary examining or sponging (preshrinking) was done, and cutting began in August. Delivery to the distribution center started in October and delivery to the stores in December. From December to June or July the spring line was sold.

Manufacturing had no responsibility for the purchase of fabric, the factory's single most important raw material. All responsibility and authority for selection and purchasing rested with the merchandising division. However, manufacturing was charged with the purchase of the numerous trim items that were combined with the piece goods to make coats or skirts. Manufacturing also kept track of the status of the piece goods inventory: quantities remaining and their locations. For trim items such as shoulder pads, fusings, and sleeve heads, there were always two sources of supply; the split between the vendors depended upon price. Commitments to vendors typically extended 6 months in advance, but the shipment of items was specified for much narrower time periods; linings, for example, were delivered every week or two, buttons every 6 weeks.

Many of the vendors had been dealing with Bank for 25 years or more. Only if a vendor's price got out of line would the company threaten to reduce the amount of orders placed with it. New vendors were occasionally chosen. Vendor qualification was handled by design/quality control, which tested the item's physical characteristics (such as stretching and pulling) as well as the way it behaved when sewn or dry cleaned. If a vendor was deemed qualified, the trim purchasing manager negotiated the price. Typically, new vendors started with small orders as a further check on quality and delivery capabilities and on the stability of the pricing structure. Only if these tests were passed would the order be enlarged for subsequent years.

Production Planning

The production plans began with broad, large-scale decisions, which were subsequently refined and made more detailed. The broadest plans involved ranges—aggregate counts of fabric needs by type. Thus, there were ranges within plains, within stripes, within herringbones, and within plaids. These ranges were then broken down into particular quantities of specified fabrics required; they helped define what was cut and assembled during the entire season. A particular week's production plan was part of a 6- to 8-week batch of work from the merchandising division. The merchandising division balanced finished goods deliveries to meet catalog and retail store sales. It was the merchandising division's responsibility to monitor sales and to adjust subsequent batch "purchase orders" accordingly.

The production schedule set was typically for an 8-week period. The first week was allocated to planning, the next 2 weeks to cutting, and the ensuing 5 weeks to the shop. What was cut in a particular week depended on three things: the expected finished goods inventory, the attempt to develop an appropriate mix of cloth (the 60/20/20 plain/stripe/plaid breakdown mentioned earlier), and piece goods availability.

Production Planning Paperwork

Once the merchandising division provided the initial batches (batches contained specific purchase orders for defined finished goods deliveries), the batches were matched to the available piece goods inventories. The paperwork was then initiated to direct and control the transformation of fabric into suits, coats, and pants. The production plan for any week triggered several actions in the cutting room office. One of them was the computerized issue of a cloth pull sheet (Figure C5), which authorized the withdrawal of fabric from inventory. Authorization to cut the cloth was also provided by the computer. It created a cutting slip and the accompanying cutting chart (Figure C6), which indicated, for each lot number, the quantities and the size combinations for the markers or patterns that were actually used to cut the fabric. Cutting was done in groups of fabrics compatible for sewing and for machine setup and operation (see Figure C7). The cutting slip and the cutting chart traveled with the job. After the materials were cut and fitted, the Soabar report (Figure C8) was issued by the cutting room office. This report indicated not only the lot number but also the make, model, and size for all the bundles of fabric to be processed. The data entry for the Soabar report generated, via a special computer program, the fitter's report, which indicated the lot, bundle, and quantities, by size, that were to be run through each shop. The fitter's report in turn generated the coupons that traveled with the job and were critical to the operation of the piece-rate system.

continued on p. 77

$25^{.4}$

1,001 UNITS
CLOTH PULL SHEET

PAGE NO. _142·67_
WK 18
75

MODEL: _S365T/S33XT_   *Coat & Pant* TYPE OF CLOTH: _Plain – Cotton/Poly_

DELIVERED BY: _____   RECEIVED BY: _____   DATE: _1-17-89_

Lot No.	Ydg. Rec'd.	Shade	Ydg.	Loc.	Shade	Ydg.	Loc.	Shade	Ydg.	Loc.	Shade	Ydg.	Loc.
35530	3.40	R											
1123 R	286/972	114.	60.	609.	115.	59.	609.	117.	60.	152.	119.	58.	549.
1124 L	214/728	124.	60.	152.	125.	60.	152.	128.	58.	151.	130.	52.	609.
		140.	59.	055.	141.	60.	055.	142.	60.	145.	145.	60.	055
	1,700	146.	59.	145.	151.	31.	610.	153.	42.	609.	154	26.	611.
		158.	20.	610.	161.	57.	145.	163.	60.	146.			
		L											
		89.	55.	055.	99.	55.	145.	101.	32.	044.	102.	23.	044.
		105.	29.	145.	106.	30.	145.	107.	4.	055.	109.	43.	044.
		110.	54.	055.	116.	60.	152.	118.	59.	152.	121.	55.	152.
		126.	59.	055.	127.	58.	152.	131.	60.	152.	132.	59.	152.
35531	3.40	R											
1123 R	292/993	97.	59.	694	99.	60.	054.	100.	56.	053	101.	59.	053.
1124 L	208/707	102.	58.	054.	109.	27.	705.	118.	60.	705.	119.	59.	705.
		120.	59.	053.	123.	58.	705.	125.	60.	705.	126.	59.	705.
	1,700	127.	57.	069.	130.	58.	697.	134.	57.	054.	136.	59.	054.
		137.	58.	697.	140.	59.	053.						
		/											

Notes:

1. This is the cloth pull sheet for group 259, coats and pants for model S365T/S33XT.

2. The sheet indicates the yards of fabric cut for each lot, the shade (bolt of fabric), and where that bolt of fabric was located (the bin number).

FIGURE C5   Cloth pull sheet.

CUTTING CHART A

#4. Cutting Shee

CUT = _____ MODEL _C 355 E   SPORT COAT_____ 589_____ MAKE = __001__

GROUP = 260_____ UNIT __PLAIN - WOOL_____ GOODS $\frac{R_{g.}}{I_{g.}}$ 60. 60, Sto + Yl. 59

LOT NO.	SHADE NO.	40 R 44R	41 R 43R	42R 42R	39R 46R	38R 48R	37R 46R		45R					
35910		30	28	21	15	8	3		4					
		42L 44L	43L 46L	41L 48L	39L 46L		40L							
35910		29	19	12	4		8							
		38S 40S	43XL 44XL	39S 42S	42XL 48XL		42S	46XL						

Notes:

1. This is a portion of the cutting chart for an order for group 260, York sport coat model C355E. The cutting chart indicates which size combinations will be used for the markers on this order and how many of each lot and shade of fabric are to be cut. The group number and shop number are given in the cutting office.

2. These coats will be cut from a plain wool fabric.

FIGURE C6   Cutting sheet used by a spreader.

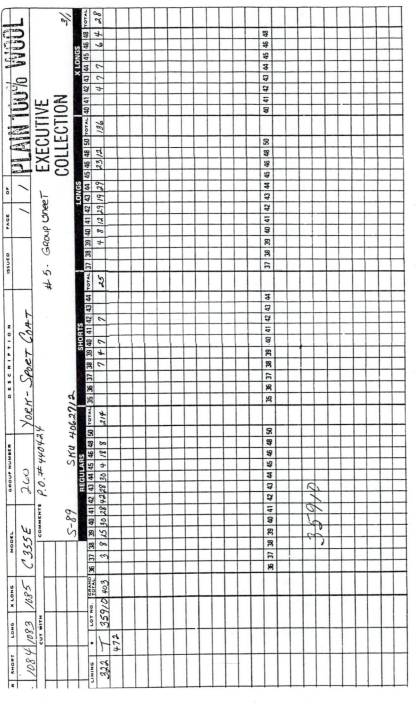

Notes:

1. This is the group sheet for a York sport coat, model C365E. The group number is 260 and the shop numbers are 1083 through 1085. After the shop number has been assigned, five copies of this sheet are given to the cutting room floor and one copy to customer service.

2. There is one lot in this group (35910) calling for various quantities of regulars, shorts, longs, and extra longs.

3. The colors to be used for UC (undercollars), linings, and * (fusings) are indicated by the numbers or letters in those columns at the left.

FIGURE C7   Group sheet.

MEN'S SOABAR REPORT

SEASON: S   YEAR: 89   LINING: 0   WIDTH: 60   DESCRIPTION: STRIPE-WOOL   DATE: 9/26/88

| SHOP# 0279 | COAT MODEL S321E | PANT MODEL S32XE | VEST MODEL | MAKE 001 | GROUP 87 | VAR 3 | DUE DATE 11/4/88 | DATE SOABARED |

TYPE: 1 STOCK

UNIT COST MFG *HC* RETAILER *θ*   UNIT COST MFG *NP* RETAILER *θ*   UNIT COST MFG RETAILER

K: 1 000
2 2PC SUIT
3 3PC SUIT   TOTAL QUANTITY

VAR: 1 REGULAR   6 PORTLEY SHORT
2 SHORT   7 PORTLEY LONG
3 LONG
4 X LONG
5 PORTLEY

LOT #	M A K E	T Y P E	COAT	VEST	PANT	29 35	30 36	31 37	32 38	33 39	34 40	35 41	36 42	37 43	38 44	39 45	40 46	41 48	42 50	43 52	44 54	46	48	PO #
		1																						
34653	2	1	57		57											5	5	4	5					44030
		1																						
34642	2	1	140		140											5	11	11	5					44030
		1																						
34631	2	1	59	.	59											5	5	4	5					44030
		1											5	21	19	15							
		1											15										
		1																						
		1																						
		1																						
		1	*Double - Pants 10-3-88*																					
		1																						
TOTALS	1		256		256			15	19	21	21	43	29	38	15	21	19	15						

HAMPSTEAD

EXECUTIVE

Notes:

1. This is the Soabar report for shop number 0279, for group 87, coat model S321E and pants model S32XE, soabared on September 26, 1988 and due out of the shop on November 4, 1988. The HC and NP entered for Mfg. indicate the Hampstead coat shop and the North Avenue pants shop, respectively.

2. There are three separate lots. The report indicates the exact sizes and how many of each should be made.

FIGURE C8   Fitters or Soabar report.

The paperwork just described served to follow up on the production planning by initiating work in the cutting room and the several shops of the factory. Other paperwork served to help control the movement of materials through the factory and to cope with irregularities (such as rework, recutting, and failed matchings).

TECHNOLOGICAL INNOVATION

Apparel manufacture, especially the manufacture of high-quality merchandise such as Bank's line, still required operator involvement and manual handling of suit parts. Innovations such as automatic thread trimmers and needle positioners, and work aids to improve operator efficiency and to reduce handling time had been implemented. There were some automatic machines for pocket cutting and other tasks, but most of the factory's sewing machines were strictly manual.

There had been other investments over the years in improved technologies. The AM-5 machines for automatically generating markers for the cutting room was among these. They eliminated waste in laying out the piece goods, and they automatically increased sizes, saving considerable time in the design of the markers themselves. New equipment for piece goods inspection, for fusings, and for steaming cloth had also been purchased. Productivity had improved each year in all product types.

Bank reviewed new technology on a regular basis, always with an eye to maintaining or improving quality. Chronically under review for application to Bank's high standards were high-speed automated spreading and computerized cutting equipment that were compatible with the AM-5 machine.

PART TWO

DISCUSSION

Jos. A. Bank Clothiers is in no way responsible for the following views and presentation. They remain solely the responsibility of the author.

THE PROCESS AND INFORMATION FLOWS

In comparison with the job shop of Norcen Industries, the flow of production at Jos. A. Bank is better defined. While there are some understandable differences between the coat shop and the pants shop, we can compose a process flow diagram for each of those shops that adequately represents the process, at least in general terms (see Figure C9). A more detailed process flow diagram, one that encompasses the actual operations described on the coupons, would reveal that there are still substantial differences between various products (such as suit coat versus sportcoat), models, and materials. Variations in any one of these lead to the inclusion of certain process steps and the exclusion of others. In general, however, the flow of materials through the process is fairly smooth and easily directed. Concern for materials routing is much less critical in this batch flow process than in a job shop.

Because of the wide variety of materials, models, and sizes, the factory must deal with a vast array of different batches. These variations underscore the still very strong need of the batch flow process for information and control. In their own way, the information flows of the batch flow process are inflexible, although compared with the job shop, the flow of information between workers and management is somewhat reduced. While workers are responsible for notifying management of machine malfunctions and quality problems, the major information flows to and from workers revolve mainly around the coupons that move with each bundle, as shown in Figure C10. In essence, the coupons serve as both process sheet and job sheet, to borrow language from the Norcen Industries example. The coupons inform

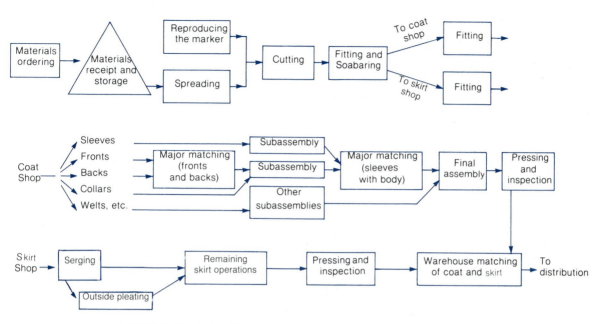

FIGURE C9   A simplified process flow diagram for a Jos. A. Bank suit.

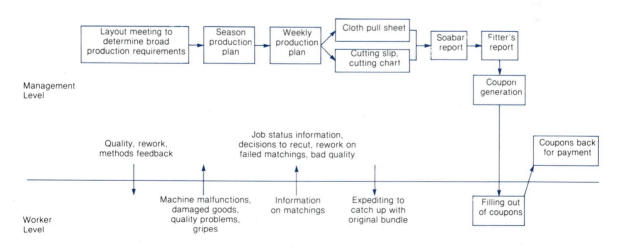

FIGURE C10   A simplified information flow diagram for Jos. A. Bank.

the worker of what must be done to the batch, and they also keep track of who did what to each batch of work.

The increased stability of the batch flow process reduces the amount of information that must be communicated from management to workers. The foreman typically has less troubleshooting and expediting to do and fewer scheduling changes to make. Therefore, it is often possible to supervise more people in a batch flow operation than in a job shop. The foreman at Jos. A. Bank has time to track quality and improve methods rather than having to make schedules and troubleshoot.

The need for continuous flow of information is reduced in the batch flow process, primarily because its product selection, while large, is still limited and well known in advance. Furthermore, it seldom has to bid for contracts, and so precise, order-specific cost information is not required.

CAPACITY IN THE BATCH FLOW PROCESS

The notion of capacity is only slightly less ambiguous in the batch flow operation than in the job shop. Nevertheless, the wide arrays of products that can be produced in any week make it difficult to specify a batch process's capacity in specific units of output without pegging it first to some standard mix of products.

The capacity of the batch flow process is influenced by many of the same factors that determine the capacity of the job shop.

1. *Batch (or lot) sizes.* Although the setup time for any bundle of materials is low at Jos. A. Bank relative to Norcen Industries, certain procedures are necessary (change of thread and needles) before a new batch can be processed. As mentioned in the process description, the larger the batch, the more

satisfied is the worker, too many low-count batches spur complaints from workers.

2. *Complexity of the products run through the operation.* As noted, plaids and stripes are markedly more difficult to handle than plain fabrics; when the production schedule includes a higher-than-normal percentage of these materials, the capacity of the entire coat shop declines.

3. *Nature of the jobs already on the factory floor.* Batch flow operations, like job shops, are subject to shifting bottlenecks and worker-machine interference. However, the definite limits to product diversity in batch flows generally mean that the severity and frequency of these two capacity thieves are reduced.

4. *Scheduling.* Scheduling is still an important consideration with the managers of the batch operation but the task is generally simpler than in the job shop. Again, the reduction of products and capabilities offered accounts for the bulk of this difference. With the batch operation, scheduling begins to shed some of its critical importance to the success of the operation as a whole. Given a reasonable composition of orders for the week (e.g., the 60/20/20 split of plain/stripe/plaid fabric), scheduling becomes much more routine.

5. *Process improvement.*

6. *Number of machines and their condition.*

7. *Quantity and quality of labor input.*

The last three major influences on capacity, like many of the other influences cited, take on less importance for the typical batch operation than for the typical job shop. This is because the batch flow process itself is better defined, with workers more apt to be assigned to particular machines and less free to float among machines. The transition from job shop to batch operation accounts already for considerable process improvement (such as specific methods, worker aids at the workstation, quicker setups). Considering its routing tickets (coupons), assigned machines, and specialized training, the batch operation is more likely to treat machines and workers as one producing unit. Thus, capacity can be enhanced significantly by increasing both in similar proportions. This is not to say that equipment improvement cannot be made in the typical batch flow operation. Jos. A. Bank, for example, was making substantial investments in new cutting tables and was monitoring advances in sewing machines.

THE ROLE OF STANDARDS AND INCENTIVES

At Jos. A. Bank, the role of standards takes on a different function than at Norcen Industries. At Norcen, you will recall, standards were used to estimate times and costs for bidding on jobs and also to provide information for scheduling jobs through the shop. Although the second function for standards is retained at Bank, standards are not used for job cost estimation because there is no bidding for new orders. Rather, standards in the form of piece rates and standard-hour (i.e., the standard-allowed minutes system) incentives are used explicitly to determine worker compensation and thus to spur worker effort and output. In a sense, the piece-rate and standard-hour incentives act to pace work through the factory.

As the process description made plain, the setting of incentives at Jos. A. Bank is serious business. Great care is taken to see that they are both accurate and fair. Considerable time and expense are spent setting new piece rates, observing workers trying out new piece rates, and testing modifications in methods. The procedures for setting and using incentives and for resolving disputes over them are well established and routine.

DEMANDS OF THE PROCESS ON WORKFORCE AND MANAGEMENT

The demands made on the workforce center around the incentive system. The system, rather than foremen, acts to pace production; thus, the demands for worker output are mainly triggered by the incentive system itself. Demands for quality output, on the other hand, come from the foremen. The foremen's most important job is to check the work that has been done and make sure that the methods being followed are proper.

At Jos. A. Bank, the ambition of workers is not great, and so not a lot of effort is expended to provide career paths for the workforce. Some other batch flow operations are more concerned with such issues. Of course, there is cross-training in a batch flow operation like Bank. Not only does cross-training help cope with absenteeism, but it also helps break bottlenecks, particularly chronic ones.

Clearly, one of management's chief concerns in a process like Bank's is the incentive system. The incentive rates should be fair to the workers but not so loose that costs get out of control. Striking a suitable balance is an important endeavor.

Apart from the incentive system, management must also be concerned with keeping the flow of work smooth. This means grouping work well and staying within guidelines for the materials mix. Not only must management be wary of the policies by which it loads the factory, but it must also track jobs through the process and act immediately to remedy any difficulties. While the flow of information is not as rigid and sophisticated as in a job shop, management must still pay considerable attention to the information pertinent to the flow of materials and jobs.

QUESTIONS

1. Compare and contrast the characteristics of the information flow in the batch flow process used by Jos. A. Bank with the information flow characteristics of the two other processes discussed in Tours A and B. Which process requires the least in the way of information flow from its managers? From its workers? Does anything replace the flow of information to workers or managers?

2. The typical duties of first-line supervision at Jos. A. Bank are divided between two people. What are the strengths and/or weaknesses of such an arrangement, as you see them?

3. Discuss the difference between the piece-rate and standard-hour schemes at Jos. A. Bank. Could the cutting room have been put on a piece-rate system? Had that been done, what complications would you have anticipated?

4. Under what conditions do you have the most confidence in the factory's ability to produce 550 coats a day? Under what conditions do you have the least confidence? Why?

5. How would you describe the market for Jos. A. Bank? What relationship, if any, does this market have to the production process chosen by the company?

6. In what ways is the union a help to Jos. A. Bank? A hindrance?

7. Could the low rate of movement of workers among jobs in the factory be related to the activities of the industrial engineer? Elaborate.

SITUATION FOR STUDY C-1

BROWN, SMITH & JONES (BS&J)

Paul Alvarez has just been hired by BS&J as superintendent of the fabricated tank division. Paul's previous experience had been with a leading manufacturer of home heating systems where the processes were highly automated. At the previous firm, the goods were also processed in a continuous manner, with a product line being set up for a year or more of production.

The products manufactured by the fabricated tank division were typically oil storage tanks made from sheet steel, which were sent to the customer much like a kit and were erected in remote oil fields. Occasionally, the firm sold the tanks in various sizes to other customers for other uses, such as to the military for the storage of diverse liquids like water and jet airplane fuel. Figure C11 is an example of a tank and some of the parts that must be fabricated. Table C1 is a partial process sheet for these parts. Figure C12 is a layout of the relevant processes.

Many of the smaller parts are common to most tanks, and they are made on a continuous basis to inventory requirements. There are three parts that are unique to each tank size: the tank side parts called staves, the triangular roof, and the bottom sections. The smallest tank, 1500-gallon capacity, requires five staves, five roof sections, and five floor sections. A 55,000-gallon tank, five rows high, requires 13 roof sections, 13 floor sections, and 65 staves. The typical order is for three tanks of the same size, but an order can be as small as one tank and has been as large as 15 tanks. The tanks are made to order, but BS&J has a backlog estimated at 1 1/2 months' production.

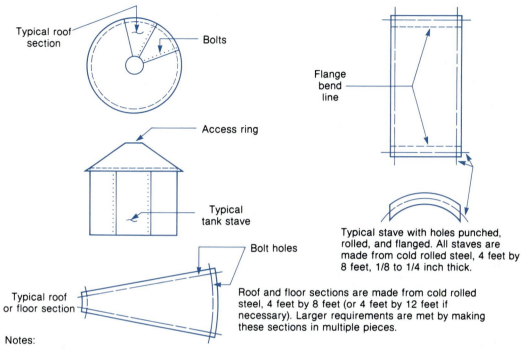

Typical roof section

Bolts

Access ring

Typical tank stave

Bolt holes

Typical roof or floor section

Flange bend line

Typical stave with holes punched, rolled, and flanged. All staves are made from cold rolled steel, 4 feet by 8 feet, 1/8 to 1/4 inch thick.

Roof and floor sections are made from cold rolled steel, 4 feet by 8 feet (or 4 feet by 12 feet if necessary). Larger requirements are met by making these sections in multiple pieces.

Notes:

1. A typical tank stave (1) is trimmed (if needed), (2) has holes punched on all sides, (3) is rolled to the approximate shape (depending on the tank diameter) on the pyramid roll, and (4) is flanged on both ends in a large brake press. The press is set up with a flanging that also causes the stave to be formed to the final shape according to the tank diameter. There is a flanging tool for each diameter tank.

2. The roof and floor sections are made from material similar to the tank staves, ranging from 1/8 inch to 1/4 inch, per the engineering design. If necessary, these sections can be made from material 4 feet by 12 feet. BS&J uses standard mill sizes to avoid the extra costs involved in having special sizes available; also, pieces that are too big would create construction problems. Two sections are usually cut from a single sheet:

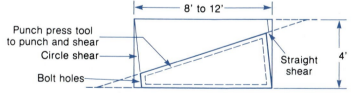

Punch press tool to punch and shear

Circle shear

Bolt holes

8' to 12'

4'

Straight shear

(The view is somewhat exaggerated to demonstrate the method.) If a top or bottom piece were too long, it would be made from two pieces:

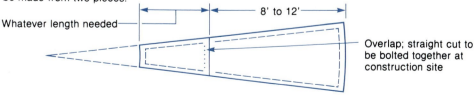

Whatever length needed

8' to 12'

Overlap; straight cut to be bolted together at construction site

FIGURE C11   Typical tank and parts.

TABLE C1 Partial outline of the process (Brown, Smith & Jones)

STAVE		ROOF AND FLOOR SECTIONS	
OPERATION	PROCESS	OPERATION	PROCESS
Shear edges true	Sheet shear	Shear edges and split each sheet on diagonal	Sheet shear
Punch bolt holes in both ends	Brake press setup with punches	Punch/shear small end*	Punch press
Punch bolt holes in both sides	Brake press setup with punches	Shear large end	Circle shear
Roll to tank diameter	Pyramid rolls	Clean and paint	Paint line
Flange both ends	Brake press setup with correct flange	Pack and ship	
Clean and paint	Paint line		
Pack and ship			

*For typical tank sizes there were punch press tools for this. Others had to be laid out, circle sheared, and single punched.

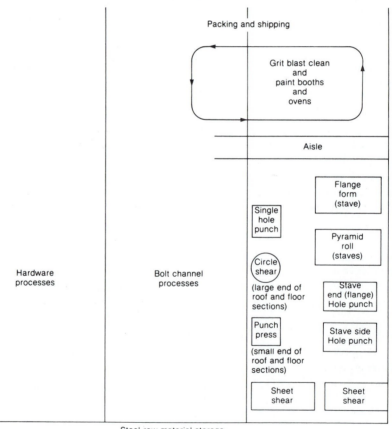

FIGURE C12 Fabricating process layout for a side stave, roof section, or floor section.

Paul was hired because the fabricated tank division has been unable to meet scheduled shipping dates, quality problems are cropping up, and the workers are unhappy about never being able to earn any incentive pay. Paul thought he would focus on the manufacture of the side staves, roof, and floor sections. What information does he need next? What information should be included on parts routing sheets?

1. Draw a process flow diagram for the two major tank parts.

2. What information would you need in order to set up a production schedule for this shop?

3. What approaches would you suggest to Paul to help him with both his quality problems and his incentive pay problems?

SITUATION FOR STUDY C-2

WELCH'S ICE CREAM

Ice cream production took place every weekday at Welch's, a shop that sold ice cream to the public. The entire process of making the ice cream was performed by Brad Gentry, an hourly employee. In addition, Brad had sole responsibility for inventory maintenance, quality control, and production scheduling. He worked about 4 hours a day during slow periods and about twice that during the peak season. Because he knew more than anyone else at the shop about production needs at any given time, and because he was decoupled from the sales portion of the business by an inventory of finished ice cream, Brad set his own hours. He usually worked from about 10 A.M. to 2 P.M.

The shop owned one ice cream machine with a 40-quart batch capacity. (The capacity refers to the finished volume rather than the volume of ingredients.) The manufacturing process involved rapid agitation and aeration of the ingredients, which nearly doubled the batch's volume. Hence, a 40-quart batch required approximately 20 quarts of mix.

The machine itself resembled a stainless steel 20-gallon water heater, lying on its side on a waist-high stand. The cylinder had a refrigeration layer on the outside, through which re-

frigerants circulated when the machine was in use. At one end of the cylinder was the motor unit, which drove the refrigerant pump and the agitation blades inside the tank. At the other end was a lower spout, through which the finished ice cream was pushed by the rotation of the blades. A table was positioned here so that buckets on it could catch the ice cream. Above the spout were two built-in funnels, through which extracts and flavorings could be added. On top of the cylinder was a stainless steel tub, which held a little over 20 quarts of liquid.

The ice cream machine was located in a small room called the process room, which also contained also a few shelves of supplies, reusable plastic buckets, scales, and a large sink. Three doors in the process room provided access to a walk-in refrigerator where the raw mix was kept, a walk-in freezer ($-30°F$) called the hardening box, and the rest of the premises.

The ingredients used in production were of three general types. The major type was the "mix," which was milk containing sweetener and a high cream content. An order of mix was delivered daily by a local dairy. This order consisted of five 50-pound cartons. Welch's placed an order with the dairy every day for delivery the next day, even though a different quantity was rarely ordered.

The second type of ingredient was the flavor bases: the various syrups and extracts that were added to the mix during agitation. The third type consisted of nuts, cookies, and some syrups that were "marbleized" into the ice cream. (Marbleization means that the ingredient is not beaten into the mix, but is poured into the stream of finished ice cream as it comes out the spout.)

The major vendor for the second and third types of ingredients was a company that usually delivered within 7 to 10 days after an order had been placed. This supplier paid freight costs but required a 15-case minimum. Brad took inventory on flavor bases once a month, and on marbleizing ingredients every 2 weeks. After taking inventory, Brad gave his boss a list of supplies needed and the boss did the ordering.

A production run began with sterilization of the ice cream machine and enough plastic buckets (a bucket equals 10 quarts) to hold the day's batches of ice cream. Each batch required 20 quarts of mix, and Brad usually made six batches a day, so Welch's received about 125 quarts of mix every day. Because the mix doubled during processing and the other ingredients also took up space, Brad used about 25 buckets per day.

While the machine and buckets dried, Brad checked the stock of ice cream in the tempering box, a walk-in freezer (adjacent to the hardening box) kept at 6°F. Ice cream in the hardening box was too cold to scoop, and so a sufficient inventory in the tempering box was necessary to ensure that Welch's did not run out of servable ice cream. After seeing which flavors were running low, Brad rotated those flavors from hardening to tempering box via a doorway connecting the two freezers. A map of ice cream locations was posted in the tempering box so that people who worked out front could easily find whatever flavor they needed. Maintaining this map was important because there were usually about 150 buckets ranging over 40 flavors stocked in this freezer. Welch's complete inventory comprised the contents of (1) the tempering box, (2) the hardening box (also an average of 150 buckets), and (3) the glass-topped refrigerators located in the service area (usually 32 buckets).

After rotating the stock, Brad took from the stock room the flavor bases and any other ingredients he needed that day. On Monday and Friday mornings, he took inventory of the hardening and tempering boxes and on the basis of this decided which flavors to make on a given day. Because he did not work weekends and Welch's sold 65 to 75 percent of their ice cream from Friday to Sunday, Brad had a target inventory for each flavor that he wanted to have on hand by Friday. The Monday inventory informed him how much of each flavor was sold over the weekend and therefore how much he needed to make above daily usage to reach Friday's target. The Friday inventory was a check that enough of each flavor was on hand for the weekend in the tempering box. By comparing usage figures from week to week, Brad could schedule flavor production to reflect demand. The target inventory was not a specific figure but rather a rough number that Brad carried in his head and altered according to his judgment. He did keep track of what he produced during the week, and he used this list to avoid duplicating batches or forgetting needed flavors. It was usually necessary to make two batches of vanilla a day, because about a third of all sales were vanilla.

Brad scheduled the batches from lightest taste and color to heaviest taste and darkest color. This way he avoided having to rinse the machine after every batch and saved 5 to 10 minutes, plus the ice cream that stuck to the blades. Vanilla was always first, because what little stayed in the machine blended well with the following batch. Brad could usually run three different flavors before having to rinse the machine.

Brad dumped 20 quarts of mix into the tub and allowed it to drain into the tank. He then closed the valve between the two and poured another 20 quarts into the tub, ready for the next batch. He turned on the agitator and added a measured amount of vanilla flavoring and cream tone. Welch's provided a complete index of recipes and instructions, but Brad had those for the most popular flavors memorized. He timed the batch—the first batch of the day for 10 minutes and the subsequent batches for 8 minutes. The first took longer because the machine was not yet cold.

When the time was almost up, he took a sample and weighed it. The batch was done if one cup weighed 90 to 95 grams, though chocolate flavors ran a bit denser. When ready, the ice cream was run out into buckets, covered with waxed paper, labeled with flavor and date, and placed in the hardening box, where it stayed for at least 12 hours before being rotated to the tempering box. Ice cream usually stayed in the hardening box for more than 12 hours; it would keep indefinitely at that temperature. When the end of the batch would not fill most of a bucket, Brad filled a few pint and quart cartons which, after freezing, were stored in a confection box at the front of the restaurant and sold. Although not a large business segment, this procedure avoided waste.

Brad repeated this batch process until he had either used up the five cartons of mix or made all he wanted to for the day. Normally he used all the mix, although it could be kept in the refrigerator for several days. When finished, he again sterilized the machine and washed the walls and floor of the process room before leaving. The cleanup took about 45 minutes.

1. Diagram the process and information flows for this process.

2. How would you plan production for such a process (i.e., how would you schedule which flavors would be produced and when, both during the day, the week, and the month)?

3. What controls on ice cream production would you use in this ice cream parlor? Why?

A MACHINE-PACED LINE FLOW PROCESS
General Motors Corporation
Chevrolet–Pontiac–Canada Group
Oklahoma City, Oklahoma

The Oklahoma City plant of the Chevrolet–Pontiac–Canada Group (C–P–C), one of the 28 domestic assembly plants operated by General Motors, was situated in the southeast part of Oklahoma City. The plant, built in 1979 on a 436 acre site, was huge, having 3 million square feet of space under roof. The plant employed a total of 5300 people, of which 430 were salaried. The nearly 4900 production workers were employed on two production shifts. (See Figure D1 for a layout of the plant.)

The plant currently assembled two nameplates of the body type A car, the Oldsmobile Cutlass Ciera and the Buick Century, in both sedan and station wagon models. In the past several years, however, as many as five different models (Buick Century, Oldsmobile Cutlass Ciera, Chevrolet Celebrity, and two versions of the Pontiac 6000 [front-wheel drive and all-wheel drive]) had been assembled there.[a] The plant delivered truckloads and rail carloads of these cars to every domestic auto dealer carrying those nameplates. The Oklahoma City plant was one of only two plants to assemble the A car, the other being in Ramos Arizpe, Mexico.

The Oklahoma City plant assembled cars of world-class quality. In the previous two years the plant had been rated as either the third or fourth best plant by J. D. Power, an independent company widely recognized as the arbiter of car quality for North America. In the latest year, the Pontiac 6000 produced in Oklahoma City tallied only 78 defects per 100 cars. This rating was exceeded only by the Lexus and surpassed that of the Toyota Camry and the Infiniti. The Buick Century's rating, 91, and that of the Oldsmobile Cutlass Ciera, 97, were better than that of the Honda Accord and of all other nameplates sold in North America.

[a]Although still selling well, the A car "platform," as it was termed, was aging and for the latest model year, the Chevrolet Celebrity and the Pontiac 6000 had been discontinued.

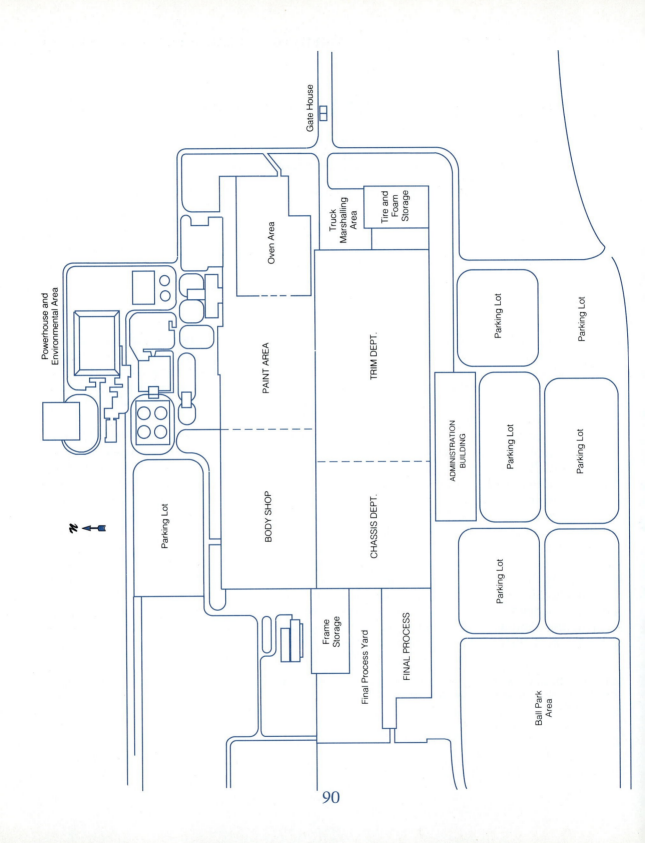

PART ONE

Process Description

HOW A CAR WAS ASSEMBLED: A SIMPLIFIED DESCRIPTION

The production process at C–P–C Oklahoma City was a classic, but modern, example of the moving assembly line so closely associated with Henry Ford and the Model T. The essence of the process was to build the car bit-by-bit by having workers perform the same tasks on each car as it moved through their work stations on a conveyor system. The A body car, with its front-wheel drive, could be viewed as the marriage of two large subassemblies: one for the body of the car and one for the engine cradle (the engine, its support structure, the front axles, and the trailing exhaust system and rear-wheel brake lines). The assembly plant was organized to build up the body and the engine cradle separately, to "marry" them, and then to finish the car's assembly and construction. The body and engine cradle lines were both fed by smaller subassembly lines. The plant was laid out with a flow that went clockwise, starting with the body shop, then the paint shop, the trim line (known as General Assembly I), and the chassis line (known as General Assembly II). See Figure D2. A more detailed version of the steps to build a car would require more space and explanation than is merited.

The entire line was composed of about 1800 cars with a single car taking about 28.5 hours to progress through the complete assembly process, a rate of about 1 car per every 50 seconds per work station. A typical work station consisted of 2 workers, 1 on each side of the line, some space in which to do the work, equipment specific to the job, and in many stations, some totes or bins stocked with the parts to be assembled onto the car. A great deal of variety existed from one work station to another. For example, a typical work station in the General Assembly 1 area might have the car moving at ground level, while at other positions in the General Assembly 2 area, the car was raised for work underneath it. An inspection station might have intense lights and raised platforms so that inspectors could easily identify any flaws and mark them for correction. Some work stations in the body shop were completely mechanized, with either robots or fixed automation. About the only consistent feature across work stations throughout the plant was that work averaged about 50 seconds per car.

For some options, such as occurred with station wagons, a worker might have to take somewhat over 50 seconds to do the job. This deviation was termed being overcycled. Naturally, a worker could not be continually overcycled without falling behind the pace of the line. To keep up, overcycled jobs had to be balanced off quickly by undercycled jobs for the workers affected. Given the existence of overcycled jobs, then, the sequencing of cars along the line, to provide a balance of overcycled and undercycled work, was an important endeavor. For example, the larger labor content station wagons were never scheduled back-to-back on the line.

Much of the overcycled work occurred along the General Assembly 1 and General Assembly 2 lines, where many of the multitude of options were added to the cars. Workers were advised what options to include on any car by reading the "broadcast," or "manifest," an instruction

continued on p. 94

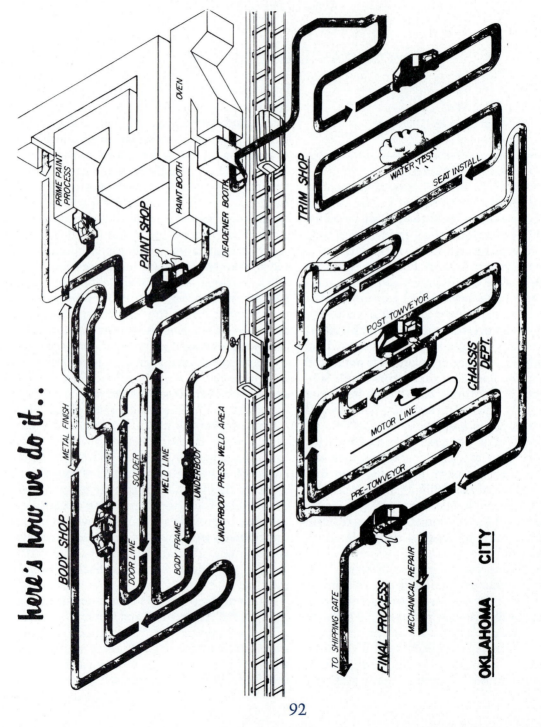

here's how we do it...

BODY SHOP

METAL FINISH · SOLDER · WELD LINE · UNDERBODY · UNDERBODY PRESS WELD AREA · DOOR LINE · BODY FRAME

PAINT SHOP

PRIME PAINT PROCESS · OVEN · PAINT BOOTH · DEADENER BOOTH

TRIM SHOP

WATER TEST · SEAT INSTALL

CHASSIS DEPT.

POST TOWVEYOR · MOTOR LINE · PRE-TOWVEYOR

FINAL PROCESS

MECHANICAL REPAIR · TO SHIPPING GATE

OKLAHOMA CITY

FIGURE D2 How a car is assembled. (Courtesy of General Motors, Oklahoma City Plant)

92

The body shop's wheelhouse subassembly area. (*Courtesy of General Motors, Oklahoma City Plant*)

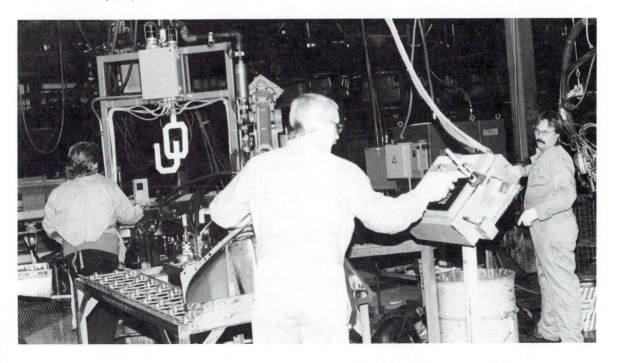

Calling for replenishment in the body shop's wheelhouse subassembly area.
(*Courtesy of General Motors, Oklahoma City Plant*)

sheet attached to the car, usually on a window. The broadcast was the primary information by which the worker determined what part or component was to be placed on a particular vehicle. In an effort to reduce error, the plant generated some "mini-manifests," which highlighted in large bold print the options that were called for in a particular department. The mini-manifests required more paperwork, but they enhanced quality by simplifying the information flow to workers along the line.

LOADING THE PLANT

Planning Production

Because cars and the parts to make them were both expensive and bulky, considerable thought was given to limiting inventories in the plant. No finished goods inventories were kept. All the cars assembled were trucked or shipped by rail to individual dealers within a short period of time after coming off the production line. Therefore, all of the cars destined for a particular dealer had to be scheduled for completion at roughly the same time to avoid significant delays.

Furthermore, all of the cars were produced to order as to make, model, color, and options. C–P–C Oklahoma City, on its own, was not permitted to ship any dealer a car that the dealer had not ordered. Roughly 5 percent of a dealer's order represented cars that were already sold to particular customers. About 25 percent were orders for fleet sales, and the remainder represented the dealer's speculation about what the dealership would be able to sell. Such production to order, given the wide range of options permitted in a car, placed tremendous demands on the plant's materials function to schedule the proper mix of cars through the line and to secure enough of the proper parts to fill the order.

The scheduling and material procurement functions were characterized by successive tiers of forecast orders and due dates that represented ever more precise refinement. At the broadest level, the corporate office in Detroit determined a rough production schedule for the year. The schedule served as a target for the company's outside suppliers and for its own internal supply groups such as engine plants and transmission plants. As dealer orders came in, the schedule became increasingly firm. The C–P–C central office in Warren, Michigan, scheduled production in the plant in order to meet a customer promise date known as *target build*. When a dealership received confirmation of an order, it also received word of exactly which week each car ordered was scheduled to be built. Meeting this commitment drove the production plan and the materials scheduled from a myriad of suppliers.

This target build program represented a change from the production planning used until the early 1980s and was part of the company's just-in-time production principles, termed "synchronous manufacturing." The plant operated with a firm car-by-car production schedule for 10–15 days in advance; it was known as the "stable schedule process." Any changes to production had to be accomplished beyond the three-week limit set by this stable schedule process. With this schedule, 98 percent of the target build sequence was accomplished when expected. Moreover, that production schedule persisted throughout the entire plant. It was only rarely that a car had to be taken out of the production sequence because problems could not be fixed on line. Thus, a car begun in the body shop maintained its order in the line throughout the paint shop and the General Assembly areas. Some cars, like station wagons, were periodically removed for extra work, but then they were repositioned to the same place in line. This schedule was announced on Mondays, so that every Monday there were 15 days of firm car-by-car schedules.

Although the line was flexible in handling many make/model and option variations, there were certain limitations. A special computer program, known as "auto sequence," helped to take account of them. The restrictions varied. For example, the plant wanted to batch colors as much as possible, but every day, every color was made, although in a specific sequence that went from white, then to light blue, dark blue, medium blue, red, brown, and finally silver, before returning to white. Never, for example, was a red car scheduled next to a white car because of the trouble in purging the paint lines. There were also restrictions caused by the number of side gates in the body shop used to hold side panels. There were 54 gates and only so many of particular models. This meant, for example, that the plant could run no more than 6 Oldsmobiles in a row. In addition, they could run no more than 7 station wagons in every cycle of 54, and these wagons had to be spaced out because of the overcycle condition they provoked in General Assembly 1. Similarly, the auto sequence program spaced out the options of power doors and windows as much as possible.

This system was very much appreciated by the factory's supplier base. The visibility this gave suppliers and the level aspects of the demands placed on them permitted some suppliers to reduce their costs, and this in turn was passed on to the plant in lower prices. The auto sequence program that created the stable schedule was communicated electronically to all of the plants' suppliers on Mondays. This communication was called the production point-of-use. Every Monday, as well, suppliers received a 20-week planning schedule from the Warren Central Office which included the firm 3 weeks that matched the production point-of-use sequence, but also included forecasts for the subsequent 17 weeks. In the future, it was

planned for these two documents to be merged into one document that the supplier would receive from the plant.

This change in production planning both removed a good deal of expediting and improved quality at the supplier and at the plant. Although the sequence was known in advance, no material was shipped from the suppliers in sequence. Oklahoma City did its own sequencing simply because it was more economic to do so. All of the plant's part numbers were scheduled in this way.

Purchasing and Raw Materials Inventory and Control

There were 4046 active parts and 493 suppliers that were used by the Oklahoma City plant. These figures represented reductions from the years when all four nameplates were manufactured at the plant and the active parts had totaled 7059. The reduction in the number of suppliers from as many as 783 suppliers to the current 493 was deliberate. The reduction in suppliers often improved both quality and price. For example, the 7 film suppliers previously used by the plant had been collapsed into a single vendor. The C–P–C Central Office in Warren negotiated all of the long-term contracts for the plant. The plant's purchasing people purchased non-production items, paints, sealers, and vehicle fluids, such as fuel, brake fluid, etc.

To avoid excess materials inventory, the delivery of materials was very tightly controlled. The plant had moved to provide reservations for both the truck and rail deliveries. It was essential that suppliers were reliable in these deliveries. For the most part, only between one or three days' worth of production items were kept in inventory at the plant, with one and one-half days being typical. For the relatively expensive items (engines, radiators, alternators), less than one day's production items were inventoried. Such tight control helped greatly, because the most expensive 350 parts accounted for 80 percent of the dollar value of inventory. Even small items like screws were stocked for only two to three days. How many days of inventory were held depended on:

1. *Volume.* The more regular a part's use, the tighter the schedule.
2. *Monetary value.* The higher the value of the part, the tighter the schedule.
3. *Physical size.* The larger the part, the tighter the schedule. And,
4. *Transportation.* The farther away the supplier, the greater the days of inventory held.

Many of the deliveries at the plant involved "milk routes," where a truck or train was filled with deliveries from several vendors and moved on a regular daily basis to the plant from as far away as the Midwest. Oklahoma City unloaded 50 rail cars and 90 truck trailers a day.

With materials delivery scheduled tightly, it was necessary to monitor the entire supplier network constantly. Failure to have on hand a key part could shut down the plant. Constant vigil was kept on the number and location of all supplies coming to the plant. Every day a list of critical parts that might turn up short or ʳ ıt of stock for the next two days was developed. The plant notified the suppliers to expedite the parts sought. Usually expediting involved securing a part from either the supplier or a sister plant and switching delivery to a faster and generally more expensive form of transportation.

Monitoring materials delivery involved not only the materials department at Oklahoma City (staff to track shipments, unload and handle materials) but also line workers and their supervisors. Even transportation carriers had electronic access to the materials system and

knew exactly what the plant's needs were. However, the plant was careful not to incur extra transportation costs just to carry lower inventory levels. Calculations were made that traded off the extra transportation costs against the inventory carrying costs that might be incurred. And, often, more inventory was kept in order to keep the total cost of procurement lower.

As a result of these improvements in production planning and in "synchronous manufacturing" (discussed in more detail below) inventory turns at the plant had risen consistently over the years. From levels in the mid-1980s of 30 to 40 turns, the plant's inventory turns had risen to a level in excess of 56 turns for 1991, with a peak month level of over 79 annualized turns. What is more, these high turn figures included the fact that the plant owned inventory in transit as well as the inventory that was physically at the plant.

SYNCHRONOUS MANUFACTURING

The Oklahoma City plant was well along with a C–P–C division goal to develop synchronous manufacturing in the plant (what many other companies call just-in-time production). Synchronous manufacturing involved a coordinated set of strategies (17 were identified; see Figure D3) that were designed to help identify and eliminate the non-value-added activities in the factory. Thus, there was an effort to rid the plant of unnecessary activities and controls, to eliminate excess inventories, to contract the working space, or work envelope, so that workers could take fewer steps, to simplify the presentation of parts to the worker so that mounting parts on the car was easier, and to help the worker ergonomically so that less stress and strain was placed on hands, wrists, arms, backs,

A car entering the ELPO bath. (*Courtesy of General Motors, Oklahoma City Plant*)

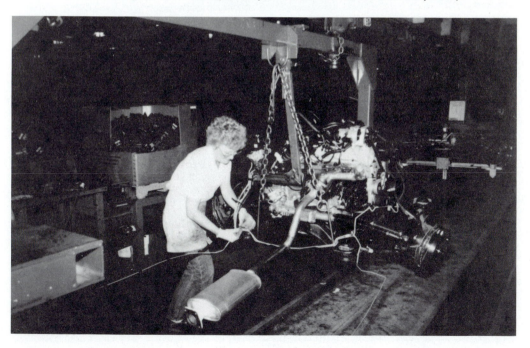

Along the chassis line. (*Courtesy of General Motors, Oklahoma City Plant*)

The marriage of the body and the chassis. (*Courtesy of General Motors, Oklahoma City Plant*)

FIGURE D3 Synchronous Manufacturing	Attachment F
KEY SUCCESS FACTORS	**DESCRIPTION**
1. Lead time reduction.	Method to identify, measure and eliminate waste.
2. Supplier involvement.	Extension of the process.
3. Reduction of variation.	Method of decreasing deviation from a target.
4. Pull system.	Replenishment based on consumption.
5. Leveling.	Providing stable & smooth flow.
6. Quick set-up.	Rapid preparation and changeover.
7. Total preventive maintenance.	Proactive planned upkeep.
8. Process/operator control.	Prevent problems from being passed on.
9. Problem solving.	Logical thought process to identify and eliminate problems.
10. Standardized systems.	Consistent and repeatable operations.
11. Small lot production.	Minimum material quantity and flow.
12. Capable systems.	Equipment/process within desired range.
13. Facility/equipment layout.	Effective layout of worksites (I.P. "U" shaped cells, etc.).
14. Workplace organization.	Orderly place for everything.
15. Audio visual controls.	Make problems noticeable/status at a glance.
16. Error proofing.	Proactive problem prevention.
17. Flexible systems.	Equipment and process adaptability.

SOURCE: Courtesy of General Motors, Oklahoma City Plant.

For exa
manufa
of spac
invente
and th
strume
minish
work-i
and the
time d
were b
new op
ufactur
time.
    Unde
with sy
a comn
be the
held at
The we
ated by
utilizin
(NUMM

R

Althoug
in the
makes,
it did h
and ma
Key rol
control,
the plar

The mo
pressure
ity. The
one had

and legs. In line with this approach to manufacturing, the Oklahoma City plant was relatively "low tech" compared to a number of auto assembly plants. It had only between 30 and 40 robots vs. perhaps 150 in a more automated plant. The plant's management pursued a strategy of more incremental automation.

Supporting this movement for synchronous manufacturing was the development of a support network to generate ideas for improvement, to analyze them, and then to implement them. Also supporting synchronous manufacturing was a change in the way materials were ordered and packaged for the line. On the line there were switches that turned on lights on a special panel to indicate to materials handlers that they were needed to fetch small bins and boxes of parts for particular positions on the line. In a standard assembly plant, in contrast, large baskets of many parts would be placed in the vicinity of the line, taking up space and forcing the workers to walk considerable distances to pick the parts needed for a particular car. No special signals would be devised either. Under synchronous manufacturing, parts were placed within easy reach of workers and would be replenished much more frequently by the use of worker-initiated signals. This was called the "pull card" system that was used to "pull" materials through the plant (as opposed to "pushing" materials onto the factory floor in anticipation of their use). Cards were used to identify parts, where they came from, where they were used on the line, how the standard quantities in the totes and bins are used, and when the worker should signal for more (see Figure D4). This system forced the coordination of materials handling to the needs of the line worker, and placed demands on both the process and the supplier network to produce high quality parts so that the line could function well. In addition, all kinds of worker aids and assists had been created for synchronous manufacturing. Special hoists and other ergonomi-

cally friendly tools and devices eliminated much of the effort that traditional assembly lines placed on workers.

The areas of the plant that had been converted to synchronous manufacturing were provided with only four hours of parts on the line. These parts were picked from so-called "supermarkets," where larger bins of the parts were kept and where materials handlers replenished the totes and small bins of parts that were found near the line. The supermarkets were laid out in mirror image to the line so that the materials handling fork lifts and cart trains could easily move in to collect the parts that the pull card or "smart light" systems had indicated were needed.[b] Similarly, synchronous manufacturing had also led to the realignment of the line so that subassembly areas were greatly reduced and placed closer to the point of their use along the main assembly line.

The move to synchronous manufacturing affected both supervision and design. The changes in the process gave supervisors "cradle-to-grave" responsibility for distinct segments of the process, say, for example, all of the assembly for a rear door. This increased the identity that supervisors, and their workers, felt for the product and the process. Contributing to this was a plant program (termed "Design for Assembly") to foster redesigns of the car itself so that assembly could be easier and of higher quality. From time to time groups of design engineers came to the plant and spent time learning from the workers how to do the job, actually doing the job on the line, discovering for themselves the problems that production workers had in doing the job, and leaving with numerous ideas for altering the way that the car was designed.

[b]The hand deliverable parts were on the pull card system; the bulk or fork truck deliverable parts were on the "smart light" (Synchronous Manufacturing Andon Retrieval Transport) system.

what corrective work needed to be done farther down the line in certain repair areas.

The quality control department's reliability group was charged with a number of tasks. They were the overseers of driver and passenger safety in the car. They also dealt with incoming quality by working with suppliers. They were also responsible for engineering change orders and for leading any product changes that had been mandated.

The audit group was responsible for grading the production quality every shift. Eighteen cars were investigated every shift, selected at random. Four of those cars were checked for everything. Fourteen others were checked systematically for the most prevalent problems. Once the more prevalent problem areas were studied, and preventive countermeasures arranged for them, then the inspection sampling for those problems was reduced and other problem areas were sampled more intensively. Three cars a month were subjected to a comprehensive evaluation and were measured in every way possible so that "variables," as opposed to "attributes," data[c] were collected on things like noise, fit, finish, and other important criteria for the customer. In addition to these three cars, a competitor's car was also evaluated in the same way.

The daily audit included a special 18-mile road test and a 12-hour cold soak. These processes allowed the auditors to check for cold starts, squeaks, and rattles. The number of defects per car was assessed. In addition, about ten times a year, unannounced and at random, a quality audit team from Detroit would perform their own audit of 20 cars. This procedure served as a check on the plant's daily audit.

By matching the voice of the customer to the voice of the process, the plant developed some statistical measures that provided the information needed to improve the process. Currently, the plant had between 70 and 80 quality control charts, about the same number of trend charts, and very many more charts of raw data that supplied insight into process improvement. Problems that had shown up repeatedly were assigned to special cross-functional teams that were charged with mapping the process with a process flow diagram and then indicating where production variability might be caused. This systematic investigation, in conjunction with some experimentation, led to effective countermeasures aimed at prevention of these problems.

In addition, any employee could shut down the line if a quality problem cropped up. Such actions were seldom taken, however. The factory had programs whereby both hourly and salaried employees acted on specific problems that had been raised by customers. Employees were also sent to supplier companies to educate suppliers on exactly what the assembly plant's requirements were. Numerous quality aids had been introduced in the process. In some cases these aids were protective devices for the car itself, such as to avoid scratches or other damage, and in others they were worker production aids that decreased effort or fatigue (ergonomics) or increased precision or reliability.

Industrial Engineering

The Industrial Engineering Department was charged with: (1) translating the engineering design of an automobile into a step-by-step procedure for assembling it; (2) laying out the line, work stations along the line, and any production aids such as equipment and fixtures for the work stations; (3) assigning work to each worker on the line and measuring that work so that it was appropriate; (4) establishing the authorized level of work and monitoring that

[c]For this distinction, consult Chapter 4 on quality management.

The point on the line where the engine is lifted up and married with the body.
(*Courtesy of General Motors, Oklahoma City Plant*)

Ergonomic fixtures in the door pad subassembly area just off the main line.
(*Courtesy of General Motors, Oklahoma City Plant*)

Small-part delivery trucks in a "supermarket." (*Courtesy of General Motors, Oklahoma City Plant*)

level; and (5) devising methods improvements or other ways to lower costs and/or increase productivity. The Department spearheaded many of the synchronous manufacturing initiatives at the plant. Ideas for changes typically sprang up from the workforce, supervision, or industrial engineers themselves. Conceptual drawings for any change were done by the Industrial Engineering Department.

As mentioned earlier, the line was designed in such a way that all workers averaged about 50 seconds' work on each car. Given any major model changes, the line would have to be thoroughly redesigned so that workers assigned possibly very different work tasks from what they were used to still had about the same amount of time to work on each car. This is

what line rebalance was about. With the adoption of synchronous manufacturing, line rebalance occurred all the time as tasks were changed and jobs (or job links) were altered, non-valued-added tasks removed, and value-added tasks reshuffled so as to put fewer workers directly on the line.

In greater detail, the rebalance of the line followed a number of stages:

1. Given the car's engineering and design, the industrial engineer described what had to be done to assemble the car. This description involved painstaking detail; for example, one could not simply specify, "mount headlight" since the task may take either shorter or longer than the desired cycle time. Mounting

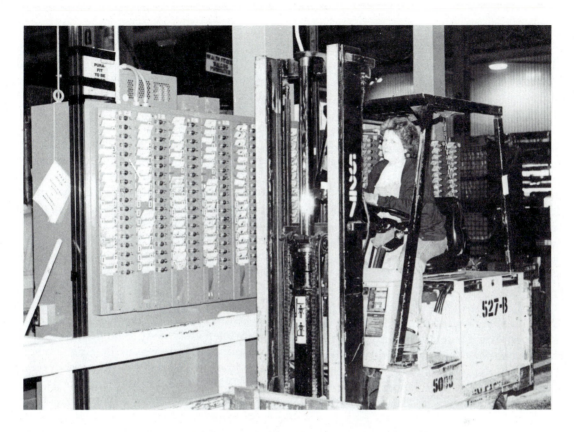

Call board for large parts. Part of synchronous manufacturing.
(*Courtesy of General Motors, Oklahoma City Plant*)

a headlight would involve a number of separate actions such as walking 5 feet to the supply bins, reaching for a headlight and screws, walking back to the line, positioning headlight in the socket, and using a power screwdriver to screw in two mounting screws.

2. Each of these separate actions (job elements) was assigned a time. These times were primarily determined by reference to standard time data established by General Motors, although sometimes they were determined by a special stopwatch where an engineer would time a worker performing a task. The standard time data typically would derive from numerous stopwatch studies, films of workers, and other sampling studies of specific worker tasks.

3. Once times were assigned to specific elements, the industrial engineer would review them with the relevant supervisor on the production line to determine whether they were reasonable. The changes would then be made.

4. Once an agreement was reached, the task, its elements, element time estimates, and whether the task was performed on all cars or only a few, were placed in computer-readable form. A computer program then calculated the work schedule, trying to bal-

ance work loads among the workers, such as by taking job elements from one worker and placing them with another, or otherwise shifting assignments to distribute the work evenly.

5. Generally, the initial computer schedule left some workers with either too much or too little to do. What was to be avoided was putting workers in an overcycled condition where they would consistently have too much work to perform for the time cycle decided on. If an imbalance in the line were serious and could not be remedied easily, the task was sometimes taken off the main line and performed as a separate activity. This course of action was considered a last resort, however.

   On the basis of the computer-run, tasks and times were adjusted and a subsequent computer run made. This run was studied for reasonableness, and again adjustments were made. Numerous iterations of this adjustment process were generally performed before the line was satisfactorily balanced, at least on paper.

6. The paper balance of the line was then ready for trial on the factory floor. Industrial engineers, supervisors, and workers all became involved in this activity. The danger was that the predicted and actual times would not mesh. If this in fact occurred, the first thought was to help the worker improve the time by changing the layout of the work station, adding fixtures or other equipment, or changing methods. Such action was usually sufficient, but, if need be, another operator could be added or a modest rebalance of the line effected.

Plant Engineering

The Plant Engineering Department directed all the construction, maintenance, repair, recy-cling, and environmental work of the Oklahoma City site's land, buildings, and equipment (except tooling, which was handled by the assembly engineering group). All the plant's requests for major expenditures and capital appropriations were coordinated by Plant Engineering.

Plant Engineering was constantly on the alert for technological improvement and was involved in all of the plant's initiatives for synchronous manufacturing. The Plant Engineering Department did the detailed engineering on equipment involved in the synchronous manufacturing effort. It did the costing and the approvals for any capital dollars required. And, it was responsible for the installation. Oklahoma City tried to do as much of its own installation as it could, contracting out, as a matter of course, only concrete work and roof work. Installations were meant to be flexible and easily repositioned. There was no bolting of machines to the floor unless safety concerns so dictated.

The Plant Engineering Department was involved in technological advances such as the use of turbo bells for painting and the use of robots for applying adhesives to the windshield or to the door paper. A new dynamic vehicle testing area was the responsibility of Plant Engineering.

The Oklahoma City plant prided itself on being able to make most line and equipment adjustments on the fly, without disrupting production.

THE WORKFORCE AND THE PERSONNEL DEPARTMENT

The plant's non-supervisory factory floor personnel were paid by the hour. All supervisory and clerical people were paid a salary. The plant currently operated two shifts of production with an hour of scheduled overtime each shift, a total of 18 hours of production a day. In addition, the plant operated two Saturdays a month. The first shift began at 7 A.M. and ended at 3:30 P.M., with a half hour break for lunch. The second shift began at 5:00 P.M. and ended at 1:30 A.M. During each half of each shift, the entire line shut down for 23 minutes so that workers could rest. This was termed "mass relief" and replaced the individual-by-individual tag relief that had proceeded it. Mass relief was seen as improving quality.

The hourly employees were represented by the United Auto Workers (UAW) union. Most features of the agreement between GM management and the plants workers were spelled out in a 597-page national agreement covering a wide range of topics, including wage payments, fringe benefits, seniority, grievance procedures, overtime, layoffs, safety production standard procedures, and numerous other topics. There was also a smaller 194-page additional agreement between the local UAW organization and the plant's management. This separate agreement provided detailed information on wages, layoff procedures, health and safety measures, and the like.

Plant relations with the union were generally cordial and constructive, fostered by daily dialogue between the parties. There were no secrets at the plant. Any union member could attend any meeting at the plant except for those relating to human resource issues. A union representative was always present at staff meetings.

Most worker complaints were resolved without recourse to the grievance procedure. Grievances, such as overwork conditions, were generally resolved at the first of four levels of the grievance procedure. Few grievances reached the final arbitration level.

The plant's personnel department was an essential factor in plant management. Not only did the personnel department oversee labor relations with the UAW, but it was also charged with training responsibilities and payroll.

The personnel department had spearheaded the drive for increased competitiveness and worker involvement with a program called the "Voluntary Input Process" (the VIP process). Teams of workers, typically between six and ten, met for half an hour every Wednesday morning to discuss improvements that could be made to the process. About 75 percent to 80 percent of the plant was involved in this effort. For their involvement, workers were paid an additional fifty cents an hour. A VIP operator had a number of responsibilities, including attendance at the weekly meetings, knowing all of the jobs that were done within the unit, agreeing to rotate to retain proficiency in those jobs, helping to maintain the cleanliness and good housekeeping of each unit area, providing training for others, and working to improve the materials scrap processing and efficiency of that area. VIP operators worked to build quality into the car in their areas through the use of statistical process control (SPC) and self-inspection. The VIP process had resulted in an increase in quality and a number of helpful suggestions for the increased efficiency of the plant. It fit well with the drive for synchronous manufacturing. In addition to the VIP operators, the program also had duties for the support people assigned to every unit along the line (see below) and for the group coordinators or supervisors that oversaw the area.

C–P–C Oklahoma City offered the hourly employee a number of possibilities for advancement and work preferences from the simple movement from one shift to another, to transfers between departments and promotions to higher-pay classifications. Hourly employees could also move to management by becoming supervisors.

Supervision

Work on the line was directly overseen by first-line supervisors assisted by three to four group leaders, called support people. Typically, the supervisor was directly responsible for between 30 and 35 workers on a shift. There was one support person for about every seven-to-ten member unit. Supervisors were thoroughly familiar with all aspects of work within their own sections of the line and of what workers could or could not be expected to do, largely because of once having been one of them. At the start of the shift, the supervisor's immediate concern was manning the production line and making sure material and tools were available.

Once workers were at all of the line positions, the supervisor spent much of the remainder of the shift in two activities: promoting and checking quality and troubleshooting any problems on the line, such as equipment malfunc-

tions, pending parts shortages, or defective materials. Very little of the supervisor's time was spent at a desk. For most of the shift, the supervisor walked the line, talking with the line's workers, trying to solve any problems they might have, and promoting quality.

Four or five supervisors in turn reported to a general supervisor, and the general supervisors reported to one of four superintendents, one each at the body shop, the paint shop, General Assembly 1, and General Assembly 2. (See the organizational chart in Figure D5.)

The superintendent's job included many aspects of the first line supervisor's, plus other responsibilities. The superintendent was concerned primarily with quality and safety, but also spent considerable time and effort on cost

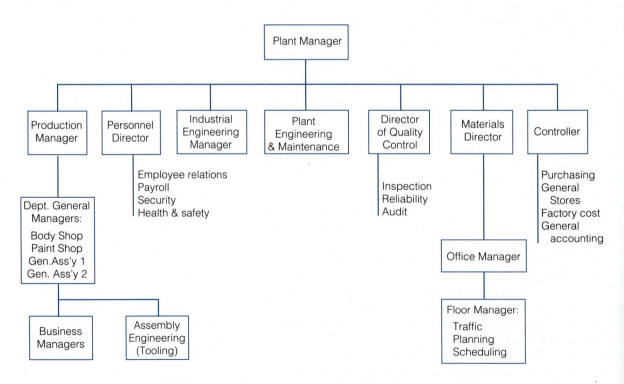

FIGURE D5   Organization chart for the C–P–C Oklahoma City plant.
(*Courtesy of General Motors, Oklahoma City Plant*)

control, human relations, and housekeeping chores. Some of these tasks were routine, such as meeting with union committeemen, checking absenteeism, and conferring with other superintendents. But there were always special plans or meetings and unexpected problems on the line to overcome.

PART TWO

DISCUSSION

The GM C–P–C Group is in no way responsible for the following views and presentation. They remain solely the responsibility of the author.

plies a great deal of communication between workers and management in the plant and between the plant, corporate level managers, and outside suppliers.

THE FLOW OF THE PROCESS AND OF INFORMATION

The process flow in a factory such as C–P–C Oklahoma City is among the most complex one can encounter. A blizzard of different tasks, equipment, and skills are required to assemble an automobile. Yet the process flow can be diagramed in a very straightforward way. Figure D2 represents a rough-cut process flow diagram. A more detailed version would consist of recounting all of the workstations along the production line; it is these workstations through which every car passes. Thus, compared with a job shop or a batch flow process, the classic assembly line has a very well-defined process flow.

With a process as complex and as closely scheduled as an automobile assembly plant, it is not surprising that the information flow is complex as well. Figure D6 portrays an information flow diagram for C–P–C Oklahoma City. While the information flow is essentially oneway, from the top down, the need to track materials both inside and outside the plant im-

CAPACITY

The notion of what capacity is in a machine-paced line flow process like C–P–C Oklahoma City is as clear as it ever gets. At C–P–C Oklahoma City, one car rolls off the end of the production line every minute. Everything in the process is geared to making that happen. It is as though the process were a huge on-off switch: when it is on, one car a minute is produced; otherwise, nothing is produced.

Similarly, the notion of capacity utilization is relatively unambiguous. When the plant is up and running, capacity utilization is 100 percent. Otherwise, it is zero. Simply by tallying the hours the plant actually runs and dividing this total by a count of hours the plant could be open gives an idea of what capacity utilization is. How many hours the plant could be open is subject to some debate, however. For example, it may be very contrary to corporate policy to schedule a third shift of production, and so a capacity utilization measure should be based on two shifts only. Another problem may lie in the determination of how much overtime is the

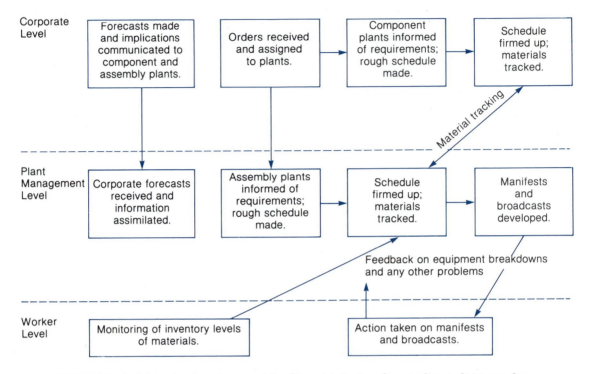

FIGURE D6   An information flow diagram of the Chevrolet–Pontiac–Canada Group, Oklahoma City.

maximum the plant could schedule without antagonizing workers. Is it an hour a day? Two hours a day? Every Saturday? Questions like these make a capacity utilization calculation fuzzy, but it is clear how much the process is capable of producing when it is up and running.

In a machine-paced line flow process, capacity in the short run is severely constrained. It can be modified only by scheduling more or fewer hours. In the medium run, however, capacity can be substantially modified (without huge, new additions of plant and equipment) by adjusting the balance of the production line. Thus while the machine-paced line flow process cannot modulate its capacity smoothly, as can occur in job shops and batch flow processes, capacity can be adjusted in abrupt steps and by varying amounts.

DEMANDS OF THE PROCESS ON THE WORKFORCE

A machine-paced assembly line places special demands on a worker. In a sense, the worker is a "slave to the iron monster," which is the moving assembly line. He or she cannot simply decide to take a break from work and wander about chatting with co-workers. (But then neither can the second-grade teacher.) Moreover, the assembly line worker must perform the same, fairly routine task repeatedly throughout the workday. Many people view that as monotonous or degrading or worse.

But not all people hold to that view, and therein lies a fundamental point about assembly lines and assembly line workers. Happily, people are very different from one another in tolerances for certain activities and in expectations about their jobs. One class of personality savors proximity to power and influence and will forgo higher salaries to do so (consider many staff workers on Capitol Hill), while another will sacrifice salary for considerable freedom of schedule and the chance to be "their own boss" (such as many college professors). If the assembly line worker can be typed in this way at all, he or she has forgone diversity in the job for relatively high wages and freedom from the anxiety many people suffer when they are confronted with decision making. For many people, that is not a bad trade to make.

Nevertheless, despite the matching of personalities to job types that goes on continuously in our economy, progressive companies like General Motors constantly search for ways to improve the quality of work life for their workers.

We have dealt more with quality of work life in Chapter 5. Suffice it here to observe further from the process description (1) the importance that the personnel department at C–P–C Oklahoma City enjoyed and the mandate it bore for worker training, safety, and promoting worker involvement in the process; (2) the challenge supervisors felt for recognizing worker achievement and integrity and for assisting their workers in solving problems both on and off the job; and (3) the care with which the industrial and plant engineers studied the tasks that make up automobile assembly and devised ways to eliminate or simplify more difficult or disagreeable ones. Within most machine-paced line flow processes, the career path of the worker is much less well defined than it is in many continuous flow processes or in the batch flow process. Lines of progression are not spelled out as directly, and most workers earn about the same pay. Most job changes involve transfers from evening or night work to day work, or from one department to another with what may be perceived as easier or more exciting work. Some promotions in job categories are frequently possible as well.

Demands of the Process on Management

The machine-paced line flow process places a number of taxing demands on management. The products it produces are typically consumed in high volumes; therefore they are likely to compete on price as well as product performance, workmanship, and perhaps even the reliability of delivery. This is a broad front on which to compete, and it means that line flow managers must devote their attention to cost reduction measures (items 1 through 4 in the following list) and to product performance and workmanship measures (items 5 and 6):

1. *Balance.* The definition and balance of the line, as discussed previously, is a critical aspect in ensuring that as little labor as necessary is placed on the line.

2. *Materials management.* Like the continuous flow process, the line flow process places very regular and steady demands on its suppliers. Because of this regularity, the line flow process can often avoid drawing on large raw materials inventories and paying the necessary finance charges, but only by carefully managing the purchase and logistics of supplies. Such materials management involves the establishment of superb information and control systems so that (1) parts in imminent danger of falling short are identified and noted and (2) parts from suppliers are tracked thoroughly and delivered on time. The process description noted how recent changes have contributed to coordinating materials more tightly.

3. *Technological change.* In processes as complex as most line flow ones there are always ways to improve their workings. Most such changes are incremental in nature, but periodically more significant steps can be taken either to speed up the process or to eliminate some stations through the introduction of new equipment. Computers,

more versatile machine tools, and increased automation have often made significant contributions to process improvement.

4. *Capacity planning.* The managers of a process as rigid in capacity as the machine-paced line flow process must be very careful to plan diligently for its future capacity needs. Line rebalance may be called for or more drastic modifications to the design of the line. Design changes must be thought through carefully from the beginning of any planning cycle.

5. *Product design.* The high-volume products of the typical line flow process must be designed to be manufactured; the more exotic the demands the product places on the design of the line and the tasks workers perform, the more likely the competition will bury the product on price. Yet some of the best assembly line products give the impression that they were custom-made, there being so many options for the customer to choose from. Automobiles are often this way. The trick, of course, is to design flexibility into the product so that the same general worker task results in a different appearance or performance in the product. This is where the Oklahoma City plant's program for "design for assembly," where design engineers are brought to the plant to be educated by the workforce on what is easy to assemble and what is hard, is so important.

6. *Workforce management.* In so many line flow processes, quality is fundamentally dependent on the workforce. Fostering pride in workmanship and creativity in the identification and solution of problems, when the tasks performed are as repetitive as they are, is a challenge, but an essential one.

QUESTIONS

1. Why is the production process at C–P–C described as "classic but modern"?

2. It has been said that industrial engineering is the most important element of control in a machine-paced line flow process. Do you agree? Why or why not?

3. What are the connections between the workforce and its supervision and product quality at C–P–C Oklahoma City?

4. Discuss in detail the relationship between the notion of capacity in a machine-paced line flow and the technique of line balance.

5. Based on different operations you have so far studied, which operation would you rather work in? In which would you rather be a manager? In which would you like least to be a worker? a manager? Support your answers with specific references to the processes.

6. Various changes in materials management were mentioned in the process description for C–P–C Oklahoma City. Trace the changes in both process and information flows that you would expect to result from these changes.

7. Suppose that you had just been designated the plant manager for a new plant about to be completed. You are in charge of assembling your own staff (such as in quality control, plant engineering, supervision, production planning). Based on the process descriptions to date, how would the composition and relative strengths of your chosen staff differ from one type of process to another?

8. Suppose C–P–C Oklahoma City has been designated to produce a new General Motors car. What aspects of the plant's operations do you think will be most affected by this change?

A HYBRID (BATCH/CONTINUOUS FLOW) PROCESS
Stroh Brewery Company
Winston-Salem, North Carolina

In 1982, the Stroh Brewery Company of Detroit acquired the Jos. Schlitz Brewing Company of Milwaukee. In the process, Stroh acquired Schlitz's Winston-Salem brewery, which had begun production in June 1969. At the time, the Winston-Salem brewery was the largest brewery ever built at one time. It occupied 1.1 million square feet on 150 acres and cost $130 million. Originally constructed to produce about 5 million barrels of beer per year (a beer barrel is equal to 31 gallons), the brewery was now capable of producing about 6 million barrels of beer per year.

PART ONE

PROCESS DESCRIPTION

THE BREWING AND PACKAGING OF BEER

Beer is a malt-and-hops-flavored drink that is fermented and carbonated. It has been popular for thousands of years and, in one form or another, exists in almost every society. Although known and enjoyed for so long, the chemistry of brewing is very complex and is still not understood in all its particulars. Brewing remains very much an art as well as a science, with rapid innovation over the past 20 to 25 years; developments in brewing automation and control have reduced the need for manual labor by 75 percent and placed much of the control of the process on instrument panels.

The brewing process itself can be divided into two main stages: (1) the production of natural cereal sugars, called wort production, and (2) fermentation and finishing. (The process is depicted in Figure E1.) At Stroh, a batch of beer typically took about a month to brew and age.

115

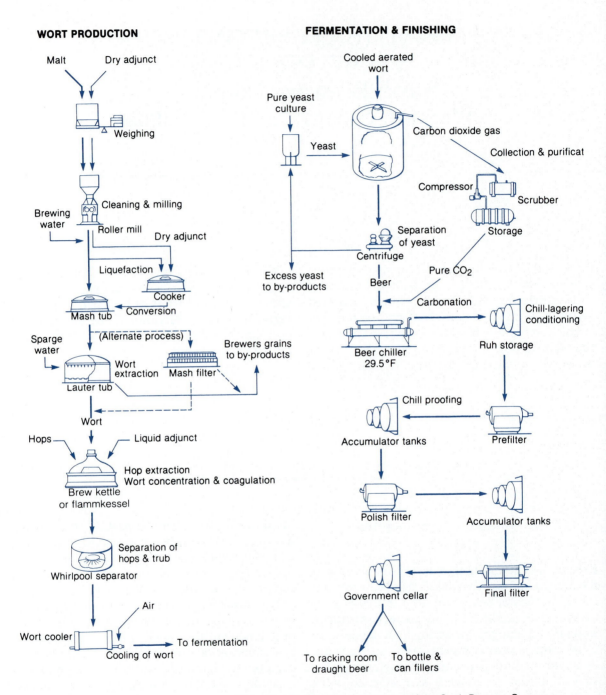

FIGURE E1   The brewing process as followed at the Winston-Salem plant of the Stroh Brewery Company.

A control panel in Stroh's Winston-Salem brewhouse. (*Courtesy of Stroh Brewery Company*)

Wort Production

Wort production starts with the weighing, cleaning, and milling of the malt, which gives beer its flavor. The malted barley and an adjunct (corn, rice, malt, and/or liquefied corn) are prepared separately. The adjunct is used because malted barley can convert more than its own weight of starch to fermentable sugars. To the milled or crushed barley, malt, and adjunct is added the brewing water, which is specially treated by filtering and pH adjustment to remove impurities.

This addition of water to ground malt is known as *mashing*. This occurs in large, stainless steel vessels in which the ground malt and brewing water can be stirred together and brought to a boil.

The Stroh's brand and its Stroh Light extension brand are famed for being "fire brewed." Instead of the wort being cooked by heat from steam coils, as was the common practice, the wort for Stroh's and Stroh Light is cooked using direct flame in the flammekessel. This step gives Stroh and Stroh Light its distinctive taste.

After mashing, the mixture is transferred to a lauter tub, which separates the liquid (the wort) from the undissolved solids of the mash. The lauter tub is a large, circular tub with a false bottom and a rotating set of "rakes" that can be raised or lowered. These rotating rakes smooth out the mash as it enters the lauter tub and makes an even filter bed. Undissolved particles in the mash settle to the false floor of the lauter tub. Once settled, the liquid wort can be

A brew kettle in Stroh's Winston-Salem brewhouse. (*Courtesy of Stroh Brewery Company*)

drawn off with the aid of hot "sparging" water, which rinses the wort off the grain. The undissolved mash is then collected and sent to the nearby Miracle Feed Company, where it is processed into a highly nutritious livestock feed.

The drawn-off wort then enters the brew kettle, where it boils for 2 hours. This boiling stabilizes the wort by killing off bacteria, deactivating enzymes, and coagulating any still undissolved particles. During this boiling, hops are introduced to the wort to enhance its flavor by extraction of desirable hop components. Boiling also increases the concentration of the wort through evaporation. Once boiled, the hops and trub (coagulated sediment) are separated out by whirlpool action in a special vessel. The hot wort is then cooled and aerated.

Fermentation and Finishing

Only after yeast has been introduced to the cooled wort and fermentation is complete can the product be called beer. The yeast that is introduced to the 50-foot-long fermentation tanks transforms maltose, glucose, and other sugars in the wort to alcohol and carbon dioxide. Stroh's fermentation is accomplished by a patented process called "accurate balanced fermentation." During fermentation, carbon dioxide gas is collected and purified. After fermenting has finished and the yeast has been separated from the beer by centrifuge, the carbon dioxide is reintroduced to the beer (carbonation), and the beer is chilled.

Once fermentation is complete and the yeast separated, the remaining finishing consists of a string of storage and filtering steps. The chief aging occurs in the ruh cellar, where the beer is held for between 15 and 21 days. Once properly aged, the beer is filtered several times through diatomaceous earth. Final storage occurs in what is called the "government cellar," where the next day's production is inventoried and where the quantity of beer subject to federal tax is monitored. Beer typically spends less than 7 days in the government cellar, the time largely dependent on packaging needs.

Out of the government cellar, the beer flows to the keg, canning, and bottling lines.

Canning, Bottling, and Kegging

The Winston-Salem brewery operated six canning lines, three bottling lines, and a keg line. Each line performed essentially the same functions: (1) filling and capping and (2) pasteurizing (for the non-draft beers). Cans and bottles were also boxed into six-packs and cases, and cases were placed on pallets for shipping by truck or rail. The process from filling to palletizing ran continuously, with no significant buildup of in-process inventories unless a piece of equipment in the line broke down. The key piece of equipment on the line was the filler (an investment of $400,000) — the limiting element for capacity. All of the machines that followed had rated capacities in excess of the filler; so any equipment breakdown after the filler did not necessitate shutting down the entire line. Small reservoirs of work-in-process were held at several places along the line in order to keep things moving in case one part of the line had to be shut down temporarily (such as a shutdown to remove a broken bottle).

The can lines could run at 1600 cans per minute, the bottling lines at 900 bottles per minute, and the keg line at 340 half-barrels per hour. With six canning lines, several brands brewed at the plant could be canned at the same time. Alternatively, the same beer could be packaged in two different size cans at the same time. Three bottling lines were needed not only to match the demand for bottles but also to permit bottles of different shapes and sizes to be run at the same time. In addition, returnable bottles were separated from new bottles for filling and packaging. A canning line shift required 6 workers, while a bottling line shift required 15.

Warehousing

The Winston-Salem plant preferred to load the beer directly from the line into railcars or trucks rather than warehouse it. (See the plant layout in Figure E2.) In fact, about half of the plant's output was shipped without any storage in the warehouse. The warehouse's fully enclosed railroad docks could store fifty 50-foot freight cars. In addition, 15 truck loading docks were available. The warehouse was designed so that output could be shipped by either rail or truck. The warehouse stored some brands that were not produced at the plant. Also, 10-ounce cans were not filled here. These items had to be supplied by other Stroh plants.

LOADING THE PLANT

Order Taking

Stroh's Winston-Salem brewery served approximately 200 wholesalers stretching over the entire eastern seaboard from New England to some parts of Florida and inland to Michigan, Indiana, Kentucky, and some parts of Tennessee. A wholesaler generally handled one of the major national brands and perhaps a smaller, regional brand. Each wholesaler serviced a range of retail accounts (such as liquor stores, bars, grocery stores) within a specified geographic area.

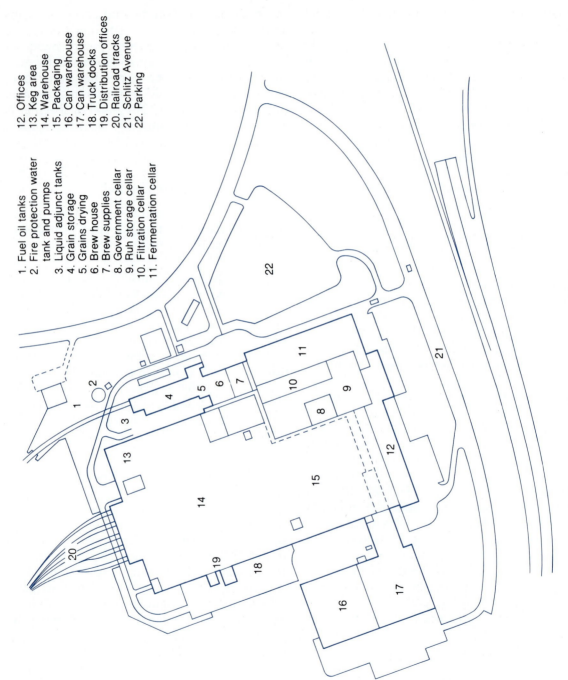

1. Fuel oil tanks
2. Fire protection water tank and pumps
3. Liquid adjunct tanks
4. Grain storage
5. Grains drying
6. Brew house
7. Brew supplies
8. Government cellar
9. Ruh storage cellar
10. Filtration cellar
11. Fermentation cellar
12. Offices
13. Keg area
14. Warehouse
15. Packaging
16. Can warehouse
17. Can warehouse
18. Truck docks
19. Distribution offices
20. Railroad tracks
21. Schlitz Avenue
22. Parking

FIGURE E2 Layout of the Winston-Salem plant of the Stroh Brewery Company.

120

At the middle of each month, every whole-saler placed an order for delivery next month. This procedure meant that the brewery had lead times of 2 to 6 weeks for each order. The order, entered either directly by computer or mailed in, specified item, quantity, and date (sometimes hour) for delivery of the beer ordered. The brewery offered a remarkable diversity of items.

Seventeen different brands of beer were brewed at the plant (Stroh's, Stroh Light, Old Milwaukee, Old Milwaukee Light, Old Milwaukee Non-Alcoholic, Old Milwaukee Draft, Schlitz, Schlitz Light, Schlitz Malt Liquor, Piels, Piels Light, Goebel, Goebel Light, Schaefer, Schaefer Light, Red Bull, and Silver Thunder). Old Milwaukee accounted for 37 percent of pro-duction and Stroh for 22 percent, with the other brands dividing up the remaining 41 percent of the brewery's capacity. This beer could be pack-aged in cans, bottles, or kegs of various sizes, with different lids and in different kinds of card-board cartons. In all, there were 759 beer and packaging variations that a wholesaler could order. Wholesalers could pick up their order by truck, paying the expenses themselves, or they could have the plant load a special Stroh-assigned rail freight car and direct it to the wholesaler's own rail siding. The truck option offered greater speed and reliability of delivery than rail, thereby cutting down on the inventory the wholesaler had to carry, but it cost considerably more. About 20 percent of the plant's volume was shipped by rail and 80 percent by truck.

The kegging line at Stroh's Winston-Salem plant. (*Courtesy of Stroh Brewery Company*)

The Winston-Salem plant monitored the inventory positions of each of its wholesalers, and it followed trends in the marketplace as well (such as promotional campaigns and their effect). The plant sometimes made suggestions to its wholesalers on what and how much to order, especially if it felt strongly that a wholesaler might not have ordered correctly.

Production Planning

Production planning was intimately related to order taking and was performed in the same department. (See the organization chart in Figure E3.) The role of the production planners was to figure out how the brewery could best fill the orders placed by its wholesalers. A good production plan was one that satisfied all of the wholesalers' demands with (1) little repositioning of the requested delivery dates, (2) few changes in the workforce, and (3) full usage of the existing equipment.

Planning and scheduling production for each month meant determining (1) how much beer of which type was required and the timing of its delivery and packaging and (2) the precise sequencing of lines and beer/packaging combinations on each line.

Because it took a month to brew beer, the brewmaster had to produce to a forecast of sales rather than to customer order. This production to forecast was a key reason why the plant kept close tabs on retail activity and made buying suggestions to its wholesalers. The packaging of beer, on the other hand, could be, and was in fact, done to customer order.

In planning packaging for any given month, it was advantageous to:

1. Group runs of the same beers together, such as packaging Old Milwaukee on several lines at the same time.
2. Group similar packaging sizes and types together, such as running all quart bottles at

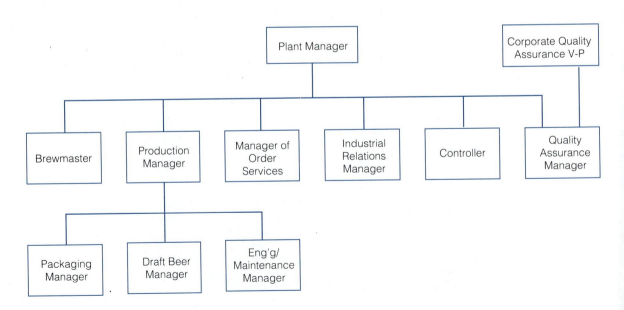

FIGURE E3 Organization chart for the Winston-Salem plant of the Stroh Brewery Company.

the same time rather than interspersing them among other production runs.

3. Run similar lines at the same time, such as running two can lines in tandem. To run a second line, given the first was running, required only four more workers rather than the eight it took to run the line by itself.

4. Run a canning line together with the keg line, since the joint workforce for such a combination could then be shifted en masse to a bottling line if need be. In that way, the groups working on any line would not have to be split up and reassembled as often.

Once the next month's wholesaler orders were received, the production planners went to work to schedule the production to fulfill that demand. This scheduling was accomplished manually, using trial and error but with reference to decision rules like the four mentioned here. After the production plan became "final," the wholesalers' delivery dates and order quantities were acknowledged on a week-by-week basis, giving the wholesalers 2 weeks' notice. About 70 percent of the wholesalers' original orders were acknowledged without any changes in dates or quantities. For the other 30 percent, all quantities were filled with timing dislocations that were always less than 2 weeks. Fully 99 percent of all the acknowledged orders were shipped on time.

Wholesalers could request changes in the schedule after their initial orders had been placed. This meant calling a production coordinator who could change the production plan or arrange swaps between wholesalers (since the brewery was aware of all wholesaler inventory positions). Major modifications of the production plan rarely had to be made. Minor adjustments were made about twice a week, but these occurred normally for production problems such as a machine breakdown. The production plan was declared fixed as to labor content one week in advance of production. It was declared fixed as to packaging variations only one day in advance of production. About one shift's production was kept as a safety stock so that snafus in demand, production, or logistics would not necessarily affect delivery.

The production plan had another role somewhat different from the weekly scheduling of machines to match orders exactly. This role had to do with anticipating the seasonality of beer drinking. There was a definite seasonal trend to beer sales. Demand peaked from May through September, with the height of the peak accounting for sales roughly double those of the winter trough. Because Stroh's pasteurized beer had no living organisms in it (milk has 500 per milliliter), the beer did not spoil. (The draft beer was specially filtered so that it, too, had no living organisms in it.) The brewery could therefore cushion itself somewhat for the peak season demand by building up inventories, both in its own warehouse and in the warehouses of its wholesalers. In this way, the brewery did not have to hire or lay off as many workers during the period when demand was changing abruptly. The brewery and its wholesalers built up some inventories during the late spring and ran them down as summer progressed.

Because beer tasted best when it was fresh, it was company policy to hold no packaged beer at the brewery that was older than 21 days. The policy for wholesalers was not to hold any beer longer than 60 days. These policies helped to ensure that consumers enjoyed a fresh product.

The precise production schedule for the various lines depended in large measure on the time it took to accomplish various changeovers with the equipment. There were three key types of changeovers:

1. *Beer changeovers.* When a different beer was to be packaged, the pipes leading to the

line from the government cellars had to be cleaned out by a "blow back" of beer to the cellars, using carbon dioxide. Only then could the new beer travel the pipes to the filling machine. For most beer switches, this changeover could be accomplished in 15 minutes, quicker than that for lines close to the government cellars and longer than that for lines far from the cellars. Because of the significantly different composition of light beers, a changeover to or from light beer involved, in addition to a "blow back" with carbon dioxide, flushing the pipes and the filling machine bowl with water. Thus, when light beer was run, the changeover entailed 20 or 25 minutes to prepare the line for the beer and a similar amount of time to clean up the line once it was run.

2. *Packaging changeovers.* On the canning lines, the chief packaging changeovers involved either a change of can lids or a change of case carton. The "ecology lid," where the tab was pushed down into the can and remained attached, was used exclusively, but these lids could carry special tax-paid statements for various states, and thus can-lid changes had to be made. There were three major carton possibilities: (1) a standard case of 24 made up of four six-packs, (2) a fully-enclosed box of 24 loose cans, and (3) a fully-enclosed box of 12 loose cans. Other carton possibilities were possible, however. A change of lids took 5 to 10 minutes on average, while a change of case cartons took about 5 minutes.

The only packaging change for the bottling lines involved a switch of cartons for the 7-ounce bottles, a changeover that averaged 10 minutes.

3. *Container changeovers.* The most complex and time-consuming changeover involved a switch of container sizes — for example, from 14-ounce to 16-ounce cans or from 7-ounce bottles to quarts. (Four can sizes were possible — 12, 14, 16, and 24 ounces — and four bottle sizes — 7, 12, 32, and 40 ounces.) Such changes involved resetting the filling equipment, the lid placement or bottle crowning equipment, the labeling equipment, and the cartoning equipment. Typically, an entire shift was devoted to these changeovers.

On a typical day, for example, a 12-ounce can line would make 8 to 10 lid or beer changeovers, a 16-ounce can line would make six such changeovers, and a quart bottling line would make three such changeovers.

The extent of container changeovers depended on the season. There were two basic types of can changeovers and two basic types of bottle changeovers. In the summer, the cycles shown in Table E1 prevailed for these can and bottle lines.

Given changeovers of various sorts and mechanical and other problems, can and bottle lines could not operate all the time. For the most part, the line efficiencies ran about 80 and 85 percent. Changeovers accounted for between 5 and 8 percent of the difference between these efficiencies and 100 percent.

Purchasing

The purchasing function for the plant was housed in the same department that handled order taking and production planning. This arrangement made sense since the production plan implied, in a straightforward way, the material needs for the entire process.

All of the brewery's major materials inputs (malt, adjuncts, cans, bottles, cardboard) were purchased on long-term contracts from major suppliers. These contracts were all negotiated by Stroh's headquarters staff in Detroit. The Winston-Salem plant negotiated on its own only those contracts for materials and services

TABLE E1   Container changeovers for can and bottle lines during summer (Stroh Brewing Company)

LINE	SHIFTS PER CYCLE
Can Line	
Type A (12-ounce cans)	Line devoted to 12-ounce cans: no changes
Type B	
16-ounce cans	15 shifts
14-ounce cans	6 shifts[*]
Bottle Lines	
Type A	
12-ounce returnables	12 shifts
12-ounce nonreturnables	3 shifts[*]
Type B	
Quarts	20 shifts
7-ounce bottles	5 shifts
Stroh taper bottles (12 ounces)	12 shifts
32 ounce or 40 oz. bottles	6 shifts[*]

[*]Cycle then repeats.

that went into the maintenance of the brewery itself and were not an integral part of the final product. Still, there were plant-specific negotiations for 2500 contracts each year. Also, even though Detroit headquarters may have negotiated for a specific material, there was often a direct supplier-brewery relationship. This was particularly true for cans and bottles. Cans were supplied by Stroh's own can plant located near the brewery, and bottles were provided by three outside sources: Anchor, Foster-Forbes, and Owens-Illinois.

The brewery placed orders for these major materials in much the same way that Stroh's wholesalers placed orders with the brewery. For example, the July order for cans or bottles would be placed on June 10. At that time, the brewery would place a firm 4-week order and an estimate of the succeeding 4 weeks' demand.

The inventory levels for any one of these major materials depended crucially on the dependability of the supplier. If the supplier had proven reliable and no special circumstances intervened, the brewery would want to hold only enough of the material to last until the next delivery. As it was, special circumstances were continually intervening, and so the brewery often adjusted the amount it ordered to take advantage of volume discounts in price or seasonal differences in sales or expectations about a strike in the supplier's plant. Some typical inventory levels for major materials were:

Bottles	1–2 days of production
Malt	5–7 days
Cans	1 week
Cardboard cases	1 week
Bottle labels	1 month

THE WORKFORCE

The brewery currently employed about 600 people, producing on three shifts a day, 5 days a week. Of these, about 100 were salaried (managers and staff) and 500 were paid hourly. The hourly workers were represented by a union, the International Brotherhood of Teamsters.

Most of the workforce had been hired from within a 50-mile radius. Half of the salaried workers were drawn from other Stroh breweries, but none of the hourly workers came from other Stroh breweries, mainly because they had to be volunteers and had to pay for their own move. During plant startup a strong effort was made to hire persons so that there was a representative mix of ages, races, and sexes.

The hourly workers were divided into two main groups: the production workers who brewed and packaged the beer, and the engineering and maintenance workers who cared for and fixed the plant's equipment. The maintenance workers were paid about 5 percent more than the production workers, since their jobs required greater expertise and wider skills.

Once in a department (brewing, packaging, engineering/maintenance), workers tended to stay, often doing the same job. This status quo was frequently by choice, since workers who complained of boredom were generally shifted to more complex jobs or made relief workers (spelling other workers who were taking breaks). Advancement through the ranks and into management was possible, especially in brewing and packaging, although the odds were short. Most movement among the hourly employees was between shifts; such moves were based on seniority.

CONTROL AND EVALUATION OF THE OPERATION

Quality Assurance

Quality assurance (QA) at the brewery was an important activity, employing 33 people in three separate labs: microbiology, brewing, and packaging. The staff at those labs performed 1100 separate tests, many of them repetitions of the same test, on each batch of beer brewed at the plant. QA staff worked round the clock, seven days a week. Quality assurance had the authority to stop operations at any point in the process. The QA manager was responsible for dealing with and rectifying any customer complaints.

Here are two examples of the specifications that the QA staff tested for, one set by the corporation's brewing staff and the other set by the corporation's packaging staff:

1. The brewing staff had set a standard of 16 million yeast cells (plus or minus 2 million) per milliliter of beer during fermentation. Quality assurance tested for this standard twice for every fermentation tank's batch. The test had to be completed within the first four hours of fermentation so that any necessary corrective measures could be taken. The test was accomplished by taking a 4-ounce sample from the tank, diluting it in three steps, and then counting yeast cells by microscope.

2. The packaging staff had established a standard that the air content in a 12-ounce can of beer be no more than 0.66 cubic centimeter, because oxygen caused flavor instability in the beer. The QA staff tested for this standard by checking each canning line five times per shift, taking three cans from each line each time. If the cans were off specification, the QA staff would quarantine all the line's beer up to the last good check and then systematically inspect the quarantined lot until the beginning of the off-specification beer was encountered. The beer that passed inspection was released, and the beer that failed inspection was discarded. As it turned out, about 98 percent of any quarantined beer was eventually released as good product.

Rarely did any of the batches of beer fail to satisfy standards, but the quality assurance department prided itself on its vigilance. It viewed itself as the early warning station for detecting any encroaching degradations of the process's integrity.

Information Flows Within the Process

Most of the information flows within the process were directed from the top down. If the process was working smoothly, workers needed to be informed of only routine things, such as the changeover in a line from one beer to another or the shifting from one line to another. Most jobs did not vary that much anyway, and so the information that was transmitted could be sparse without any detrimental effect.

Top management was eager, however, for the thoughts of the workers on all matters of plant operations. The plant had begun a total quality management (TQM) program that was involving the workforce in process improvements. Of particular concern were breakdowns in the process. After worker signals of process breakdown, the engineering and maintenance force would be called in. These troubleshooting jobs were generally regarded as the most complex at the brewery and the most pressure-filled. A good engineering/maintenance department was a real asset and a chief way to keep costs low by maintaining high speed and high yields. The TQM program was also instituting supplier certifications to improve quality even more.

Evaluating Plant Performance

Each week management at the brewery developed an operations summary that listed goals and actual results for an entire list of performance measures such as productivity (barrels per worker), cost per barrel, packaging line efficien-

cies, material losses, beer losses, beer rejected by QA, deliveries made on time, shipment errors, wholesaler complaints, and worker absenteeism. Each week, too, the plant's beer was evaluated by taste tests in Detroit and elsewhere. More than any other test, this was the one the plant always wanted to pass.

In many respects, the plant's performance could be fine-tuned only from week to week. The major elements of plant performance were either already decided (plant design) or beyond the scope of plant management (the plant's sales volume). As the plant manager admitted: "The heaviest decision in our industry is capital equipment investment." Major cost and quality advances were very much a function of the equipment the company's design people in Detroit decided to incorporate into the plant.

Over the past 20 to 25 years, breweries had also been built larger than before. There were real cost savings implied by larger brewery size: vats and tanks could be larger and still make quality beer at lower cost per barrel, and packaging line speed and capacity could be used fully. The size for the Winston-Salem brewery was determined as a sort of "lowest common denominator" for different "lumpy" capital investments. Specifically, the plant's lauter tub could process 3 million barrels of beer a year, and the mandatory assortment of packaging lines (lines for kegs, cans, one-way bottles, and returnable bottles) could process 5.2 to 6 million barrels a year. With the addition of other canning lines and another bottling line, packaging capacity could then precisely match the output of two lauter tubs—hence a brewery capacity of 6 million barrels a year.

What the plant manager worried about depended a lot on volume. As he noted, "Volume solves everything." When volume was high, all the manager had to worry about was whether the workers would accept the necessary overtime

A worker inspecting cans of Schlitz along the Stroh's Winston-Salem canning line.
(*Courtesy of Stroh Brewery Company*)

and whether maintenance could hold everything together. At capacity, quality and meeting shipments were chief concerns, with product cost lower in priority. When sales volume dropped, however, meeting cost targets became relatively more important, and that meant tightening up on staff and laying off workers. The plant was operated as a cost center, since it had no responsibilities for revenue raising (e.g., no marketing at the plant) and its geographic market area was fixed. Plant management was concerned chiefly for the maintenance of the plant and the motivation of the workforce; with them came good-quality beer, high yields, and on-time shipments.

PART TWO

DISCUSSION

The Stroh Brewery Company is in no way responsible for the following views and presentation. They remain solely the responsibility of the author.

THE PROCESS FLOW

Much of the Stroh brewery's operation is reminiscent of the continuous flow process at International Paper's Androscoggin Mill. Even though there are about 420 beer and packaging variations, most of these modifications require setup times that are tiny in comparison with the run length. The process flow is well defined, and every product goes through the same steps in the process. (See Figure E1 for a process flow chart.) Over time, equipment advances have speeded up the process and have driven labor out of the product's value.

The job contents of the direct labor in the process are of two kinds, polar extremes. Most workers have well-delineated tasks, most of which are repeated time and again as the product is manufactured. These jobs, typically, are not very demanding. At the other extreme lies the brewmaster. Despite great strides in automation and control, the brewmaster's duties still lie within the realm of art. Brewing is still imperfectly known enough to require great experience to produce a quality product.

Requiring nearly comparable levels of skill and experience are the plant engineers. Plant engineering and maintenance are crucial to an operation such as a brewery, where the capital investment is enormous and the success of the process depends on meeting quality standards and delivery schedules and on maintaining high yields of output. All of these goals are influenced importantly by the design and upkeep of the equipment in the plant. Moreover, all of the equipment must be functioning smoothly for any of the product to meet its specifications. Breakdowns or below-specification performance of any of the equipment is likely to lead to poor quality, poor shipment performance, or excessively high costs (such as low packaging speeds).

Despite these important similarities to the continuous flow process at the Androscoggin Mill, the Stroh brewery is not strictly a continuous flow operation. This is true primarily because the brewing phase of the process is done on a batch basis. True, these batches are large, but it is only because of their sequencing and the accumulation of a work-in-process inventory just before packaging that the batch operation in brewing can supply a steady flow of beer to the continuous flow that is packaging. The work-in-process inventories in the ruh and government cellars separate the two different types of processes. Without such an inventory, even though the daily or weekly capacities of the two processes (brewing and packaging) may be matched perfectly, the lumpiness of the batch flow operation's output cycle would cause severe problems for the smooth-running continuous flow operation.

THE INFORMATION FLOW

The inventory between brewing and packaging does more than even out production. It also separates the information needs of the two processes. The brewmaster need only know how much beer of which kind to brew, and the packaging department need only to know what, when, and how much it is to package.

Moreover, the timing of the information flows is much different. The precise packaging department schedule is set as final only one day prior to packaging. Up to that time, adjustments to the schedule can be accepted. Needless to say, the brewmaster cannot react so quickly. Since it takes about a month to brew a batch of beer, the brewmaster can only work to an estimate of demand, not from firm wholesale orders. The work-in-process inventory between brewing and packaging, then, acts as a safety stock of beer as well, so that last-minute changes in demand can be accommodated. It also serves as the dividing line between production triggered by estimate (brewing) and production triggered by firm orders (packaging). This difference in information requirements, as much as anything else, sets aside the Stroh brewery as a hybrid (batch/continuous flow) process.

The separation of information needs and flows at the brewery is depicted in an information flow diagram (Figure E4). Note that the information basically flows in only one direction (top down) except for the usual signaling of equipment breakdowns and acknowledgments of orders shipped. In this way, the information flows are reminiscent of the Androscoggin Mill.

CAPACITY MEASURES

The capacity of the brewery is a firm and easily understood number, 6 million barrels of beer a year. Barring a major breakdown of equipment, the capacity figure is primarily what the existing plant and equipment permit. Neither product mix nor scheduling has much impact on capacity. Other than to maintain the equipment and keep quality up, the plant can pull only so many levers to increase the quantity of good product brewed and packaged.

By the same token, capacity utilization is a well-defined concept. The capacity of any piece of equipment is known because it was engineered that way, and the current capacity is also easily measured. Moreover, because the plant's designers want to leave as little waste or spare capacity unused as possible, the capacity utilization for any single piece of equipment is often very close to the capacity utilization figure for the process itself. Since the process's capacity utilization is determined by the bottleneck operation, one can say that all equipment capacities are likely to lie close to the bottleneck capacity.

STANDARDS AND INCENTIVES

The standards that matter at the Stroh brewery are not the type of standards that managers of

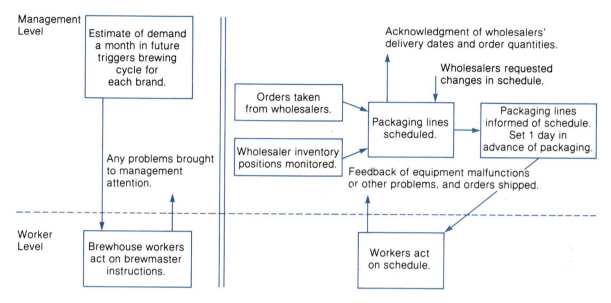

FIGURE E4   An information flow diagram of the Winston-Salem plant of the Stroh Brewery Company.

batch or job shop operations get concerned about. Labor standards (output per worker per unit of time) do not exist at the brewery. Rather, it is machine standards (units processed per hour) and quality standards that capture managers' attention and influence their behavior. These are the standards management strives to meet.

Similarly, labor incentives are absent from the brewery. The plant's output is so overwhelmingly related to machine performance rather than worker performance that worker incentive schemes make little sense.

Demands of the Process on the Workers

The process at this Stroh brewery places a variety of demands on a variety of different work groups within the brewery. Art, science, and routine are all found. For the brewhouse work-

ers, even with the panels of controls that now abound, the brewing process still requires art, a "feel" and a "taste" for what makes quality beer. In many breweries, it still is true that the brewmaster's skills have been handed down from generation to generation.

While science may not have overtaken all aspects of the brewing art, it rules the quality assurance operations of the brewery itself (although the Detroit taste test is still the single most important check on the brewery's quality performance). Science is evident everywhere in quality assurance, from the chemistry involved to the statistical sampling. The training for the quality assurance department can thus be long and rigorous.

Science and art are mixed in the plant's maintenance activities, which are an important and prestigious activity. The capital intensity of the process dictates heavy reliance on maintenance and the ability to troubleshoot problems quickly so as not to waste time and output needlessly. Only with the line jobs in packaging does routine best characterize the process. Still, switching from canning to bottling to kegging provides a measure of diversity in the job from day to day.

DEMANDS OF THE PROCESS
ON MANAGEMENT

Stroh's Winston-Salem brewery and International Paper's Androscoggin Mill place many of the same kinds of demands on management. The high degree of capital intensity they both share dictate concern for (1) selection of the proper technology and (2) the balancing of capacities in all segments of the process. Over time, technological advance has dictated numerous advances in the process itself (centrifuges, stainless steel tanks, panels of process controls) and in the scale of the process (larger tanks than ever before). The design, choice, and matching of equipment are critical decisions for a brewer like Stroh.

Scheduling production, while a nontrivial matter, is not as critical to a brewery's success as it is to a job shop. As important, or even more so, as the positioning of orders within any work shift or within any week's production is the accurate forecasting of demand. A Stroh wholesaler who is out of a particular beer or package risks that the consumer will merely choose a different brand. It is up to the brewery to track sales reliably and to forecast sales, especially seasonal sales, accurately.

Good forecasting also plays a significant role in managing suppliers' deliveries and inventories (e.g., cans and bottles) well. Since individual breweries do not negotiate price, delivery becomes the key aspect of brewery–supplier contact.

HYBRID PROCESSES

Hybrid processes, mixes of two or more of the purer process types (job shop, batch flow, line flow, continuous flow), are common occurrences. Numerous plants are organized with line or continuous flow processes on their front ends, say, to assemble a product or to package it. On their back ends, these plants often have components fabricated or materials processed by job shop or batch flow processes. Much of food processing, drug manufacture, many complex consumer items (such as, appliances and furniture), and other products combine production in lots with assembly/packaging in lines— the kind of hybrid process represented by the Stroh brewery.

QUESTIONS

1. What similarities are there between the Stroh brewery operation and the Androscoggin Mill operation? What dissimilarities?

2. What did Stroh consider to be the elements of the satisfactory production plan and the requirements for good package planning? What particular elements of Stroh's hybrid process planning might be applicable to the hybrid process in general? Why?

3. Describe how quality control may differ between the two main processes involved in a brewery.

4. Compare and contrast the demands of the process on Stroh workers and management with the demands on the same groups in two other processes you have studied.

5. It was stated that the brewery had a capacity of 6 million barrels of beer per year. If the plant were to can, bottle, and keg 6 million barrels in a year, what would be the capacity utilization of the packaging equipment, given the speeds mentioned in the case? Feel free to make assumptions about the relative demands for cans, bottles, and kegs.

6. How could the capacity of the brewing process itself be increased without a physical expansion of the brewery? How attractive is such a change?

7. Given the chapter's information on the relative demands of different brands and the summer cycle of container changeovers, concoct a month's production schedule for each major Stroh company brand. In an average week, what fraction of time would be devoted to changeovers of various types?

SITUATION FOR STUDY E-1

COUNTRY GELATIN COMPANY

Thomas Brewer is the plant manager for Country Gelatin Company, maker of powdered gelatins for human consumption. The main component of gelatin is collagen, a fibrous substance that is mostly protein. Steerhide, a major source of collagen, is the main ingredient in the gelatin powder produced at Country's Kansas City, Kansas, plant.

Figure E5 shows the process that Country uses to produce its gelatin. First, the steerhides are treated (acid is added to remove the hair, then neutralized), weighed, and put into storage. Enough steerhide is treated at one time to provide 2 days' worth of production. The hides are then stored for about 2 weeks so that they begin to "break down" and can be blended with other ingredients. This storage is called "aging."

Once several batches of steerhides (1500 kilograms each) have aged properly, enough batches are ground (to about the consistency of hamburger) to run 1 week's production. These mixed batches (5500 kilograms each) are then aged again for a few days before they are mixed into a gel blend (8000 kilograms, of which about half is water). One gel blend is enough for 1 day's production of gelatin.

After being mixed and aged, the mixed batch undergoes microcutting, a process that cuts the material into very small pieces. It then is mixed with water and an acid to form the gel blend. Next the gel blend is forced through a dryer to make it a powder. Under proper conditions, the powder can be stored almost indefinitely, until it is needed for final production.

Final production consists of two stages. First, the powder is mixed with sugar and a powdered flavoring (unless the final product is to be an unflavored gelatin); second, the product is measured and packaged. Final production, although continuous, is done to customer order. All stages in the process are highly mechanized, and workers are needed only to monitor the machines.

Tom feels that quality control at Country can be adequately handled by three types of highly trained process control workers: solutions technicians, powder technicians, and line technicians. The solutions technician is responsible for the proper acid balance, salts, density, percent of solids, and the like of the gel blend. The powder technician's main responsibility is proper mixing of the final product—

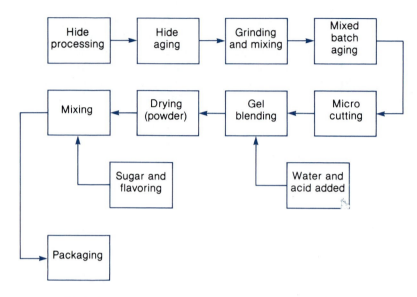

FIGURE E5   The production process at Country Gelatin Company.

that is, the proper proportion of powder, sugars, and flavoring. The line technician is responsible for packaging.

Tom is wondering how he should schedule production at the various stages in the process, including the scheduling of labor and machines. In addition, he is uncertain how much inventory should be carried, and in what form.

He feels he could begin to answer his concerns about scheduling and inventory control by (1) analyzing the characteristics of the process, and (2) asking himself what aspects of the process would help him in scheduling production and controlling inventories and which ones would hinder him.

SITUATION FOR STUDY E-2

BUCHANAN TOBACCO COMPANY

Buchanan Tobacco employed 2000 people in a plant that stretched 15 acres. Ten different cigarette brands were made at the site, each with its own blend of bright, burley, and Turkish tobaccos and various other flavorings.

After the tobacco (the whole dried leaf) had been purchased by the company's buyers at various tobacco markets, it was brought to the stemmeries. Here it was cleaned with moist air

and dried, and the stems were removed. The tobacco was then cut into small pieces and stored for 2 to 3 years in hogsheads before being brought to the plant for blending. The hogsheads were loaded onto flatbed tractor-trailers, and the tobacco arrived at the west end of the building in the containers in which it was aged.

In the blending area, the tobaccos were blended and flavorants were added in order to produce the correct blend for each brand of cigarettes. At each stage in the blending process, the tobacco was exposed to certain relative humidities and temperatures. At the completion of each stage, the blended tobacco was aged through drying. This aging allowed the tobacco to absorb moisture and flavorants.

After being aged, the tobacco went through the "casing and cutting" process, where certain liquids (casings) were added and the tobacco was shredded and blended for the particular brands being made. A pneumatic vacuum system transported the blended tobaccos to one of the 100 making machines (makers) designated for its brand. Each maker required one operator.

The sealed vacuum tubes ran above the machines, and so the tobacco fell to the bottom of the makers by gravity. The tobacco entered at the rate of 10 pounds per minute. The action of turning drums pulled the tobacco up through the machine. This action also vacuumed out dust and particles such as stems. As the tobacco came out of this section of the maker, it entered a small tube at such a constant rate that one continuous rod of tobacco was formed; this rod stretched almost the length of the machine.

At this point, the paper was wrapped around the tobacco. The paper, which was produced by a subsidiary, came in rolls over 6 miles long. Each roll contained enough paper for 95,000 cigarettes. The paper was threaded through the machine, and the cigarette brand name was printed on it. As the paper was folded around the continuous rod of tobacco, a wheel applied glue to one edge. The paper was then sealed around the rod of tobacco.

After sealing, the continuous cigarette was cut by a revolving knife, which cut 4100 cigarettes per minute and was timed to cut the exact length required.

The cut cigarettes next went to a drum. Vacuum pressure held the cigarettes on the drum

as they slid into pockets. Simultaneously, the filters for the cigarettes, which were made in another area of the building and were precut to the appropriate size, were blown over on a tube. The cigarettes in the pockets were directly opposite each other, and a filter simply fell between them so that a cigarette, double-length filter, and another cigarette were all sealed together. At this point, the double cigarette passed over a sealer, and the filter was sealed to the paper on both ends. At the same time, corking paper, which was fed from a roll into the maker, was cut to the proper length and wrapped around the filter by the action of the drums. The "tipping" picked up enough glue to cause it to adhere to the filter. The double cigarette was then moved to a knife and cut into two 80-millimeter filtered cigarettes.

There were various automatic quality checks during the making process. Any cigarette with a defect would be automatically rejected. Common defects found at this point included air leaks and pin holes. All defective cigarettes were broken down and completely recycled through the process.

Immediately after cutting, the cigarettes that passed inspection were moved on a belt, with cigarettes on the back part of the drum being turned so that all were now facing the same direction. This belt carried the cigarettes to a special reservoir that created a buffer between the making and packing processes.

This reservoir loaded cigarettes onto a conveyor for up to 17 minutes. If the maker went down, the packer could continue running for up to 17 minutes by using the reserve cigarettes from overhead. If the packer went down, the process simply reversed and cigarettes fed onto the conveyor directly from the maker. If either machine was inoperable for more than 17 minutes, both machines had to be shut down.

From this point, the cigarettes were fed by gravity into the packing machine or packer. As the cigarettes were fed into the machine, they automatically fell into three rows of seven, six, and seven cigarettes. A plunger pushed the 20 cigarettes into a foil pocket, which was formed as a series of turning drums took the foil that was fed off a roll and wrapped it around a form identical in shape and size to a pack of cigarettes. This foil was the interior of a pack of cigarettes.

Next, the label was taken from the front of the machine and formed into a pack and sealer was applied. Another plunger pushed the foiled pack into the label. A stamper picked up glue and applied a closure (stamp) to the pack. The pack slid on chains to the film machine.

The film fed off of a roll and was cut to the desired length to wrap a pack. Just before the pack was pushed into the film, the tear tape was laid across the film and sealed to it. Mechanical folders folded the film around the pack and electric heaters caused it to seal.

The packer packaged 210 packs of cigarettes a minute (4200 cigarettes); it was operating at a slightly faster rate than the maker. There were approximately 110 packers in the plant, each one operated by one worker.

The packaged cigarettes were then fed on conveyor belts past an inspector. The inspector looked for missing closures, missing tape, or any other defective packaging. Packs were fed to the inspector from two packers; therefore, an inspector saw about 25,000 packs an hour.

After the visual inspection, the packs proceeded on belts to the carton boxer machine. There were approximately 50 carton boxers, each one receiving from two packers; thus, two belts came together at the boxer. The cartons were fed down by a series of rollers and automatically opened. The packs from the two belts (five packs from each belt) lined up. The pressure from the last pack activated a switch, which in turn activated the plunger, pushing ten packs into a carton. The flaps of the carton were turned down by guides. When the carton emerged at the back of the boxer, it was sealed. At this point, an electronic inspector (operating on the basis of the metal in the foil) was used to detect missing tape or packs. The carton boxer's speed was determined by the speed of the packers, but generally it boxed 200 packs, or 20 cartons, per minute.

Next, the cartons proceeded up the elevator to the carton conveyor and down to the case packer. Usually at least five packers sent cartons to a single case packer; however, a single case packer could receive from as many as 20 packers. There were five case packers at the plant.

Flattened cases were stacked and fed down through one end of the machine, where guides opened them automatically. The cases had been preprinted with the brand name, but print was now applied to the cases to specify the date and the name of the plant. Cartons came down overhead sides from the carton collector and were conveyed into the back of the machine. The cartons were stacked in layers. As soon as 10 rows of six cartons each had accumulated, a switch was activated to plunge the 60 cartons into one case. Thus each case contained 12,000 cigarettes. The filled case was then moved forward. Glue was applied from rollers to the end flaps. When the machine cycled again, these flaps were sealed down with pressure. The case stayed in this compartment until the glue was dried and sealed, which was less than a minute. Each caser had the capacity of packing approximately five cases per minute.

The sealed cases crossed an automatic scale before going up an elevator. This scale inspected for light cases; being underweight indicated that a pack or carton was missing. A heavy case was not rejected, because extra weight merely indicated the presence of collected moisture.

After reaching the top of the case elevator, the case traveled on a conveyor to the transfer room. Here all brands were assembled on pallets by brand. Each pallet had an identification number, which the computer married to the brand's code number to permit tracking these cases to the warehouse. After the cases had been palletized, elevators lifted the pallets to the conveyor to the shipping center. All of the shipping was done from the new, completely computerized central distribution center. The cigarettes were produced strictly to order. Everything produced during the day was shipped out at night so that there was virtually no work-in-process or finished goods inventory.

1. Diagram the process flow.
2. Speculate, as best you can, on the flows of information in the process.
3. Why might this operation be classed as a hybrid? What type of hybrid is it and how does it compare with the Stroh brewery?
4. What do you see as key challenges for management in this process?
5. What kinds of changes to the process would occur as new makers are purchased with speeds twice as great or more than those already in the plant?

A WORKER-PACED LINE FLOW PROCESS AND A SERVICE FACTORY
Burger King Restaurant
Route 37
Noblesville, Indiana

The Burger King Restaurant on Route 37 in Noblesville, Indiana, was one of over 6000 fast-food restaurants operated worldwide by Burger King Corporation, a wholly owned subsidiary of Grand Metropolitan, and by the corporation's franchisees. Service was available from 6 A.M. to 2 A.M. every day. The dining room was open from 6 A.M. until 11 P.M., Sunday through Thursday, and from 6 A.M. until midnight on Fridays and Saturdays. Breakfast was available from the opening until 10:30 A.M. and consisted of a choice of bacon, ham, and sausage bagels, biscuits, and croissan'wiches, with or without eggs or cheese, French toast sticks, mini-muffins, breakfast buddies, biscuits with gravy, hash browns, and a scrambled egg platter. The regular menu consisted of a wide selection of hamburger sandwiches (regular hamburger and cheeseburger; a special Whopper sandwich with or without cheese; hamburger deluxe; double burger, double cheeseburger, and double Whopper; and a bacon double cheeseburger) as well as some specialty sandwiches (chicken, ham and cheese, fish), BK broilers (broiled chicken sandwiches), chicken tenders, and prepacked salads. To accompany these selections, the res-taurant offered various choices: french fries, onion rings, soft drinks, shakes, Breyer's frozen yogurts, Snickers ice cream bars, Kool Aid cool pops, apple pie, cherry pie, and lemon pie. Occasionally, there were promotional items such as Burger Buddies.

The restaurant, the highest sales volume Burger King in Indiana, was located on Route 37, a busy thoroughfare between Marion and Indianapolis. The restaurant was opened in May 1987 on the site of a former farm. The restaurant was owned and operated by a franchisee, Douglas Brucker of Marion.

The restaurant was rectangular, freestanding on 2 acres, and was constructed mainly of wood planks, bricks, and glass. The building was situated toward the front of the lot, freeing the sides and rear for 64 parking spaces. A "drive-thru" was operated on one side of the restaurant, with the order board at the rear and the pick-up window toward the front. Within the restaurant 96 seats (either benches or free-standing chairs) were arranged in groups. There were 16 tables of four, 1 table of three, 8 tables of two, and 13 single places within the restaurant. The eating area was tastefully appointed in oak wood, with a handsome color scheme, an atrium off to the side of the main eating area, ceiling fans, and many hanging plants. In the eating areas there were service counters for napkins, straws, and so on, and several large trash cans for customer use. The rest rooms were located next to the main door. The eating area occupied about half of the restaurant's square footage; the other half was occupied by the counter, the kitchen, and the storage area.

PART ONE

PROCESS DESCRIPTION

RESTAURANT OPERATIONS

Order Taking (The Front Counter)

After entering the restaurant, customers walked between the railings of the queuing line (or, as Burger King calls it, the "customer guidance system"). While awaiting their turns to state their order at the counter, they could consult the brightly lit menu above the counter area. At the right-hand side of the counter were two cash registers with screens (point-of-sale devices). An order-taker greeted each customer there and took the order. As the customer spoke, the order-taker keyed the contents of the order on a register (e.g., pressed the key for the Whopper—a large hamburger with lettuce, tomato, onions, pickles, ketchup, and mayonnaise), read the printed total for the order, took the customer's payment, and gave the customer change and a receipt that listed the order. Each register could accommodate one or two cashiers simultaneously and could handle up to three transactions at the same time.

At the other end of the counter, a printer printed a duplicate copy of the order. Using this copy, an expediter proceeded to assemble the order. Assembling the order meant going to the counter and the chutes that lay between the front counter and the kitchen to gather the sandwiches, fries, or other items that flowed from the kitchen. When shakes were ordered, the expediter was responsible for drawing them from the nearby dispensing machine. After assembling the kitchen items of the order, the expediter presented them to the customer either on a tray (for inside use) or in a bag (to go). The expediter also gave cups to the customer so that he or she could fill them with the desired soft drinks, tea, or coffee.

Several features of the front counter's operation were comparatively new and merit highlighting. The most important innovation was the split made in the duties of the order-takers and expediters. The system in use at the Noblesville Burger King was known as the "multiconventional" line-up. It was a throwback to the early years of Burger King when the "conventional" line-up was used. That system consisted of a single line of customers served by a single cash register where orders were taken. Expediters assembled the orders and presented them to the customers farther along the counter. The present system operated in much the same way, although up to six orders could be taken at the same time, and several expedit-

The front counter. (*Courtesy of Burger King Corporation*)

The dining area. (*Courtesy of Burger King Corporation*)

ers could handle those orders. The new, multi-conventional system was thus far faster than the old system.

The multiconventional line-up was a more radical change from the "hospitality line-up" that had replaced the old conventional system. With the hospitality line-up, cash registers were evenly spaced across the entire front counter and customers had to choose which of several lines they wished to wait in. Cashiers both took orders and assembled them. The hospitality line-up, although somewhat more labor intensive than the old conventional line-up, could handle peak hour demand more efficiently than the older system. With the advent of the multiconventional line-up, however, the labor intensity of the hospitality line-up was reduced without sacrificing its peak-period capacity advantages. Customers preferred the new line-up as well. With a single line, they did not risk becoming annoyed because some other line was moving faster than theirs. In addition, they were frequently better prepared to give their order to the order-taker, and this speeded up the process for everyone.

Another innovation involved the self-service drink dispensers. With their installation, customers could fix their drinks precisely the way they wanted (whether with lots of ice or no ice). By moving the drink dispensers out of the kitchen, time and some labor costs were also saved. Because free refills were possible, materials costs were somewhat higher, but not appreciably so.

Order Filling (The Kitchen)

Burger King differed from McDonald's and some other fast-food restaurants in that comparatively little finished goods inventory was kept; sandwiches were assembled continuously. While certain orders might not have been delivered as quickly as when larger inventories were kept, this approach offered the distinct advantage of producing to order when appropriate. As an old Burger King slogan put it, you can "have it your way," say, by ordering a Whopper with double cheese and mustard but no pickle, or a hamburger with extra onions.

Providing this kind of customer order variation with minimum customer waiting demanded a production system that was extraordinarily flexible. In fact, two kinds of flexibility were required: flexibility to meet special customer orders and flexibility to meet large surges in customer demand during lunch or dinner hours. Many aspects of the production system contributed to this flexibility.

THE "LINE": LAYOUT AND JOB DESCRIPTIONS

The process of making sandwiches and filling orders at Burger King was explicitly recognized as an assembly line. Production of the hamburger sandwiches (burgers, for short) followed a straight path from the back of the kitchen to the front counter. Along this path were a series of workstations (see Figure F1).

Any of the various burgers was begun either by taking a broiled meat patty and toasted bun out of an environmentally controlled holding compartment called a "steamer" or by placing a frozen meat patty (Whopper size or regular) and bun onto the chain drag at the feed end of a specially constructed, gas-fired broiler at the back of the kitchen. The meat patties were drawn from a freezer below the broiler. The broiler cooked the meat at approximately 800° F, allowing the grease to drip into a special compartment, and it also toasted the bun.

Next in the assembly line came the "board," where buns and meat were transformed into Whopper sandwiches, burgers, hamburger de-

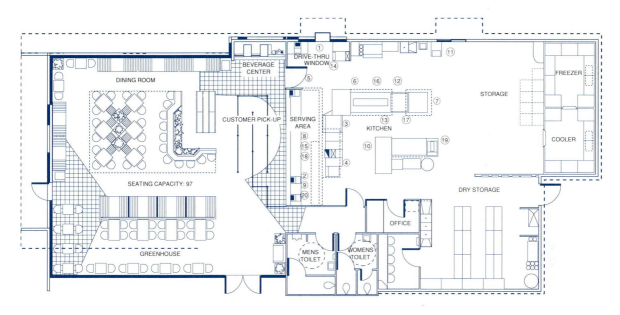

FIGURE F1   Layout of the Noblesville Burger King. The circled numbers indicate the sequence of additions of workers to the kitchen as demand increases.

luxe sandwiches, double cheeseburgers, and the like. This was the key portion of the line, where the burger could be assembled "your way." The board itself was a long, stainless-steel table in the center of which were bins of condiments (refrigerated cheese slices, bacon, pickles, onion, sliced tomatoes, shredded lettuce, mayonnaise) kept at room temperature. Below the table were racks for holding spare quantities of condiments and supplies and also places for waste disposal. There were two work areas, one on each side of the center inventory of condiments. Above each side were two microwave ovens that could be used for keeping assembled sandwiches hot, stacks of various wrappers into which the sandwiches were placed, and a special series of touch controls that were part of the information flow system of the kitchen (more on this later). Beyond the board, on the pick-up counter, were chutes that

held completed sandwiches ready for assembly into customer orders.

On one side of this main burger assembly line were the frying vats and the specialty sandwich board. The four frying vats were computer controlled, two just for french fries and two for other products (such as onion rings, chicken sandwich portions, chicken tenders, or fish portions). Near the frying vats were racks of thawed or thawing french fries (1- to 2-hour thaw times maximum). Behind the frying vats was the specialty sandwich board, which had its own assortment of condiments, buns, and wrappers. To one side of the specialty sandwich board were two warmers (one for items such as cooked chicken patties and the other for chicken tenders) and to the other side was a bun toaster.

On the other side of the main burger assembly line were the automatic drink machines for the drive-thru operation. A worker simply placed an ice-filled cup under the appropriate drink spout and pressed a button for small, regular, or large drinks; the machine then dispensed the proper quantity of soft drink, freeing the worker to do something else while the cup was being filled. The shake machine (for chocolate, vanilla, and strawberry) was located nearby, close to both the drive-thru window and the front counter.

Around the periphery of the kitchen were sinks and storage areas for food and supplies. There were also cooler and freezer rooms, an office, a training room, and a crew room where workers could congregate.

THE DRIVE-THRU OPERATION

Because the drive-thru at the Noblesville Burger King accounted for approximately 50 percent of the restaurant's business, its smooth operation was critical. Work assignments at the drive-thru depended on how busy the restaurant was. In very slow times, a single worker (order-taker/expediter) could handle the drive-thru alone. When business picked up, two people were assigned to the drive-thru — one as an order-taker and one as an expediter. At peak times, five workers were assigned to the drive-thru: order-taker, window pusher, expediter, drink assembler, and cashier. (The Noblesville Burger King had two windows in the drive-thru lane, the first to handle the money and the second to "push out" the order.)

PEAK VERSUS NONPEAK OPERATION

Employees were allocated to the workstations at the restaurant according to the pace of demand. When demand was slow, a smaller crew operated the restaurant: an order-taker/expe-

diter at the front counter, a drive-thru order-taker/expediter, and two kitchen workers. One worker took the broiler and the burger board, while one worked at the fry station and the specialty board. At peak times, there were as many as 24 employees working in the restaurant plus two or three managers. Management knew from historical data exactly when the peak hours would be at the Noblesville restaurant and so could plan worker arrivals.

Before the daily peaks in demand at lunch and dinner, considerable preparations were made, such as stocking the freezer under the broiler with hamburger patties, taking frozen fries out for thawing, and slicing tomatoes. If things worked as planned, minimal restocking would be needed during the peaks.

As demand picked up, more workers were added, and job assignments became more specialized. In slow times, for example, one worker split duties between the fry station and the specialty sandwich board; during peak periods there were separate workers for these two work areas. During slow periods, one worker handled the broiler and all burger sandwich preparation; during peak times, one worker "fed" the broiler, one or two "caught" patties and buns and monitored the steamer, and up to four workers assembled sandwiches at the burger board. At the Noblesville Burger King, the burger board was divided during peak times into cheese and noncheese sides. (At other Burger Kings, this division might be Whopper-sized sandwiches on one side and small sandwiches on the other. Such a split frequently depended on the composition of demand at the particular restaurant.) During peak periods as well, two workers helped keep the dining area clean.

During very slow periods, much of the sandwich and drink production was triggered by the customer order itself. The burger given to the customer might actually be the one placed on the broiler chain in response to punching in the

From behind the front counter. (*Courtesy of Burger King Corporation*)

Slicing tomatoes in preparation for the noon peak period. (*Courtesy of Burger King Corporation*)

At the burger board. (*Courtesy of Burger King Corporation*)

The fry station. (*Courtesy of Burger King Corporation*)

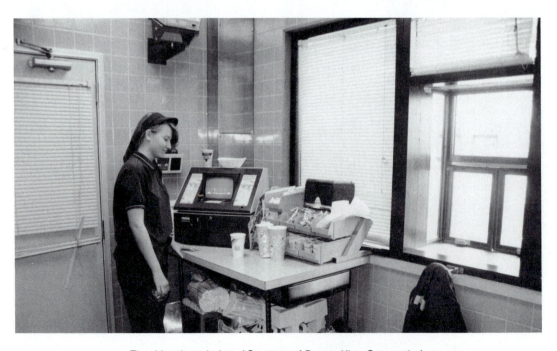

The drive-thru window. (*Courtesy of Burger King Corporation*)

146

order. Some items could be held in inventory. An inventory of the most popular sandwiches (such as regular burgers and Whoppers) were usually kept in the chutes, but only for 10 minutes; if no customer requested them, they were discarded. Each sandwich wrapper was marked with a "time to discard." The system used the numbers pointed to by the minute hand on the clock. Thus a Whopper wrapped at 20 minutes after the hour (the 4 on the clockface) would have a 6 marked on the wrapper, because at 30 minutes after the hour (the 6 on the clockface) its 10-minute hold time would have expired. French fries were handled in a special way. Fries took approximately 2 minutes and 30 seconds to cook—too long to have a customer wait. As a result, fries had to be waiting in finished goods inventory. Here, too, the restaurant kept track of the time fries were waiting. If no one claimed fries within 7 minutes, they were discarded. (The fry station computers helped by keeping track of the time between batches so that fries were not sitting out too long.)

As demand picked up, it became more and more likely that a finished goods inventory of the major burgers and specialty sandwiches would be kept and that the broiler feeder would be loading the broiler in response to the inventory situation rather than in response to the particular orders displayed on the video screens. To guide production and to maintain inventory levels as demand increased, the Noblesville Burger King operated "stock level charts." There were four stock level charts—one each for the broiler-steamer, sandwich board, specialty sandwich board, and specialty sandwich warmer. The chart featured a stock-level light indicator on which there were seven lights. Corresponding to each light was a volume of sales range to which were pegged inventory standards for the various items. Each change in the level (e.g., from level 4 to level 5 or from level 6 to peak) was announced by a

special bell and the light switched so that all workers could infer, for example, how many sandwiches of particular types should be in the finished goods chutes and how many patties and buns should be in the steamer. The workers at the board were constantly tracking how many sandwiches were in each chute as well as keeping an eye on the video screen for any special order variations entered by the cashiers. When a worker finished such an order, he or she pressed one of the special touch controls above the station (mentioned earlier), which removed the call for that sandwich from the video screen. The worker then marked the wrapper to identify it to the expediters.

For the manager, the choice of a "level" represented a trade-off between meeting service standards with quick deliveries, on the one hand, and keeping too much in inventory and risking waste on the other. The manager always wanted to raise the level just before a surge in demand and to lower it just before the surge evaporated.

Coping with Bottlenecks

Surges in demand or runs on particular items could strain the production system and cause it to miss its established service standards. Three service standards were routinely tracked: (1) door-to-door time—the time elapsed from the moment the customer entered a line to place an order until the customer was served, (2) drive-thru time—the time elapsed from the arrival of a car in line until the customer was served, and (3) drive-thru transaction time—the time elapsed between a car's arrival at the pick-up window and its receipt of the order. The Noblesville Burger King restaurant tried to keep these service standards at company-mandated levels: 3 minutes average for the door-to-door and drive-thru times and 30 seconds average for the drive-thru transaction time. This last time was tracked automatically by the store's computer.

To reach these goals consistently the restaurant's managers had to avoid bottlenecks in production. By providing both guidance to the crew and a set of spare hands, a manager could help ensure a smooth operation. (The Noblesville Burger King's sales volumes were high enough to warrant the creation of a "production leader" position for work in the kitchen, and a head cashier position. These workers were active in guiding the crew and anticipating bottlenecks.) During peak hours especially, it was not uncommon to see the production leader or a manager stepping up to the board to assemble a sandwich or drawing a shake from the machine or bagging fries or replenishing materials. The managers also encouraged crew team work. For example, workers with some slack time helped those who were overloaded—a cheese sandwich worker might assemble some non-cheese burgers. In fact, the manager's mandate for each of the workers was (1) to be aware of which "level" was being operated and what was on the video screen, (2) to be aware of any materials that would soon be out of stock, (3) to keep the workstation clean, and (4) to help anyone needing help. This mandate to keep production smooth and efficient placed special demands on a manager. The manager's job was not only to break any current bottlenecks but also to anticipate any potential ones. The manager constantly sought information from the workers on where bottlenecks were, how many cars were in line, and which materials were running low, and encouraged the workers to handle as much of any surge in demand themselves without intervention.

Adequate prepeak period preparation also meant a great deal in coping with bottlenecks. If the shake machine was not completely filled with ingredients or if the cash register tape was close to running out, the operation was in danger of some bottlenecks that might affect service adversely. The restaurant manager had to check the status of items like these to be sure that incomplete preparation did not detract from the success of the operation.

PURCHASING AND MATERIALS MANAGEMENT

For any item, the quantity ordered was the amount needed to bring the restaurant's existing inventory up to a certain established level. This level was the quantity of the item the manager expected to be used between receipt of the order and receipt of the next order (3 to 5 days at a maximum) plus a safety stock amount equal to 20 percent of the expected usage. This safety stock helped ensure that the entire menu was always available. The expected usage was calculated from the previous week's demand but was adjusted to reflect special trends or such conditions as holidays, school vacations, and newspaper promotions.

Orders were typically placed 1 day in advance of delivery. Materials were generally received in the afternoon. All materials were dated on receipt, and the oldest materials were always used first. However, usage levels were so high that the restaurant never needed to worry about spoilage, even for produce or dairy products. Orders for meat, paper products, and certain other supplies were placed three times a week with the Chicago regional office of Burger King Distribution Services, Burger King's supply subsidiary. Fresh produce was ordered from either Burger King Distribution Services or an independent supplier 6 days a week. Baked goods were ordered 6 days a week and dairy products 5 days a week.

THE WORKFORCE

The restaurant employed 45 workers. A typical worker put in 35 to 40 hours each week, spread over 5 or 6 days. Most lived in the area of the restaurant. At night and on weekends, high school students and second-job workers were often employed. The area was considered one that was hard to find staff for.

The crew for the Noblesville Burger King was hand-picked by the assistant managers. Almost none had worked at a Burger King before. Workers were paid for the hours worked, with overtime given after 40 hours each week. The average hourly wage was $5.20, with some workers receiving a minimum wage of $4.25 and the best-performing worker receiving $5.80. The fringe benefit package was modest. Labor turnover at the restaurant ran at 40 percent.

A worker's hours were likely to differ from day to day, although there was a set crew for the breakfast shift. The schedule for any week, however, was worked out about a week in advance. The schedule did try to reflect worker preferences about the amount and timing of their work. Most work assignments were shuffled daily. The prime reason for shuffling assignments was to promote worker cross-training, which increased the operation's flexibility. A manager might also be forced to shuffle assignments because of worker scheduling or absentee problems. For these reasons, the order-taker knew how the kitchen operated, and the kitchen knew how to take orders. The cross-training also had the welcome benefit of heightening the tolerance any worker had for the momentary troubles of other workers.

The daily rise and fall of peak and off-peak demand required continual changes in crew size, so that neither too few nor too many workers worked at any one time. The flexibility needed in the schedule was achieved by using the part-time labor force and by scheduling their arrivals and departures at different times. Some, for example, reported to work just 15 minutes or so before the noon rush hour. Workers worked at least 3 to 4 hours at a time. A worker's departure from the restaurant was at the discretion of the manager. If sales were light, the manager could let some of the workers out early; if demand was heavy, it was understood that workers would be asked to stay past the scheduled departure time. The best crew, however, was generally scheduled for the peak times on Friday and Saturday.

The production leaders and the head cashier were responsible for training new workers. There were seven main stations on which to be trained [sandwich board, specialty sandwich board, fry station, broiler-steamer, order-taker/cashier, drive-thru, and hostess (clean-up)]. Training for any one of these stations took about 3 hours and consisted of reading some prepared material, watching a videotape on the station's work, doing a worksheet based on that video, reading a manual on procedures on the workstation, watching the trainer demonstrate procedures at the workstation, performing on a trial basis from 1 to 2 hours, taking a written test, and then having performance evaluated by the trainer. A new worker trained first on the broiler and steamer and then progressed to every station in the kitchen, finally winding up at the front counter and drive-thru operations. The fry station and the burger sandwich board were generally acknowledged to be the toughest tasks at the restaurant.

QUALITY

Periodically, about once a month, a team from the corporation would visit the restaurant unannounced to perform a quality inspection. They used a form for rating the food, the service, the appearance of the restaurant, and some other factors. In addition, the district manager for the franchisee made weekly visits to the restaurant to audit quality. Twice a year, management performed a 3-day restaurant operations consultation during which every aspect of the restaurant's operation on every shift was analyzed. The results of such audits were taken very seriously. In addition, much of the managers' time was spent in the dining room talking with customers and assessing how well the service was being delivered.

MANAGEMENT

The Noblesville Burger King was a franchise store. It was part of the company's Chicago area. Supervising the Noblesville Burger King were a manager and five assistant managers. One of these six was always at the restaurant. During peak times managers would overlap, so that two or three sets of extra hands and eyes were available for breaking bottlenecks. The five assistant managers worked 5 days a week, but on a rotating shift.

Any manager's primary responsibility was to ensure that a good-quality product was promptly served in a clean environment within company guidelines. Although a manager's ability to control costs was valued, meeting the corporation's service, quality, and cleanliness goals came first. Meeting these goals meant developing the capabilities of the production crew and maintaining its morale. Thus the manager was first and foremost a crew foreman, teaching new hires, guiding work assignments, checking quality, breaking bottlenecks, and providing an example for the crew. Layered on these responsibilities were others—ordering materials, receiving deliveries, checking and posting standards of performance (such as the door-to-door or transaction times), checking on the preparations for the day and for the peak periods, and scheduling the part-time workforce. Of the restaurant's five assistant managers, three specialized in the functions of ordering, scheduling, and breakfast operations.

Burger King headquarters provided restaurant managers with a number of aids. Chief among these aids for the week-by-week operation of the restaurant were the charts, formulas, and decision rules for scheduling the workforce, given the restaurant's particular configuration. The corporation had developed aids that showed, for different sales levels and hours of operation, how much labor each restaurant should have and where that labor ought to be assigned. These charts, formulas, and decision rules greatly aided the managers in controlling labor costs, which was the second highest cost that could be controlled.

The restaurant's POS system (computer/cash register network) was also a useful management tool. From the computer, the manager could obtain information, by half-hour increments, on sales, product mix, and discounts. The POS system also kept track of the restaurant's service standard performance.

FACILITIES AND TECHNOLOGY

This Burger King was a design called BK87. According to Larry Levensky, the franchisee's district manager, the BK87 was an excellent design for a high-volume restaurant. The layout was very efficient, workers did not waste many steps in performing the tasks required of them, materials were readily available, and there was ample storage space. Workers at nonpeak times could easily cover more than one workstation.

In addition, the Noblesville Burger King included several technological improvements that had been initiated by the corporation. For example, computerized frying vats had been installed with temperature probes that automatically adjusted the frying times so that french fries or other fried foods were cooked perfectly. Buzzers indicated when the fries should be shaken or removed from the vats. The automatic drink machines were another advance; these permitted workers to engage in other tasks while soft drink cups were being filled automatically. A new shake machine mixed shakes automatically as well. The addition of TV screens to indicate variations on the standard sandwiches was another advance; these reduced the cacophony that could strike the kitchen during peak periods. The kitchen included a new breakfast grill and hood, a specially designed unit that could be set up for the breakfast business and then transformed into a

work area the rest of the day. The heat chutes for finished sandwiches were coated with Teflon and were enclosed to keep the sandwiches warmer. The extra window for the drive-thru was still another innovation, helping to cut 12 seconds off the line time for drive-thru customers. Burger King was always inventing new ways for delivering better service.

PART TWO

DISCUSSION

The Burger King Corporation is in no way responsible for the following views and presentation. They remain solely the responsibility of the author.

THE FLOW OF THE PROCESS AND OF INFORMATION

In most service industries, the time delay between service provision and service consumption is necessarily very short. Put another way, one can rarely inventory a service, at least not for very long. Hotel room-nights cannot be inventoried, nor can timely tips on the stock market, nor can tasty hamburgers. Hence a whole degree of freedom is removed from the service manager, which heightens the importance of capacity choice in most service industries.

It is also frequently the case that services must be particularly flexible so that they can be customized to individual consumer needs. Think of the travel agent, the salesperson, the cab driver, and, yes, the fast-food restaurant.

These two basic features of many service businesses place substantial demands on the

process design and information systems of an enterprise like Burger King. Flexibility in both product and volume is paramount, and Burger King has adopted some classic policies for yielding such flexibility.

Figure F2 is a process flow diagram for assembling an order. It is simple, and that is one of its advantages. Responsibilities are clearly demarcated, and yet all of the key tasks for customizing the hamburger or specialty sandwich rest with the worker who actually assembles the sandwich at the board. This fact, in turn, simplifies the information flow so that only one worker need pay strict attention to the punch-in of a special order. (An information flow diagram is found in Figure F3.) In this way, with a clear delineation of tasks and direct information flows, rapid product changes can be facilitated.

Flexibility in changing production volumes is achieved by a continual rebalancing of the sandwich production line. The time pattern of demand is well known from past experience, and this knowledge has permitted the staggering of work hours for the part-time workforce so that varying numbers can be on hand at any one time. The workforce ebbs and flows from

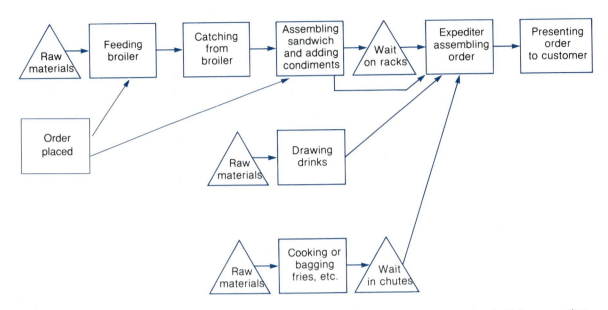

FIGURE F2   A process flow diagram (nonpeak period) for the Noblesville Burger King restaurant's kitchen operations.

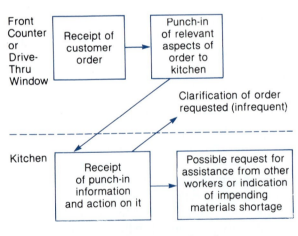

FIGURE F3   An information flow diagram (nonpeak period) for the Noblesville Burger King restaurant.

More and more, production is keyed by the levels of the finished goods inventory and of the work-in-process inventory of broiled burgers and toasted buns. Instead of reacting to the order punched in, the broiler feeder reacts to the manager's posted list of burgers to be held as work-in-process, feeding the broiler so as to maintain the desired inventory level. Similarly, the board workers respond to the level of finished goods inventory, although these board workers must also respond to any special orders that are punched in. Special orders, of course, must take precedence over the maintenance of the finished goods inventory. The peak period changes in the process and information flow diagrams are pictured in Figure F4.

four during slack periods to 24 during peak periods. As more workers are added, the job contents narrow and, importantly, the flow of information changes. No longer is production keyed completely to the punch-in of the order.

DEMANDS OF THE PROCESS ON THE WORKFORCE

The flexibility of the Burger King fast-food operation demands flexibility from its workers.

Process Flow Diagram for Burgers

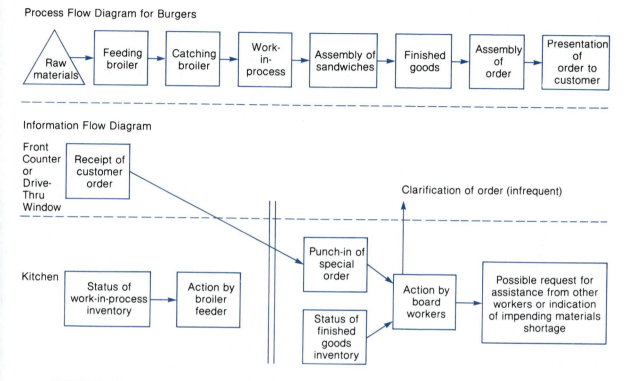

FIGURE F4   Process and information flow diagrams (peak period) for the Noblesville Burger King restaurant.

The job contents and the production pace vary markedly throughout any worker's shift during the day, requiring a special tolerance. Workers on a machine-paced assembly line get used to the rhythm of the conveyor. But, on a worker-paced line, and particularly one in a service industry, any rhythm may soon dissolve.

What is especially true of worker-paced lines is that the crew on the line views itself as a team, largely because they are so dependent on one another. This fact often permits worker-paced lines where the demand is steady (unlike at a fast-food restaurant) to be paid according to a group incentive scheme. Some standard of production—X units per time period—is established and the crew on the line, if it can better the standard, is paid extra for doing so. This kind of group incentive pay scheme can tie a crew together as a team even more thoroughly than usual.

DEMANDS OF THE PROCESS ON MANAGEMENT

An operation like a Burger King restaurant places specific demands on management both because it is a service operation and because it is a worker-paced line flow process. As a line flow process, many of the issues that were discussed in Tour D with respect to General Motors surface:

• Balance of the line.
• Materials management.

- Technological advance.
- Capacity planning.
- Product design.
- Workforce management.

Managers of worker-paced lines should be sensitive to all these issues, since to fall down on any one could seriously jeopardize the entire operation.

The issue of technological advance is particularly acute, since such an advance may enable a smoother, more regular flow of the product. After all, a worker-paced line flow usually remains worker, rather than machine-paced, because there is as yet no easy way to guard against a succession of overcycle conditions striking a worker all at once (such as a run on "Whoppers, hold the pickles"). If the mix of product options can somehow be smoothed out or if particular advances can be made in product or workstation design, a worker-paced line can easily be transformed into a machine-paced line. In other words, the worker-paced line is somewhat more vulnerable to radical, rather than incremental, change than is a machine-paced one.

The technological changes evident at the Noblesville Burger King all contributed to a smoother flow of product. The automatic drink machines, the computerized frying vats, the TV monitors of information, and even the new BK87 layout all act to speed up and smooth the delivery process.

A Burger King's status as a service operation only heightens the importance of capacity planning, since service firms cannot ordinarily inventory their product. The new BK87 design is testament to the importance the corporation assigns to planning capacity. The importance of workforce management is also heightened, because the worker-customer interaction is part of the service. Ordinarily, one cannot hide the service process as readily as one can hide the manufacturing process. Keeping the workforce productive and interested in their jobs is a key challenge for managers in service operations.

QUESTIONS

1. Visit a fast-food restaurant with a friend to perform an experiment. While one of you times the other's entry and exit and the time from the placing of the order to its receipt, the other should observe how many workers are actually involved with the order. Visit the fast-food restaurant at a slack time and at a peak time, and compare the differences in time and number of workers.

2. Watch for bottlenecks the next time you are in a fast-food restaurant (or any worker-paced service operation). Where do they arise and why? How might they be remedied?

3. Suppose that Burger King were to introduce a new type of sandwich. What aspects of the restaurant's operations would be affected, and how?

4. Why is flexibility one of the key features for success in a worker-paced assembly line operation such as Burger King?

5. How would you define capacity at a Burger King? What factors influence the establishment of a limit to capacity?

6. Would you prefer to work on a machine-paced assembly line or a worker-paced one? Why? Which would you prefer to supervise? Why?

7. Visit a Burger King close to you. It is unlikely to be a brand new one with all the advances incorporated into the Noblesville Burger King. Consider the ways by which the Burger King you visit could be modernized. Consider as well what could be done at the restaurant to increase capacity as sales increase. Prepare plans of action that specify which things ought to be done, and in what order, to modernize the restaurant and/or increase its capacity. Defend your choices.

8. Consider an alternative kitchen layout to the one at the Noblesville Burger King. In what ways is your alternative better or worse than the one discussed in the tour?

SITUATION FOR STUDY F-1

LEGACY HOMES

Tom Stoddard had been employed part-time as a "rough carpenter" by Legacy Homes while he completed his degree at Interstate Tech University. After his graduation, Legacy hired Tom as a construction superintendent; this job combined the duties of foreman, scheduler, and expediter.

By building only to order, Legacy took a conservative approach to the ups and downs typical of the home construction industry. Legacy offered a limited number of home designs; Tables F1 and Table F2 show the work involved on most of them—usually about 90 days' worth. When a buyer arranged a home loan from a lending institution, the local practice was to allow the construction company to receive the money in partial payments (cash draws) depending on the degree of completion of the home. Thus, for Legacy to receive the money, Tom needed to finish a home as fast as possible.

Legacy had a nucleus crew of highly skilled workers that it wanted to keep working most of the time. Other workers could be hired to supplement this crew when necessary. Table F3 shows this crew and the various tasks they were capable of performing. Each crew member knew well a primary function such as plumbing but could be counted on to help with other functions such as rough carpentry. The crew who installed the plumbing, for example, also installed the heating and electricity. This overlap of skills was possible for two reasons: (1) most of the work on a Legacy house was rather straightforward and did not entail the total skill requirements of journeymen in any of the trades, and (2) Legacy hired nonunion workers.

Table F1 shows the minimum and maximum crew sizes for completing each task. For example, task 8 requires a minimum of two workers because one person working alone cannot position the furnace or handle the ductwork; two people working on separate houses would take much longer to complete their work on both houses than if they worked together on one house at a time. At the maximum crew size, of course, it can happen that workers interfere with each other's work. Tom assumed that additional workers could work at the same rate as workers already on the job; he therefore scaled the number of workers up or down proportionately. For example, in task 1 if two workers can do the job in 1 day (i.e., 2 labor-days are required), three workers can do the job in 2/3 day (2 labor-days divided by three workers available), and four workers can do it in 1/2 a day. All operations have been designed to require a low level of skill; thus, any worker can shift to another operation with only a negligible loss of efficiency. Usually one worker is used as parts chaser and relief. The supervisor can help with

TABLE F1 Crew size and times for various tasks (Legacy Homes)

TASK	DESCRIPTION	WORK TYPE*	MINIMUM/MAXIMUM CREW SIZE	DAYS TO COMPLETE (with minimum crew)
1	Concrete footer	A	2-4	1.00
2	Foundation	F	Subcontract	1.00
3	Grading	A	2-4	0.50
4	Framing	B	5-8	2.60
5	Roofing	F	Subcontract	1.00
6	Concrete	A/B	3-5	1.50
7	Wiring	C	2-4	1.00
8	Furnace and ducts	C	2-4	2.25
9	Plumbing	C	2-3	2.50
10	Insulation	B	1-3	2.25
11	Dry wall	F	Subcontract	1.00
12	Siding	F	Subcontract	5.50
13	Sewer line	A	2-3	2.00
14	Painting	F	Subcontract	1.50
15	Finish carpentry	D	2-4	2.50
16	Tile	D	1-2	5.00
17	Electrical trim	C	1-2	1.50
18	Finish plumbing	C	1-2	3.50
19	Heating trim	C	1-3	2.50
20	Carpeting	F	Subcontract	2.00
21	Cleanup	E	1-3	2.00

*A, excavate; B, rough carpentry; C, plumbing, heating, electrical; D, finish carpentry; E, part-timeclean-up; F, subcontract.

TABLE F2 Precedence relationship (Legacy Homes)

JOB	PRECEDING OPERATION(S)
1	
2	1
3	2
4	3
5	4
6	2
7	4
8	5
9	5
10	7, 8, 9
11	10
12	10
13	9
14	11
15	14
16	14
17	14
18	15
19	14
20	6, 12, 13, 16, 17, 18, 19
21	20

TABLE F3   Labor force (Legacy Homes)

TYPE OF WORK	CURRENT LABOR AVAILABLE	TASKS PERFORMED*
A Excavate	3	1, 3, 6, 13
B Rough carpentry	5	4, 6, 10
C Plumbing, heating, electrical	4	7, 8, 9, 17, 18, 19
D Finish carpentry	2	15, 16
E Part-time cleanup	1	21
F Subcontract		2, 5, 11, 12, 14, 20

*See Table F1 for an explanation of these numbers.

the parts chasing but is not expected to take part in operations except as a troubleshooter.

Although the products (houses) do not move, Tom feels that the principles of worker-paced lines can be applied with beneficial results.

1. Design a process flow for Tom.
2. What is the minimum time requirement to build a house? How many houses should be built to keep the permanent crew busy?

What is the maximum number of houses that should be under construction at one time?

3. Is the workforce balanced? If not, which crew sizes should be changed?
4. Design an information flow for Tom.
5. Set up a sequence for raw material flow for Tom.

SITUATION FOR STUDY F-2

SMALL CITY NEWSPAPER

Small City Newspaper (SCN) was a family-owned paper with a circulation of 43,000 in the morning and 22,000 in the evening. There were three editions of the morning paper and two editions of the afternoon paper; the earlier editions of each paper were for delivery further away.

Newspapers have two content inputs: news and advertising. For SCN, as with most daily newspapers, advertising determined the size of each issue, which in turn affected the length of the production run. To maintain an average of 43 percent news content and 57 percent adver-

tising, the number of columns of news was allocated according to the number of columns of advertising sold for a particular issue. A minimum number of news columns (front page, sports, editorial, comics, and so on) was required for the morning paper (96 total columns) and for the evening paper (80 total columns). Information about the number of columns of advertising was communicated to the editors and the production manager by the advertising department.

Advertising was divided into three categories: display, classified, and national. Display was used primarily by local retailers and ad agencies, who often had camera-ready copy prepared for the paste-up department. On occasion, the advertising and art departments worked with the customer in preparing the advertisement. Three days' lead time was generally required of the client when placing a display ad; however, flexibility in this procedure allowed for changes to be made until press time. Classified ads had to be submitted by 5:00 P.M. the previous day and could be prepared for paste-up on the computer. National advertising copy was usually camera-ready and followed much the same procedure as the display ads. To expedite the use of both display and national ad copy, an inventory of these ads was maintained.

The morning news department had a staff of 40: city desk, copy desk/AP wire service, sports, style, editorial, and cartoon. The afternoon paper had a staff of 22 (no cartoonist). The library kept microfilmed copies of newspapers, publicity brochures, and a master file of news clippings (filed alphabetically) on important individuals. A personal computer that was tied into the Associated Press news retrieval system was also located in the library.

The managing editor assigned reporters and photographers to cover newsworthy events. Editorials as well as style and feature articles had the earliest deadlines (5:00 P.M. for the morning paper and 9:00 A.M. for the afternoon paper) and so were often written the day before they were to be published. Front page stories and sports coverage demanded up-to-date reporting; the deadlines for these articles were 11:00 P.M. for the morning paper and 11:00 A.M. for the afternoon paper.

Flexibility in the entire operation was a must, to allow for reporting late-breaking news. Because these stories could significantly disrupt the process, reporters were encouraged to prepare as much of their other copy as far in advance of press time as possible. To facilitate this, the newspaper had adopted a flexible time schedule for its reporters, who were generally on the job from 3:00 P.M. to midnight (for the morning paper) and from 7:00 A.M. to 4:00 P.M. (for the afternoon paper). In spite of this effort, half of the newspaper was made up in the two hours before press time.

Generally, a reporter composed a story at a video display terminal (VDT). The story appeared on a screen (CRT) as it was typed. Errors could easily be corrected, and additions and deletions did not affect the rest of the story. Typewritten copy could enter the computer through the use of an optical character reader (OCR), which sensed typewritten copy if it was prepared in a compatible typeface. Once the reporter was satisfied with the story, a single key command put the story in line in the computer. If this was done close to the deadline and the reporter considered the story to be especially important, the reporter could supersede this queue by notifying the editor.

The editor had a list of all stories in the queue. He accessed the stories and made revisions using special keyboard commands. Once he was satisfied, the editor added the headline via the keyboard, specifying the type size of the heading (in points), and designated where the story should go in the paper. The story was then transferred by computer to page paste-up, where a hard copy was printed.

Syndicated features and wire service copy were transmitted to the paper in a form compatible with the VDT system, replacing the old teletypewriter and eliminating the need for rekeyboarding. At the copy desk these stories were reviewed and a determination was made concerning which stories to use; then the copy was forwarded by computer to page paste-up. The laser photo service was another external input. Photographs were beamed to the newspaper along with a subtitle and/or a short explanation. The photo came to the paper ready for paste-up.

Advertising copy, news stories, and photographs were pieced together on a page the size of a newspaper page. Reusable by-lines and photos of syndicated columnists were kept at the paste-up tables. Efforts were made to smooth the flow through paste-up by having advertising, feature articles, and as much of the news as possible to paste-up as early as possible. The paste-up operation for the morning paper normally ran from 5:30 P.M. to 11:00 P.M. Paste-up for the afternoon paper generally ran from 8:00 A.M. to 11:30 A.M. The time difference for the papers was due to the latter's smaller size and the advance preparation the morning paper paste-up had to do for its Sunday edition. Changes for the final edition of each paper could be made after the presses began the earlier edition(s).

Once the pages had been laid out, they were photographed. An aluminum-backed, polymer-coated plate was placed in an exposure unit beneath the page negative. After a 45- to 70-second exposure, it was put through a wash unit, which used water and a small amount of biodegradable defoaming agent to remove the nonexposed polymer areas. After drying, the plate had a raised mirror image surface, which was curved to fit the rotary press cylinder. One page could pass through the engraving process in 22 minutes standard time, though several plates could pass through simultaneously. Once the plates had been prepared, a press room employee picked them up on the fourth floor and carried them to the press on the first floor.

The current printing process replaced several steps of the old letterpress system. It was compatible with both the rotary press and the offset press systems. An offset press, although it wasted as much as 4 percent newsprint per run, offered computerized printing capabilities, better quality of print, and flexibility with the use of color.

Press runs for the morning paper were approximately as follows: first edition (outlying counties) 12:10 to 12:40 A.M., second edition (adjacent county) 1:00 to 1:25 A.M., and final edition (city) 1:45 to 3:20 A.M. Press runs for the afternoon paper were approximately as follows: first edition (all counties, except the immediate one) 12:50 to 1:30 P.M., and final edition 2:15 to 3:15 P.M. The capacity of the press was 80 pages (16 per deck) per run. When full color was used, only 64 pages could be printed per run, because two half-decks had to be devoted to overlap the four colors necessary for full color. To circumvent this bottleneck, the Sunday feature section was printed on Saturday and many of the inserts were preprinted during slack time. The Sunday comics, for example, were printed externally and were delivered early in the week.

The press cylinders were on the first floor. Rolls of newsprint were loaded on the press in the basement, and the cutting and folding mechanism was on the second floor. The newly printed newspaper was carried by conveyor to the mailroom.

Maintenance could be performed by disconnecting the individual decks; however, all five were operated simultaneously by a central drive system. A problem with the electrically powered drive unit, which had happened recently, could prevent the press from operating. Fortunately, this situation was corrected in time to get the paper out, but it pointed up a weakness in the functioning of the entire operation.

In the mailroom, the sections and inserts were assembled. The papers were counted, bundled, labeled, and dropped through a chute to an alley where they were picked up by carriers or were trucked to drop points.

Timely delivery was very important. The evening newspaper had to reach the customer before the evening TV newscast, or it would not be read. The morning paper had to be to the carriers (who usually held day jobs) in time for them to make deliveries before they went to work. In meeting these objectives, the earlier editions of the morning paper were to leave the headquarters by 2:00 A.M. and the final edition

was to be to the drop points by 4:00 A.M. The earlier afternoon edition was to be ready to go by 1:30 P.M., with the final edition due at the drop points by 3:30 P.M.

1. Diagram the process and information flows for this process.
2. In what ways is this a worker-paced line flow operation and in what ways, if any, is it not?
3. How do the concepts of line balance and rebalance apply to this situation?

A SERVICE SHOP
Ogle–Tucker Buick
Auto Service and Repair
Indianapolis, Indiana

Ogle–Tucker Buick was located on Keystone Avenue in northeast Indianapolis. It was located on 7.25 acres of land and occupied 43,000 square feet of space. The service department consisted of 27 stalls available in the service area, 24 stalls in the body shop, 6000 square feet dedicated to parts storage, and the associated office space for these operations.

The dealership was owned by Robert Ogle and Thomas Tucker, who had grown up on farms and had moved to Indianapolis after World War II. The dealership had been at its current location since 1969. It sold Buick cars exclusively.

PART ONE

PROCESS DESCRIPTION

WRITING THE SERVICE ORDER

The service operation began at 7:00 A.M., Monday through Friday. At that time, the two service advisors who were responsible for developing the repair orders began greeting the customers who had lined up for service. The service advisors' responsibilities were to detail (1) the symptoms of the problem experienced by the customer, and/or (2) work the customer wanted to have performed. This called for skill-

ful listening by the service advisor and the knack for asking the right questions to glean the proper symptoms to explain to the mechanic assigned. The service advisor was also responsible for suggesting additional services the customer might want but had not thought of, such as oil changes, new brake linings, or front-end alignments. The service advisor was the operation's chief contact with the customer through the service process. If the customer needed to be informed about the progress on his or her car, or that additional work was needed, or that the car might not be ready in time, the service advisor communicated that information.

Upon greeting the customer the service advisor logged in necessary identification information to the service department's computer, and a customized repair order form was generated (Figure G1). When the customer finished detailing the work to be done on the car, he or she signed the repair order, giving the service operation authorization to work on the car. The service advisor then assigned a control number to the job and placed an oaktag control number on the rearview mirror of the car and also attached a tag with the same number on the keys to the car.

The repair order consisted of four paper "soft" copies plus an oaktag back "hard copy." The four soft copies were of different colors. The top sheet, white copy, was the accounting copy. The yellow sheet was the customer's copy. The pink sheet was kept by the service advisor. The green sheet was a control copy that was used by the person who followed up with customers on their repairs and was then routed back to the service manager whose secretary filed them. After the service advisor filled out the repair order, he detached the green sheet and sent the other soft copies, together with the hard copy, to the dispatcher in the "tower."

DISPATCHING

By keeping the soft and hard copies together,[a] Ogle–Tucker was able to reduce some double entry of information by the tower and yet still keep control over what was done, so that mechanics could not enter work that was not ordered by the customer. The service advisor sent the repair order into the dispatching office (the tower), the nerve center for the service operation. Here the dispatcher (the tower operator) logged in the control number, the name of the customer, the type of car, the time the service advisor promised the car for delivery, the repair order number, and the work that was to be done, together with the number of the mechanic who was supposed to do that work. Figure G2 shows a dispatcher's route sheet.

Jobs were classified by category. The categories included lubrication and filter changes, tune-ups, front-end work, rear axle work, transmission work, brake work, and the like. Ogle—Tucker's mechanics (termed "technicians" at the dealership) were specialized by task. For example, one did transmission work exclusively, two did front-end work, three handled tune-ups, while others devoted themselves to other tasks. When the tower operator logged in a repair, he noted which technician in which specialty was to do the job. When that job was completed, another technician might take over the car to work on a different aspect of its service or repair. An x-ed out entry on the route sheet meant that the technician had completed his work.

Routine items such as tune-ups and oil changes could be assigned to technicians without requiring a diagnosis about what was wrong. For a number of cars, however, some diagnostic work had to be done before the car could be fixed. Whether diagnostic work was needed was generally determined from the service advisor's wording on the repair order. Key words such as "hesitating sometimes," "occasionally stalling," and so on, were tip-offs. Technicians were responsible for diagnosing problems as well as fixing them. On particularly tough assignments, the service manager was consulted. The dealership referred to the

---

[a]Many dealerships separated the soft copies from the hard copy that went to the mechanic.

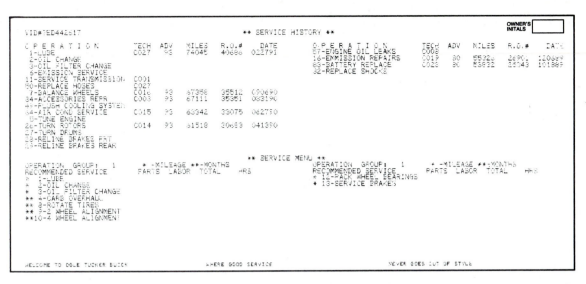

FIGURE G1   A repair order.

165

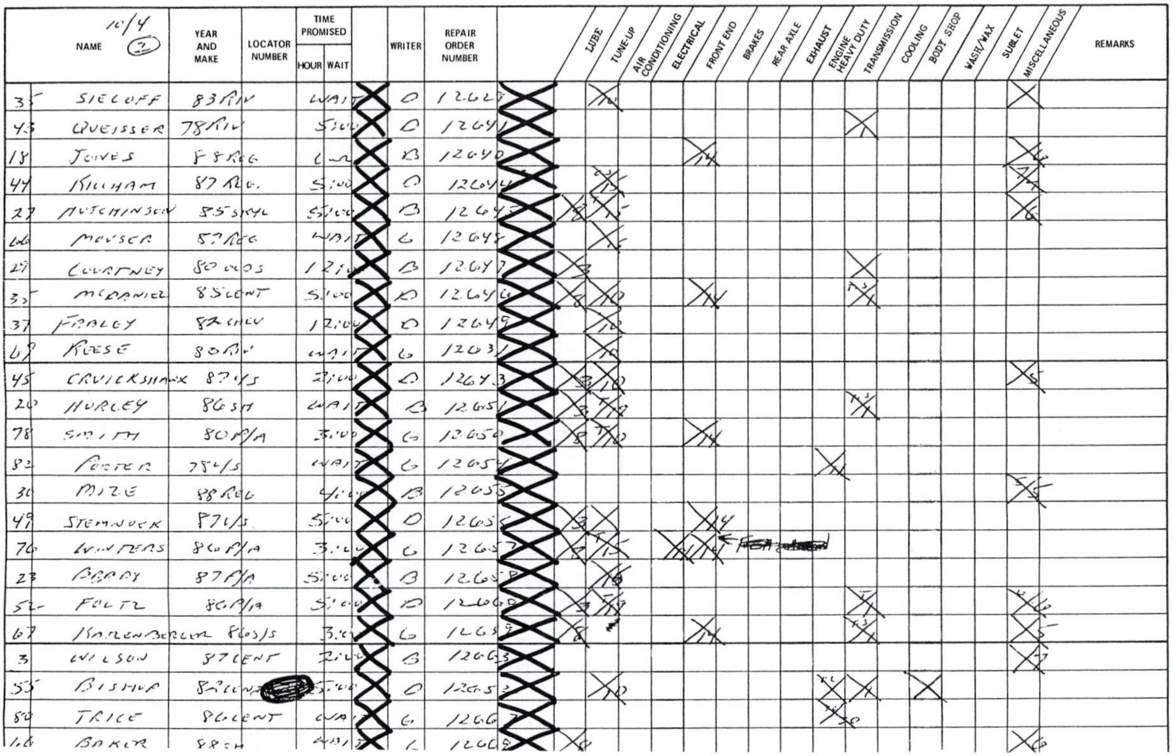

FIGURE G2   Dispatcher's route sheet.

"3 C's" of "complaint, cause, and correction" that were listed on the repair order. The service advisor was responsible for detailing the complaint and the technician was responsible for determining cause and performing the correction.

Shop Operations and the Workforce

The service floor had 27 stalls that were divided among the 13 technicians currently employed. Most technicians were assigned two stalls. Most of the shop's technicians (mechanics) had some post-secondary school education, generally technical school training, and they frequently had a rich family heritage of working on mechanical things. The better-established mechanics could make over $30,000 a year and carried at least $20,000 worth of their own tools. Established technicians earned a higher total income than younger technicians who did not have as many tools or as much knowledge. Younger technicians built up their collections of tools on a continual basis. Tool salespeople came to the shop every week to peddle their tools and collect payments from any technicians who were buying tools on credit.

The technicians were paid on a flat-rate basis. A manual indicated what the time standard should be for every particular kind of job. The technician was paid according to the standard for the job and not according to the time spent on it. Thus, if he spent less time than

The service entrance. (*Courtesy of Ogle–Tucker Buick, Indianapolis, Indiana*)

The dispatcher's tower to the left and the main desk for the service advisors.
(*Courtesy of Ogle–Tucker Buick, Indianapolis, Indiana*)

A line of service bays. (*Courtesy of Ogle–Tucker Buick, Indianapolis, Indiana*)

that indicated in the manual the technician could "beat the book" and earn increased wages. If he spent more time at the job than indicated, the technician would not earn as much. Any rework was directed back to the technician on an unpaid basis, and the shop's policy was that any rework had priority over other work. There were also some skill-level differences incorporated into the wage structure. The most inexperienced worker received $10.50 for every "flag hour" (standard hour), and the most experienced worker earned $14.50. Thus a technician could earn more annually in two ways: (1) by improving his skill level or (2) by being more efficient. When technicians had to wait for a part, it was to their advantage to go to the tower operator and get assigned some quick work that they could perform while waiting. In this way technicians were able to convert

more of the time they were in the shop into flag hours for which they earned income.

After a mechanic finished working on a car, he road-tested it, and if satisfied, wrote the mileage on the back of the repair order's hard copy and filled in both the cause of the complaint and the correction he made. He then returned the repair order to the tower. There, the dispatcher reviewed what the technician had written, and in consultation with a standard reference, determined what the flag hours should be for the repairs made. The dispatcher then filled in and attached a gummed segment of the time sheet (Figure G3) to the back of the hard copy.

The repair order was routed to the cashier for payment and accounting, the pink copies were retained by the service advisors, and the hard copies filed. White and green copies were filed

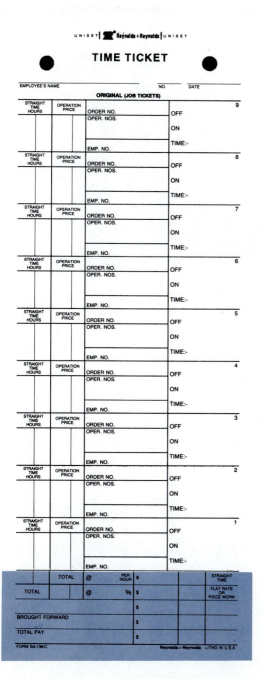

FIGURE G3   A worker's time chart. (*Courtesy of Ogle–Tucker Buick, Indianapolis, Indiana*)

by repair order number; hard copies were filed by car serial number. Customers returning for their cars went to the cashier to pay, and there received the yellow copies of the annotated repair orders and the keys to their cars. Within a few days of repair, customers were called by the dealership and asked to comment on the quality of their repair. If customers were not at home, a letter was sent. Postcard surveys were also left in each car repaired, with customers encouraged to mail their responses back in. The service manager viewed these customer surveys as an important aspect of the service department's operation.

Cars typically arrived during the morning. On an average day, 70 cars might be worked on, with a typical range of from 40 to 85. The day's chief period of stress came after 4:00 P.M., when most people came to pick up their cars. This was when customer complaints surfaced about cars not being ready or about the bill being too high. The service advisors were pulled in many different directions during this time.

QUALITY CONTROL

Quality was enhanced in several ways. There were, of course, the road tests done on each car. And because technicians had to do rework for no pay, there was an incentive to do things right the first time.

Shoddy workmanship was grounds for termination. If, in the opinion of the service manager, there were three instances in one month where poor workmanship was involved with no mitigating circumstances, the technician was terminated. The technicians, of course, were alert to this policy, and each instance of shoddy workmanship was discussed between the service manager and the technician.

From time to time, technicians were sent to training schools, usually either in Indianapolis

A service bay with an oil change in progress. (*Courtesy of Ogle–Tucker Buick, Indianapolis, Indiana*)

A technician updating a service order. (*Courtesy of Ogle–Tucker Buick, Indianapolis, Indiana*)

The parts department counter. (*Courtesy of Ogle–Tucker Buick, Indianapolis, Indiana*)

or in Cincinnati, where the zone's main training center was located. Most schools lasted between 2 and 4 days. The dealership paid for the school's fees plus food, lodging, and transportation. Technicians were also encouraged to take the twice yearly Automotive Service Excellence tests for accreditation in major aspects of automotive service and repair.

THE PARTS DEPARTMENT

The parts department employed six people: a manager, a computer operator, a truck driver, and three countermen. The parts department was charged with purchasing all the parts used by the technicians, maintaining that inventory, handling damaged parts, and filing claims and other returns. The department maintained an

inventory of $320,000 worth of parts, an inventory that turned over three times a year. In a typical day perhaps 300 parts would be used to serve the needs of the technicians in the shop, but only two or three of those parts would be out of stock and have to be special ordered.

The parts department could place orders with General Motors Service Parts Operations (GM-SPO), outside jobbers, or other dealers. The parts department liked to turn a part around (sell it) every 30 days, but with an actual inventory turn ratio of around three they were only able to turn parts on the average every 120 days. Exactly which parts should be purchased at any time was determined jointly by the parts department and a computer program developed by Reynolds and Reynolds. The computer system and its software were reasonably standard for the industry. This computer software used past sales histories to generate suggestions for which items should be purchased to replenish the inventory. Each day, the parts department manager made sure that parts that had been used or sold were removed from the perpetual inventory record kept by the computer. In this way the computer knew what was needed for replenishment, although the parts department manager could override the suggestions made by the computer to take into account special circumstances.

There were several ways by which parts were ordered:

1. *Stock orders.*   The stock order was the regular way to order parts. Parts were ordered every week at a set time (Tuesdays). Parts ordered through GMSPO by stock order received a 7 percent purchase discount and an 8 percent credit on returned parts. The credit was useful because it permitted Ogle–Tucker to return slow-moving parts at no cost, thereby improving the way the dealership's inventory dollars were spent. Stock orders were issued for regularly used parts and for parts whose demands were known with considerable lead time. There were also "target orders" (placed on Mondays) for the fast-moving parts. Extra discounts were available for these parts. Target orders could mean a 22 percent extra discount, and on special promotions the discount could be 27 percent plus 16 percent return privileges.

There were several other ways to order parts. These were more costly than stock orders, but provided faster service.

2. *Car Inoperative Orders (CIOs).*   CIO orders were handled faster than stock orders and, consequently, no discounts or returns were given. For CIO orders, GM checked the six closest depots in that region for parts. (The distribution channel for parts went through three types of depots. The most local were termed Parts Distribution Centers (PDCs), the closest being in Chicago. The next level up, Field Processing Centers, carried more inventory. Lansing, Michigan, was the nearest Field Processing Center. The last resort were the parts plants themselves, controlled from Flint, Michigan. If the part could be located in any of the depots checked, it was sent. If the part could not be located, the dealership was so informed and would have to resort either to waiting for the part or giving it higher priority.

3. *VIP (Very Important Parts) Orders.*   VIP orders called for all depots in the country to be checked for parts. The cost charged was $2.00 per item plus the dealer cost plus 5 percent.

4. *SPAC (Special Parts Assistance Center) special orders.*   If all else failed, and if GM had a formal customer complaint, SPAC could be initiated. A SPAC special order called for action within 48 hours and dealers across the country could get involved.

5. *Partech.*   For problem parts, Partech could be consulted. Partech helped with part number problems such as no part number or part number misprints in catalogs.

6. *Other dealers.*   Ogle–Tucker also bought parts from other dealers through informal relationships. The parts manager sometimes phoned other dealerships and asked whether they had specific parts that could be shipped by bus or some other means. Typically, the cost was dealer cost plus 22 to 25 percent.

Within the first floor storage area of the parts department, there were both small bins and large bins. In the upstairs area, bulk materials such as sheet metal parts were stored. Parts were stored in numerical order by group number. For example, 2000 series numbers were for electrical parts, 3000 series numbers for fuel and exhaust, 4000 series numbers for transmission and brake parts, and so forth. Ordering parts, however, depended not on the group number, but on a specific part number of six to eight digits in length. The workers at each counter were responsible for identifying the proper part for the job, tracking it down in the storage room, and delivering it to the technician or the purchaser, with the proper paperwork done. At each counter, there were manuals for each model or body type of Buick. Each manual had both text and illustrations to aid the search. Prices were kept on the computer. When a part was billed out, the computer automatically deducted it from inventory and kept its accounting straight.

Body Shop

The body shop's major task was to repair cars that had been in accidents. These cars had smashed some sheet metal parts or even the car's frame itself. The shop employed nine: a manager, four bodymen, a painter, a painter's helper, a car washer, and a porter (who did waxing, detailing, and kept the shop clean). There were 15 stalls designated for the four bodymen and 9 stalls for the painter.

The body shop was a full-service body shop that could handle both ordinary sheet metal tasks and framework — the shop was equipped with the hydraulics, chains, and other equipment necessary to straighten automobile frames. The dealership provided benches, welding equipment, painting equipment, some special tools and the consumables such as sandpaper that were used in the course of the shop's work. Each bodyman, however, owned his own tools, which were valued between $15,000 and $20,000.

The bodymen typically worked on two cars at any one time, one that could be classified as a "heavy hit" and one that demanded much lighter work. Often the major job proceeded in fits and starts as parts became available. The smaller job thus served to keep him fully occupied. The painter often worked on six or seven cars in a day.

Within the body shop, the bodymen continually helped one another with problems, such as opening smashed doors or attaching frame straightening equipment. Even though they were paid for their individual work, they recognized the need for assistance when one of them ran into trouble. Within the paint shop, the painter was aided by a helper who did much of the required sanding and the taping of those parts of the car that were not to receive paint. The painter was primarily responsible for "shooting" the paint and ordering supplies. The other two were mainly cleanup people.

The typical car spent 1 or 2 days in body repair and 2 to 3 days in painting. (Painting required the application of a base coat and a clear coat, with time in between for drying, sanding, and rubbing out.) Some cars with major damage spent much longer in the shop. They required much more work and were sometimes delayed until parts were received. Typically, the body shop did not begin work on an automobile until all the parts were received. Thus, if the owner could still drive the automobile, he or she continued to drive it until all the parts were received and an appointment was scheduled. However, if the car had sustained major damage and could not be driven, it remained outside the shop until all the parts were available. With major damage, however, there was always a substantial chance that hidden damage would be revealed as the car was worked on. Hidden damage took even more time to fix and often required the purchase of additional parts. This took time, especially if

In the body shop with a "major hit." (*Courtesy of Ogle–Tucker Buick, Indianapolis, Indiana*)

the car was a foreign make. The body shop had two constituencies: car owners and their insurance companies. Almost all of the shop's work was paid for out of insurance claims, which meant that the shop had to agree with the insurance companies about how much a particular job was worth. The estimates by both the insurance companies and the shop itself were aided by reference to standard books that periodically updated prices and gave standards on the time it should take to remedy certain problems. The shop, in particular, followed the "Mitchell Crash Book" and had very few disputes with insurance company adjusters. Most of the disputes centered around which parts ought to be straightened rather than replaced. (It was standard practice to replace a smashed part with a brand new one on new cars, whereas on older cars, the existing parts were more often straightened or replaced with used parts of the same kind and quality as used on the car.) The shop contacted insurance adjust-

ers either by telephone or when adjusters came by to check jobs in progress or to obtain estimates for potential jobs.

Adjusters could not insist that repairs be made by a particular body shop, but they could recommend shops. Thus, keeping the insurance adjusters happy was an important aspect of the body shop's efforts. The body shop manager kept the adjusters up to date on what was happening and indicated when hidden damage was found. They could check this type of damage themselves and then reach agreement with the shop on a supplement to the original estimate. The shop tried to do its work quickly. Often the insurance company had to pay for rental cars for inconvenienced owners. Thus, the quicker work was done, the more likely the insurance company would not have to pay extended rental charges. To make life easier for the adjusters when they came to visit, the body shop maintained a small office and stocked it with supplies and a telephone.

The body shop manager also spent considerable time with car owners. Typically, there were many occasions for such customer contact. The first occurred if an estimate of the damage was requested. An estimate was made by systematically examining the car, in the same fashion as an insurance company adjuster, and by using the pertinent information in the crash book. Once the owner received the estimate, the body shop manager typically followed up by phone to answer any questions about the estimate or about the insurance process itself. Often in these follow-up calls the shop was informed that it or some other shop had been selected to do the work. However, sometimes it took two or three follow-up calls before a determination was reached about what to do with the car.

After the car was brought in, the body shop manager went over with the owner what was going to happen and what the probable time for repair would be. The body shop manager instructed owners to call the shop before the car was due, in case there were any schedule problems, hidden damage, or the like. When the car was ready, he went over the car in detail with the owner, telling the owner what had been done and letting the owner check the quality. The shop delivered cars to owners in as close to showroom condition as possible. Every car was road-tested and thoroughly cleaned.

How Workers Were Paid

Workers were paid in different ways. As discussed previously, technicians were paid on the basis of a flat-rate hour. The best technicians generally were the fast ones. They were the best at diagnosing problems, they did not squander time, and they knew exactly how to do each job. Technicians could also receive "spiffs," bonuses for working more than a set number of flat-rate hours. A bonus of 25¢ per hour was paid each week to technicians who had more than 35 hours time logged. A bonus of 50¢ per hour was paid to those with over 40 hours, and a bonus of 75¢ per hour went to those with over 45 flat-rate hours for the week.

The bodymen and painter were paid in a similar way. If they were able to beat the standards set for their work, they were able to make more money. If they could not meet the standard, they made less. Some standards naturally were looser than others. In the body shop, for example, sheet metal standards were generally looser than other types of work: thus, sheet metal jobs were the most prized. The parts countermen were paid a salary, although they received a bonus if sales reached some target level. Service advisors were paid commission. That is, they got a set percentage of the service business brought in. This was an incentive for them not only to do a good job so that people were satisfied, but it was also an incentive to suggest additional repairs that the owner might not have thought of. They also received spiffs for special sales (e.g., tires, antennas) that were documented on their pink job order sheets.

The Duties of the Service Manager

The service manager was constantly on the move. In the early mornings and in the late afternoons his main interactions were with customers. He helped the service advisors at the start of the day so that particularly concerned and/or aggressive customers could be handled individually by him. This saved time for the service advisors and contributed to a routine flow of cars into the shop. In the late afternoon, the service manager spent time with customers who complained about work or registered dissatisfaction with the size of the bill.

He listened to customers and then, typically, educated them as to the real problems with their cars and/or the reasons for the costs charged.

During the day the service manager made the rounds of the repair floor, the body shop, and the parts department. He checked the dispatching and the efficiency of technicians. He did diagnostic work and road tested completed cars. On heavy days the service manager was particularly stressed. The tasks were the same, but heavier days were more demanding on everyone, especially if the shop was short-handed.

PROMOTIONS AND SPECIALS

The flow of work into both the service area and the body shop was not even from day to day or month to month. People drove their cars more during the summer months and thus incurred more repair problems during that time. Periodically, in an effort to smooth the flow of work it received, the dealership publicized some service specials. These were typically cut-rate prices on services such as oil changes and lubrications, cooling system winterizing, or total paint jobs. These specials were timed so that they did not interfere with normally busy periods.

PART TWO

DISCUSSION

Ogle–Tucker Buick is in no way responsible for the following views and presentation. They remain solely the responsibility of the author.

THE FLOW OF THE PROCESS AND OF INFORMATION

Figures G4 and G5 display process flow and information flow diagrams for a car in the course of its repair at Ogle–Tucker Buick. Similar diagrams could be drawn for the operation of the body shop or indeed for the operation of the parts department. (The development of those diagrams are left as exercises at the end of this tour.) Note that the customer's car may wait at almost any point in the process. The only wait shown in the diagram is between logging in the job and its diagnosis; it is but one of many such waits that could exist. What is most striking about the flow of the process and

of information at Ogle–Tucker versus a service factory like Burger King is the extent to which there is communication between customer and management and between management and technicians. Because of the customization that is required in auto repair, the flow of information at Ogle–Tucker is much more frequent and less structured than that at a Burger King. Management is very much an intermediary between the customer and the technician. At the same time, management is also very much the source of control for the process.

One can see from this information flow diagram why peak days are so tough on management. There are no shortcuts in the information flows that must occur on busy days. The only source of help is to draw on others, such as calling on the service advisors to do road tests or to give diagnostic work to technicians themselves.

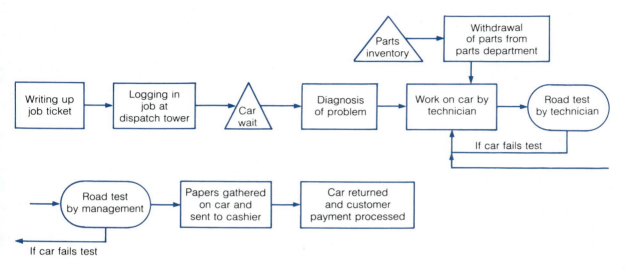

FIGURE G4   Process flow diagram that follows a car in the course of its repair at Ogle–Tucker Buick, Indianapolis, Indiana.

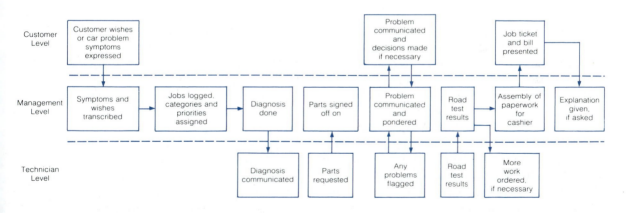

FIGURE G5   Information flow for a car in the course of its repair at Ogle–Tucker Buick.

Of interest is the fact that Ogle–Tucker represents an example of a fixed position layout, where materials are brought to a particular location. Chapter 2 had occasion to discuss this type of layout more and contrast it with other types.

DEMANDS OF THE PROCESS ON THE WORKFORCE

Most of the repair workers at Ogle–Tucker Buick are paid on an incentive basis. The technicians, bodymen, and painters all are paid according to the ratio of their performance relative to a time standard. The base wage against which that ratio is applied depends on their level of skill, which in turn depends on their willingness to learn and the experience they have accumulated. If a technician wants to get ahead and if he wants to be able to be promoted to more prestigious jobs in the shop, he must be willing to go to school. The increasing sophistication of cars demands this. The increasing sophistication of auto repair work is reflected in the fact that Ogle–Tucker's mechanics are not called mechanics but technicians. The use of that term is a reflection on how the workforce and management alike consider the demands of the job.

Working hard as a technician means more than simply beating the standard as set in the book. Working hard also means being able to juggle several different jobs at once so that little time is spent waiting for parts or otherwise removed from the actual repair job. In this regard, the technician is responsible for the pace of his own work. That pace is not dictated by the dispatcher nor by the flow of work along a line. The pace is dictated solely by the technician and his level of skill and effort.

The high level of individual responsibility evident for the technician job carries over to the considerable inventory of tools that everyone is expected to carry. Indeed, the capital-to-labor ratio implied by this tool inventory nearly equals 1 (about $20,000 in tools and somewhat over $20,000 in annual wages, for an average technician) without counting any of the plant, equipment, or parts that are made available to the technicians by the dealership itself. As owners of their tools, technicians are almost like independent operators rather than employees of the company. They have considerable freedom to come and go on their own, for they are paid only for what they do and not for how many hours they spend in the shop per day. Nevertheless, being part of a dealership's service operation has its advantages. The work is steady, training is provided, and the technician does not have any of the headaches that would be involved in establishing and directing a business.

Ogle–Tucker represents a significant contrast to a Burger King. The jobs involved in auto repair are more individual and varying, and, despite some specialization within the workforce, there are fewer job niches. Although some team work is required, the element of team work at the dealership is much less than that which has to apply in a service factory.

DEMANDS OF THE PROCESS ON MANAGEMENT

As the information flow diagram leads one to suspect, auto repair places some significant demands on management. Some of those demands deal with the control of the process, which essentially means control over the rather independent operators. The elements of control include dispatching, diagnosis, the periodic checking of efficiencies, and the quality checks made for both part ordering and road testing. Control over the workforce is a continual endeavor, and one that is fairly loosely defined.

In addition, management must deal with complaints from technicians about their pay or what has been assigned to them. Management must also keep track of the training possibilities for the technicians and who should be assigned to which school.

Monitoring technician training is just one aspect of keeping up to date. Other aspects deal with equipment and information. The use of computers is now standard in most auto dealerships, and computer facilities are steadily being improved. This permits more of the paperwork and information needs of the dealership to be put on computer. Keeping up-to-date with the increasing sophistication of cars requires added investments in plant and equipment and in manuals and documentation. It is important for management to have the right kind of equipment and enough of it so that workers are not cramped for space or equipment and thus do not impede the capacity of the shop. An important aspect of the capital requirements of the dealership is the parts department. Dealers, of course, want to have enough of the right parts available so that they do not stock out too often, but they do not want to drown in inventory. The use of the computer helped to strike this balance, as did the discipline that was applied in keeping track of the parts on hand.

Another whole realm of management effort is devoted to dealing with customers. Manag-ers were in repeated contact with customers— taking orders, handling complaints, and explaining the shop's actions. Senior managers, in particular, were safety valves for the service advisors so that when all the service advisors were occupied with customers, the flow of the process could continue unabated.

Management is also responsible for generating a steady flow of work into the shop. That means trying to perk up business in the off peak times of the year through promotions and specials. And, once a customer does come in, the service advisor informs the customer about other services that his or her car could really use.

QUESTIONS

1. How does the payment scheme for the shop's technicians compare with other incentive pay schemes discussed in previous tours?

2. How does the Ogle–Tucker Buick dispatcher compare with the foreman at Norcen Industries?

3. Why are the hard and soft copies of the repair order split the way they are?

4. What kinds of parts orders suggested by the parts department's computer program would likely be overridden by the parts manager?

5. Why was the parts manager so dedicated to updating each day the perpetual inventory records kept of each part?

6. In what ways was managing the body shop similar to managing the service shop? In what ways were they different?

7. In what ways is the Ogle–Tucker service manager's job like that of the Noblesville Burger King manager? In what ways is it different?

8. Develop process and information flow diagrams for the body shop.

9. Develop process and information flow diagrams for the parts department.

SITUATION FOR STUDY G-1

BIG CITY HOSPITAL EMERGENCY ROOM

The emergency room of the Big City Hospital served about 100 patients a day. Some patients' arrivals were unannounced. Others, however, were announced through communication with ambulance drivers or physicians. The pattern of admission was routine except for patients who were obviously in medical distress.

Each patient entering the emergency room was met by one of two clerks at the front desk. The clerk was the first to assess whether the patient needed immediate medical attention. The clerk would announce "patient here" over the loudspeaker and a triage nurse would take over, reviewing the paperwork that had been done, taking the patient's vital signs, and gathering additional information. The triage nurse then determined whether the patient had to be seen by a physician immediately or whether he or she could wait. If a patient arrived by ambulance, the communication from the ambulance would indicate an estimated time of arrival and some word of the patient's condition. If the patient could give some preliminary information on arrival to the clerk, that would be done; if not, the patient was wheeled directly into the emergency room treatment area.

There were several treatment areas to the emergency room. These included the acute trauma room; a large open area with seven bed slots with curtains to close off each of the slots; four other, separate holding slots; an ear, nose and throat room; an OB GYN room; a cast room; and a family room. The acute trauma room was kept always set up in anticipation of a patient with a severe problem. Up to 20 people could be mobilized to help stabilize a patient in acute trauma.

The open area with the seven bed slots was used for general admission patients. If the patient's condition warranted continual observation, he or she was placed near the nursing station. Patients not needing constant surveillance were placed at more of a distance. The ear, nose, and throat; the OB GYN; and the cast rooms were used for isolating patients with those conditions. The family room was used either for psychiatric patients or for the families of patients who were critically ill.

Once patients were seen by the triage nurse and then by the resident nurse, they were evaluated by a surgical or medical intern, and, if necessary, by an attending resident or physician. Upon examination, the patients were either treated and discharged or admitted to the main part of the hospital. The time goal for admitting, treating, and discharging a patient was 4 hours. Nurses handled any transfers to other areas of the hospital.

Each patient generated substantial amounts of paperwork: personal medical history, notes from physicians and nurses, diagnoses, orders and instructions, laboratory tests performed, and any supplies used. This paperwork was necessary for recording instructions to be used by other hospital personnel, or by departments for billing and for the creation of a permanent medical record. Given these various purposes, the record forms included space for personal data, the nature of the complaint, the physician's name, the type of insurance, notes from the physician, orders from the physician, diagnosis from the physician, and instructions for the discharge. Separate records were kept for nursing, the physicians, and insurance. Lab work was tracked using individual tickets that were kept grouped with the emergency room reports. After a specific time, these reports were entered in the hospital computer for storage.

1. Diagram the process flow.
2. Diagram the information flow.
3. How would you determine how the emergency room ought to be staffed with clerks, nurses, and physicians?

MASS SERVICE
Thalhimers—Cloverleaf Mall Store[a]
Richmond, Virginia

The Cloverleaf Mall store of Thalhimers was one of 25 that the company operated in Virginia, North Carolina, South Carolina, and Tennessee. Thalhimers was a general department store chain, begun in Richmond in 1842, and the fifth generation of the Thalhimer family was presently in the senior management of the corporation. Through the years, Thalhimers grew both by acquiring stores and by building new ones. In 1978, the firm merged with the Carter-Hawley-Hale group of stores, headquartered in California. By dollar volume, the firm's largest store was at Cloverleaf Mall, located in one of the fastest-growing areas in the Richmond market, and situated in one of the 15 fastest-growing counties in America. The store was built in 1972 and had been remodeled twice—extensively in 1978 when a second floor was added to the initial one-floor layout. It now occupied 130,000 square feet. As a general department store, Thalhimers carried a broad selection of merchandise for women, men, children, and the home.

[a]This tour describes operations at Thalhimers in the summer of 1988. Since that time Thalhimers was purchased by the May Department Stores.

PART ONE

SERVICE PROCESS DESCRIPTION

LAYOUT

The ambiance and design of the store was recognized as an important feature in attracting and appealing to customers and generating sales. A good layout accomplishes several things. It provides entertainment and excitement for the shopping experience. The customer is led in a logical pattern from one area to another. A good layout allows a store to

The cosmetics counter. (*Courtesy of Thalhimers—Cloverleaf Mall Store*)

present fashion merchandise in an accessible manner with proper adjacencies, to change the fashion statements each season, and to present the merchandise assortment in a meaningful manner and thereby maximize each area's sales potential.

Traditionally, department stores were designed with long central aisles that effectively divided the store into large quadrants of merchandise of a particular category. Through the years, the old-fashioned layout was supplanted by more architecturally pleasing designs. The Cloverleaf Store, for example, did not have the straight aisles. It was an open store with aisles that led the customer from one fashion world to another using soft wall treatments to designate particular areas or shops. The adjacencies of the areas and the merchandise presentations created the feeling that the customer was shopping in an area with a complete assortment of women's, men's, children's, or home merchandise. It incorporated shops—small, distinctly identified, sometimes partially enclosed areas that dramatized particularly important fashion statements. The Cloverleaf layout did not follow the "world concept." (In that concept of department store design, the consumer enters a well-defined arena or "world" of a particular category of merchandise—such as a "children's world," a "junior's world," or a "men's world." A world concept surrounds the customer with one category of merchandise and catches the customer's eye with dramatic wall treatments, color schemes, and fixtures.)

When Thalhimers designed a new store, space requests would be submitted by the Merchants as well as the Stores Division. For example, a request would be submitted for ladies' accessories for a certain square footage based on a history of results from other stores. Sim-

Signature Sportwear with the Liz Claiborne shop in the background.
(*Courtesy of Thalhimers—Cloverleaf Mall Store*)

ilar requests would be submitted for men's furnishings, the home division, and other areas, each broken down to the level of detail of individual departments within each area. Management then examined the current sales trends for the various segments of the business and the sales per square foot that were generated in each area in the current stores. Decisions were then made concerning space allocation for the new store. Together with the Thalhimers' architects, management then decided on the character of the store's environment; a store in Charleston, South Carolina, would probably be different aesthetically from one in Fayetteville, North Carolina. At this point, decisions were also made about which departments should be adjacent to one another, and what the proximity should be to the various store entrances. The different entrances generated different levels of traffic and it was important to keep that in mind in developing

the plan for the store. Plans and space allocations were changed from one store to the next, depending on the performance expectations of the various areas of the business.

There were substantial differences in the sales per square foot generated by the different departments. For example, fragrances enjoyed an annual sales volume per square foot that was 12 times the store's average. Men's ties produced sales per square foot of 7 times the store's average. Electronic sales were well above the average also. On the other hand, some areas, such as infants' clothing or men's robes, generated sales that were substantially less than the storewide average. Nevertheless, all elements of the store were important to the image of a department store with broad assortments of merchandise.

A tour of the store can help dramatize the importance of the layout. On the first floor, the Cloverleaf store had four entrances. The entrance

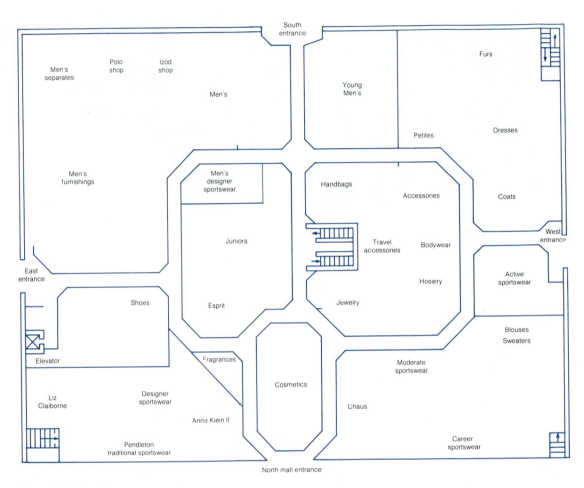

A. First floor layout.

FIGURE H1 Thalhimers—Cloverleaf Mall Store.

with the most traffic was the north or mall entrance. The cosmetics department was located there. The cosmetics counters produced high dollar volumes per square foot. It was an area that created excitement and generated impulse purchasing. To capture the attention of the customer entering the store, immediately adjacent and to either side of the cosmetics counters were a series of fashion shops featuring well-known designer sportswear (Liz Claiborne, Anne Klein II, Chaus, and Pendleton). These designer fashion shops were appropriate complements to the excitement generated at the cosmetics counters.

As demonstrated by both the cosmetics counters and the designer sportswear shop, the interior design of the store was dramatic, creative, and yet very pleasing to the eye. One could look at the presentations of the merchandise and sense a statement of fashion. The distinctiveness of these statements of taste and

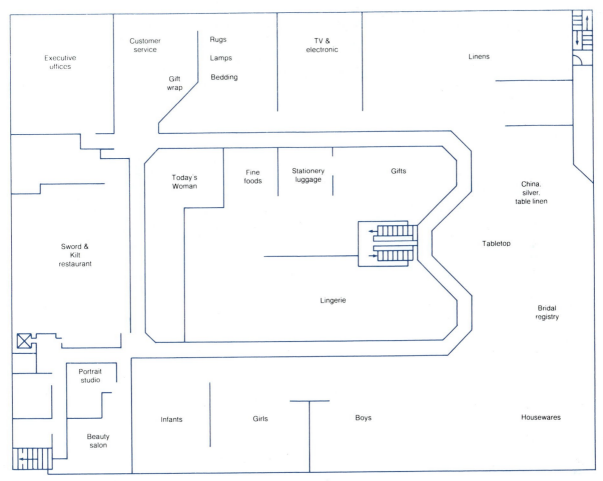

B. Second floor layout.

FIGURE H1   (continued)

fashion were important aspects of the sales performance of the store.

Moving west from the cosmetics counters and the designer sportswear shop, a customer would find both fashion and fine jewelry, and on the right, a large selection of moderately priced and career sportswear, blouses, sweaters, and active sportswear. In general, designer fashions and the more expensive labels were located closer to the front of the store. As one continued moving west toward the west entrance (the third most important entrance) (see Figure H1), one could see the bodywear and accessories departments on the inside of the aisle and women's coats, dresses, and petites' clothes on the other side of the aisle. Each of these areas maintained its own fashion statements.

The men's area was located between the south and the east entrances. The south entrance was

The Juniors area. (*Courtesy of Thalhimers—Cloverleaf Mall Store*)

The south entrance. (*Courtesy of Thalhimers—Cloverleaf Mall Store*)

The Polo shop for men. (*Courtesy of Thalhimers—Cloverleaf Mall Store*)

the second most important entrance, and the east entrance was the least trafficked entrance. As with the other areas on the first floor, the fashion statements were presented both on the aisle and with important wall treatments in the rear of the department, acting to draw the consumer's eye into that area of the store. The menswear area had its own brand name shops, including Izod and Polo.

Several areas in the store served as "swing" areas. Some, for example, offered sweaters for the fall and winter seasons and bathing suits for the spring and summer seasons. Other areas of the store were assigned even more temporary space, such as seasonal merchandise for Christmas. These trends and seasonal changes meant that the layout changed constantly.

The store's second floor was as fashion conscious as the first. On entering the second floor the customer viewed a broad assortment of fine china, silver, and glass stemware from around the world in the tabletop area. To the right of this area was the gourmet housewares area, which dramatically presented a broad selection of both imported and domestic merchandise. Other areas on the second floor were the children's departments, gourmet foods, ladies' lingerie, large-size women's clothes, the restaurant, television and electronics, and the linen and bedding shops.

MANAGEMENT AND THE WORKFORCE

The organization chart for the Cloverleaf store is displayed in Figure H2. Reporting to the store manager were the assistant manager, the

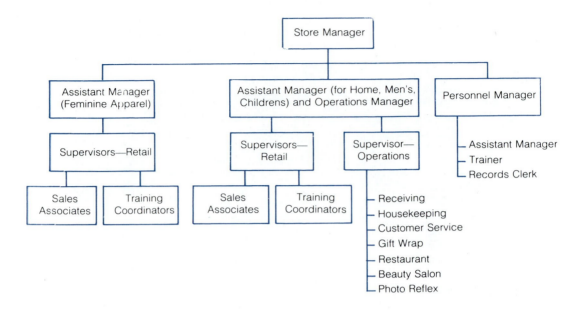

FIGURE H2   Organization chart for the Cloverleaf Mall Store of Thalhimers.

operations manager, and the personnel manager. The store manager also retained direct supervision of the home and children's areas. Reporting to the assistant manager were the sales managers for the other sales areas within the store. Reporting to the operations manager were the lease departments, the restaurant manager, the customer service supervisor, and the supervisors for housekeeping and merchandise handling. Each selling center (made up of multiple complementary departments) of the store was managed by a sales manager, and selling center sales associates reported directly to their sales manager. Also reporting to the sales manager could be an assistant sales manager (three intern-interim training positions for sales associates working their way up through the ranks).

Ensuring customer satisfaction was the primary focus of all associates. Each level of management periodically attended training seminars devoted to teaching, reinforcing, and perpetuating the culture of customer satisfaction of the Cloverleaf store. Monitoring and evaluating all elements of customer satisfaction for all associates was an ongoing function of management. Customer service was an element on which each employee was annually reviewed.

There were 250 employees in the Cloverleaf store, roughly half of whom worked full time and half part time. The store was open from 10:00 in the morning until 9:30 in the evening, Monday through Saturday, and from 12:30 to 5:30 on Sundays. With the store open so many hours during the week, employing part-time personnel was essential to providing maximum staffing. Full-time people were required to work two nights a week and to work every other Sunday. The part-time people worked a fixed schedule: mornings, evenings, and weekends.

During the Christmas season, additional temporary employees were hired (180 for the 1988 Christmas season). This temporary workforce was hired in late September and early October, trained at the end of October and began

The china and crystal area. (*Courtesy of Thalhimers—Cloverleaf Mall Store*)

The Market Place shop. (*Courtesy of Thalhimers—Cloverleaf Mall Store*)

work on the floor in early November. This hiring and training process ensured that every temporary employee has sufficient experience on the floor prior to Thanksgiving, the beginning of the strongest part of the Christmas buying season.

In addition to the store's part-time employees, there was an additional group of sales associates. The group was known as "flyers," and they formed the "flying squad." These substitute employees on the flying squad were called on short notice to work a particular day or period of time. Depending on their individual schedules, they would or would not be available to work. They were all fully trained to fill in in various departments throughout the store.

The store's employees were paid in different ways, although the same employee benefit package applied to all. Support personnel were paid between $3.35 and $7.00 an hour, based on experience and background. Sales associates, on the other hand, were paid a commission based on their individual sales. The commission rate varied from one department to another. The typical commission was 6.5 percent for most areas of the store, but it could reach 8.5 percent for accessories and 10 percent for shoes and the bridal gift areas. Each employee was paid a base hourly rate depending on experience and his or her ability to generate sales, which was applied against the commission earned. In other words, each associate was paid a commission on the merchandise he or she sold, which constituted his or her total earnings. The commission arrangement was new for the store except for shoes and electronics. It showed great promise for generating higher sales for the stores, encouraging individual effort, and for using product knowledge and individual selling expertise.

Both hiring and training were extremely important activities. The right sales associate for a particular department was critical to that department's sales performance. Different personalities were required for different departments. For example, cosmetics required sales associates who were aggressive and enthusiastic as well as highly knowledgeable about the product. China and silver, on the other hand, required sales associates of good taste and great patience, capable of serving the bride and the mother of the bride. Younger sales associates could interact more effectively with teenagers in the juniors' department. If certain clothes were selling well, it was advantageous to have sales associates who could relate to the merchandise and enjoy wearing that style of fashion.

For these reasons, the hiring decision was important and took on elements of theatrical casting. There were three required visits before a new employee could be hired, after which the employee was given 24 hours of training off the floor, 2 weeks of training on the floor, and then a 90-day period of evaluation. In addition, training sessions for sales associates (meetings and videotape viewings) were held weekly. Training was important not only for acquiring knowledge about the merchandise and the operation of the department, but also for learning selling skills. Thalhimers engaged in several innovative programs to train its sales associates. Everyone played the "Selling Game," a monopoly-like game specifically developed to teach selling skills. Through the play of the game, and by viewing accompanying videotapes, sales associates learned the best ways to approach the customer, to interpret verbal and nonverbal buying signals, to present the merchandise, and to close the sale, among a host of other things. Sales associates also attended product seminars that Thalhimers hosted from time to time. At these seminars, the store's vendors displayed the merchandise that Thalhimers had ordered for the next season and provided the sales associates with the latest product knowledge.

The sales managers were essential to successful operation of the store. Each year for a week they attended a sales leadership development seminar, focusing on the latest in store operations and in motivation and communication techniques. The 15 sales managers were responsible for a number of important activities, among which were:

1. Scheduling the sales associates in the department, both full and part-time, and determining when to use the flying squad.

2. Overseeing the training of sales associates.

3. Monitoring all sales transactions.

4. Receiving inventory, checking it against the paperwork, and reconciling any errors in its shipping or paperwork (explained later).

5. Adjusting prices and preparing the department for sales and promotions.

6. The store's management was very supportive of sales manager initiatives to make the Thalhimers shopping experience as enjoyable as possible. Fashion shows, cosmetics make-overs, special senior citizen promotions, focus group meetings with customers, and clientele books with customer preferences noted, among other things, were routinely employed to enhance Thalhimers' already enviable reputation in the community as the fun place to shop. Figure H3 displays two courtesy notes that Thalhimers' sales associates sent customers.

Some of the sales managers began their careers as sales associates. Others were management trainees, employed out of college, who served in the store for 2 years before entering the merchandising arm of Thalhimers as assistant buyers.

THE TRANSACTION — AND SUPPORTING IT

At the heart of the store's operations was the sales transaction itself, and the information it generated. Scattered throughout the store in the various departments were point-of-sale devices or registers. These registers were all tied into the store's computer, and via that computer, they were tied to the computer at Thalhimers in Richmond and the computers of Carter-Hawley-Hale in California. All transactions, once they were rung on the register, were immediately sent on to the computers in California and in the Richmond headquarters. Each transaction consisted of the following items of information: the type of payment to be made (cash or charge), the personnel identification number for the sales associate (the "pin number"), the department's number, the class of merchandise being sold, the stockkeeping unit number for the item (the "SKU number"), and the price for the item (see Figure H4). Once these bits of information were entered into the register, the sale could be completed, the drawer opened, and if change was required, change would be returned to the customer. With these registers, immediate credit information was available. Credit card numbers could be traced immediately and information relayed to the register on whether or not to complete the transaction. With the registers tied in to the company's computers, up-to-the-minute sales reports, or return reports, by department, could be generated at any time.

Supporting the store's transactions was a staff in the customer service area. The customer service department was responsible for

FIGURE H3   Courtesy notes sent to customers by sales associates.

opening up each register each day (including supplying it with $75 reserve change). Sales associates were required to log into the register upon arrival and to log out of the register when they had finished working for the day. At the end of the day the customer service staff was responsible for accounting for all cash and charges, and for checking any discrepancies. The money and the charge account media were taken to the registers by a sales associate and returned to the credit office in the evening by a sales associate. They were verified by the sales managers before being turned in to the customer service office.

The customer service department also ran the customer service window, through which it received payments, adjusted bills, sold tickets to various theater events, provided extra coins or cash to registers throughout the store, handled some customer satisfaction issues, and

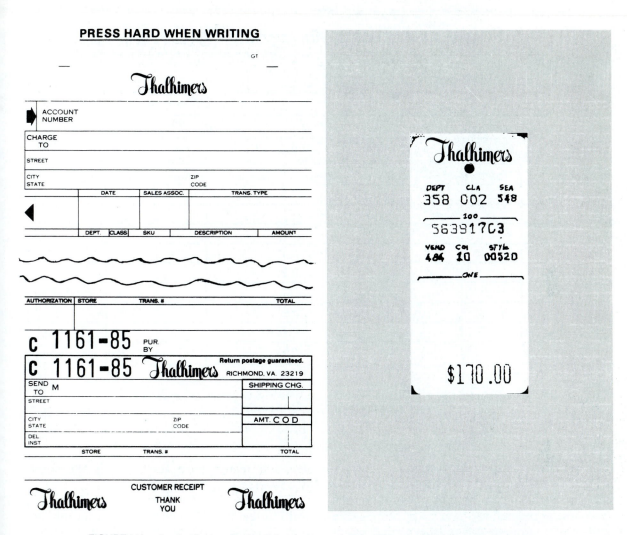

FIGURE H4   A price tag and sales ticket form used at the Cloverleaf Mall Store of Thalhimers.

cashed checks. Customer service was a vital center for the store's transactions.

MANAGING AND CONTROLLING THE INVENTORY

Providing the merchandise for the Cloverleaf store was the responsibility of Thalhimers' merchandising staff located at the Richmond headquarters. The buyers purchased the merchandise that would be sold at Cloverleaf and determined how much merchandise was to be purchased, when the merchandise was to be delivered, and for what price the merchandise would sell. Many of the items in Thalhimers were fashion sensitive, with lead times between ordering and receiving of 6 to 12 months. Thus

THALHIMERS RELAY TRANSFER MANIFEST 292101

DATE		TIME OUT		TIME IN		

DRIVER				SEAL No.

FROM		TO		TRUCK No.

DISPATCHER			RES. CLERK	

NO.	DEPT.	RECEIVING NO. OR ROSTN. NO.	HAMPER NO.	SEAL NO.	NO. OF CARTONS	NO. OF UNITS	Chk.
1							
2							
3							
4							
5							
6							
7							
8							
9							

FIGURE H5   A shipment manifest used in transporting merchandise at the Cloverleaf Mall Store of Thalhimers.

a buyer often had to make decisions months in advance on what would sell during a particular season. If the buyer bought the wrong merchandise or ordered too much, the store's sales and profits suffered. If the buyer erred on the other side and did not order enough merchandise, the store suffered a loss of potential revenue. The buying decision was thus a very important one, but one that was essentially outside the control of a branch store such as Cloverleaf. Of course, the store could provide feedback to the buyers on what merchandise was selling well, the type of customers who seemed to be buying it, and how it could be effectively presented, but the merchandising decision rested with those at the corporate headquarters.

Thalhimers' new computer system, dubbed IMIS (Integrated Merchandise Information System), was a key resource that helped relieve the store of its past labor-intensive burden of recordkeeping. IMIS kept up-to-the-minute track of every item in stock at all of the company's stores, including such information as the quantity on hand or on order, sales, returns, price changes, and transfers to other stores or returns to the vendor.

Even automatic reordering of merchandise was possible with the system to maintain inventories within a minimum-to-maximum

MOVEMENT LABEL
SERV. BLDG.
RICHMOND, VA.

DEPT.	Receiving Apron No.	RTW Pieces	SPECIAL INSTRUCTIONS
			This of Cartons
			is -Pieces
			Wheeler Container **NO.**

			Sent by	Location	Date

FIGURE H6   A movement tag that accompanies merchandise between the service center and the store.

range that was preagreed to between the buyer and the store manager.

Receiving

All items received at the store were sent from Thalhimers' Distribution Center (DC). At the DC, items were checked, sorted, priced, and marked. Deliveries to the Cloverleaf store were made between 4 and 6 A.M. The receiving crew started work at 6 A.M. and delivered all of the merchandise that was received that morning to the floor by 9 A.M. Several checks were made of the merchandise received to ensure that the merchandise received and accounted for was what was expected and had, in fact, arrived. Each truck was physically sealed and the number on the metal seal had to match the manifest that accompanied the shipment (see Figure H5). After the seal was broken, the crew grouped those boxes that were shipped together and checked their numbers against the manifest. Hanging garments in canvas rollers, termed "hampers," were similarly checked. Each group of boxes or "hampers" had been labeled with a movement tag (Figure H6). The movement tag indicated the store department to receive the merchandise, the purchase order number, the hamper number, and the seal number (which indicated the truck shipment). The movement tags came in triplicate; the white tags stayed with the hamper or box, yellow tags were kept by the receiving store, and pink tags were kept by the service building.

After the truck was unloaded, the merchandise was moved onto the selling floor. The merchandise handling group knew exactly where each department received its merchandise, usually near its register. The merchandise moved out to the floor was accompanied by the white movement tag and the paperwork on the purchase, typically the purchase order (see Figures H7 and H8 for examples of this paperwork).

Every morning the sales manager and the sales associates in each department checked the merchandise delivered against the accompanying paperwork to ensure that all of the items they expected to receive were, in fact, received. Each department checked the seals on their hampers and boxes, circled the counts to indicate agreement, stamped the paperwork "received," and then filed that paperwork appropriately. The stock was then displayed in the appropriate place in the department.

The records of the inventory received were kept in a "journal room." The journal room was also next to the office of the inventory controller and the mailboxes for all the supervisory personnel. It was the nerve center for processing the merchandise paperwork for inventory.

Variations on the Standard Receipt of Material

While most of the merchandise received at the store followed the standard procedure, there were a number of errors and changes that had to be recorded. These errors and changes were generally kept on the computer, although some hard-copy "books" were kept as well.

1. *Interstore transfers.* Often items of merchandise were transferred from one store to another. When this occurred, those stores involved entered the information on the store's computer and the appropriate records were updated (see Figure H9).

2. *Errors in shipment.* If there were errors in a shipment received by the store (what was received did not match the paperwork), these errors were noted.

3. *Report of changes in retail price.* This computer record tracked changes that had occurred to the retail price, for example, missed markdowns or markups, and month-end special sale liquidation of inventory.

4. *Merchandise transfer.* If merchandise had been incorrectly charged to the store or had been incorrectly charged to another department, these errors were corrected on the computer records.

Through the use of computer records for changes and errors, the store kept excellent track of exactly what inventory it had and that with which it should be credited. Price changes were also kept track of by the sales managers and the inventory controller. Figure H10 offers an example of a price change document.

Shipping Items Out of the Store

It was Thalhimers policy not to ship items between stores or back to the service building unless the dollar value of the transfer justified the expense. In general, unless a shipment was worth $1000 or more, no transfers were made.

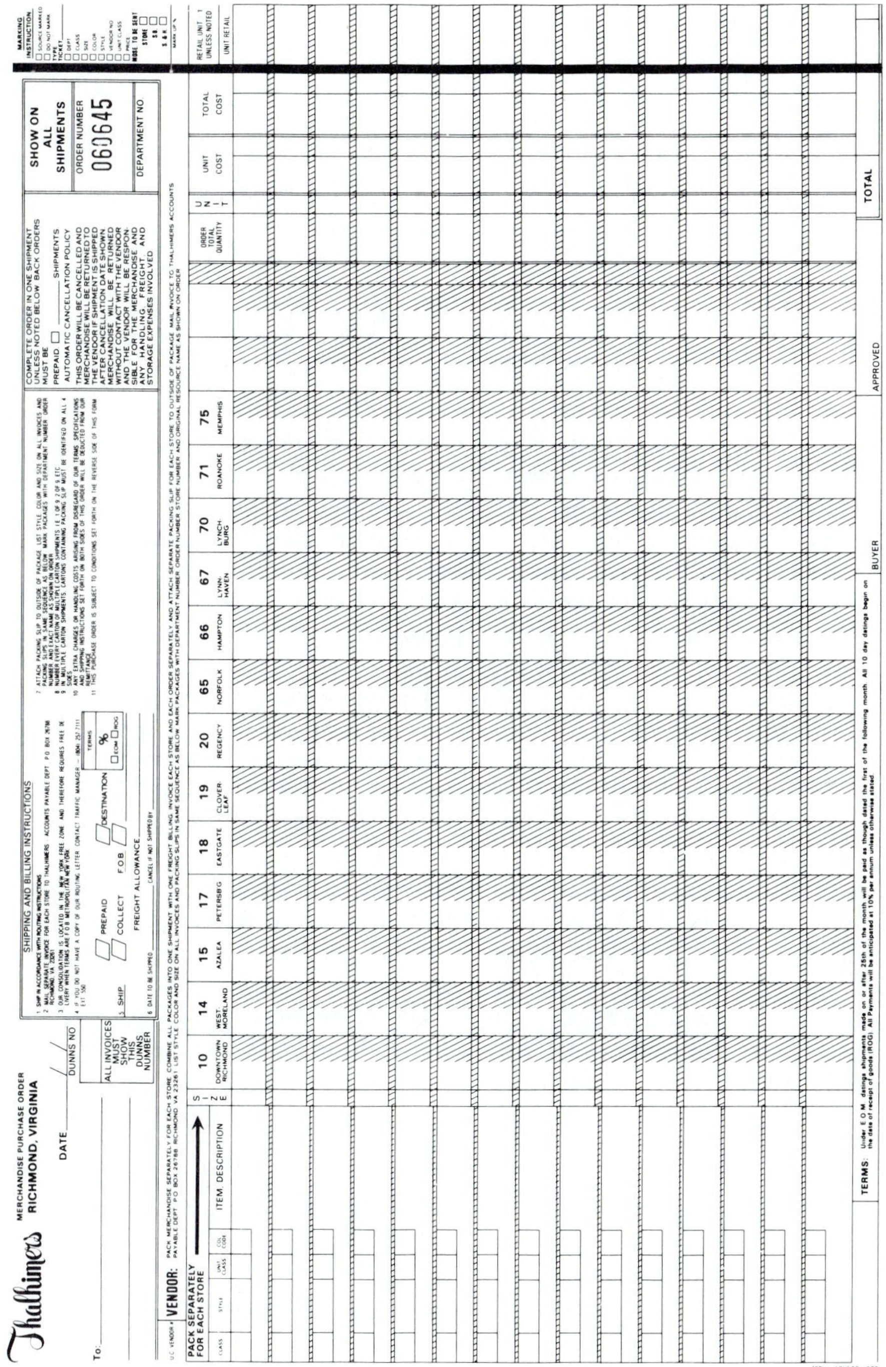

FIGURE H7   A purchase order sheet that is filled out by a buyer and that accompanies merchandise to the Cloverleaf Mall Store. Note that Cloverleaf is Store 19.

```
  11        99999        11        99999    •••••• MARKING AND TRANSFER ••••••      PRINTED 12/17/85  TIME 06:22     PAGE    1
 111        99 99       111        99 99
  11        99 99        11        99 99    MRKNG SEC/LOC _____ MRKNG LINE _____ MRKER ID ___ TKT PRT T3C@            OP ID TP00021
  11        99999        11        99999    RCV 12/16/85                       DOC : N         DOC TYPE P
  11           99        11           99
1111           99      1111           99    VENDOR   878 . JOSIAH WEDGWOOD AND CO

DEPT   281 # OF STYLES    2  SKUS     2
RCVNG  281530               UNITS    2

PO  20155396

   MFG-STYLE STYLE CD COLOR     SIZE   RCVD   REA LINE   SSKU     DESCRIPTION           RTV  CLASS   RETAIL UM     EXT-RTL

      6 00006 00                          1   ___ 0601  56147314  OCEANSIDESANDWICHTRA    0     5    25.00 EA        25.00
      8 00008 00                          1   ___ 0801  55948658  OCEANSIDETANKARD       0     5    17.50 EA        17.50
```

FIGURE H8   A computer-generated marking and transfer sheet that performs the same function as the purchase order sheet. It, or the purchase order sheet, accompanies goods to the store. It is generated by a buyer and is store-specific. Note the 19 in the upper left corner.

One day a month was allocated to transferring merchandise to other stores to balance inventories. There were some exceptions to this policy; vendor returns, damaged goods, alterations, and monograms could be returned to the service center or moved between stores on a daily basis. Shipping of this merchandise invoked the same care and controls that were shown for the receipt of the merchandise.

EVALUATING THE STORE'S PERFORMANCE

The store was evaluated as a profit center. The profit plan for the store involved the determination of sales for each department and a calculation of the proposed selling cost. (Selling cost was calculated as the compensation paid divided by the sales in the department for the time period under consideration.) The sales for each department were forecast by the merchandising arm of the company. The merchandisers were responsible for analyzing the sales trend for the store as a whole and any trends for individual areas within the store. A sales plan was developed for each department of the store and stock levels were planned to vary seasonally. Different "thrust" areas were also singled out for unusual attention; separate plans were developed for increased inventory, increased promotional activity, and additional personnel to achieve a substantially larger-than-normal increase in volume. There were daily, weekly, and monthly reports that monitored the progress of these departments and any variances from the projected sales and profit plan.

The store carefully monitored the "penetration" of particular departments. Penetration of a specific area was calculated by dividing the sales of the area by the total sales of the store. If this fraction for a particular area at Cloverleaf differed significantly from those of other Thalhimers stores, the store manager could then investigate reasons for that difference. In this manner, the store manager could move more aggressively to direct business opportunities.

The Cloverleaf store manager spent a great deal of time on the selling floor, observing the operation and communicating personally with the employees. His priorities for ensuring the store's profitability were clear: assuring complete customer satisfaction in all areas of the store, monitoring sales, selecting the proper personnel and the development of that personnel, presenting the merchandise in an appealing way to attract customers, and finally, monitoring expenses.

DIV: THALHIMERS
ON-LINE REPORT ID: HNAS0600

PAGE: 1 OF: 2
REPORT DATE: 09/23/88
RUN DATE: 09/23/88

STORE: 22

I N T E R - S T O R E   T R A N S F E R   S Y S T E M
TRANSFER DOCUMENT

DEPT: 7521   TRANSFER NO: 10362192   X-REF:
REASON: 26 CENTRL STK VERSION: SEND-BY DATE: 09/23/88
MSG:

```
TO    11    99999
STR   111   99 99
      11    99 99
      11    99999
      1111  99
```

CUST: PHONE: EMP:

DESCRIPTION:	CLASS:	VNDR:	STYLE:	***COLOR*** NUM: DSCRPTN:	**SIZE* NUM: DESC	SSKU/UPC NUM:	MFG/STYLE:	RETAIL:	RQST QTY:	SENT QTY:	RCVD QTY:
LIBERTY 5 PC.PL	30	82	1207	0	0	59901524		105.00	1	1	0
STERL.COVE CUP	50	142	5702	0	0	72479750	5	24.50	1	1	/
STERL.COVE SAUC	50	142	5703	0	0	72479769	5	12.00	1	1	/
STERL.COVE SALA	50	142	5704	0	0	72479777	5	17.00	1	1	/
STERL.COVE BREA	50	142	5705	0	0	72479785	5	12.50	1	1	/
STANFORD CT.20	50	709	1708	0 0	0	59320432		340.00	2	2	2
STANFORD CT.OVA	50	709	1711	0	0	59278142		65.00	1	1	/
STANFORD COURT	50	709	1712	0	0	59287591	1	105.00	1	1	/
ROTHSCHILD 20 P	50	709	3308	0	0	59320351		278.00	1	1	/
CARLYLE 5 PC.PL	60	134	1007	0	0	70968029		198.00	12	12	12
CARLYLE 20 PC.S	60	134	1008	0	0	59910868		792.00	2	2	2
CARLYLE COMPLET	60	134	1009	0	0	70968037		520.00	1	1	/
CARNATION GRAVY	60	134	1119	0	0	71781364		48.00	1	1	/
SHERBROOKE DINN	60	134	1301	0	0	59623370	1	34.00	4	4	4
SHERBROOKE CUP	60	134	1302	0	0	59282026	1	24.00	4	4	4
SHERBROOKE SAUC	60	134	1303	0	0	59282093	1	18.00	4	4	4
SHERBROOKE OPEN	60	134	1311	0	0	59505874		78.40	1	1	/
SHERBROOKE COVE	60	134	1317	0	0	72471342		160.00	1	1	/

FIGURE H9 A transfer document.

```
BATCH REPORT HMMS5411-01              P R I C E   C H A N G E
DIVISION: BOYLE 27-TABLE TOP
DEPT    PC NUMBER     XREF NUMBER    XREF TYPE     REASON
7521    5556503                                    12
COUNTED BY --------J.Koles---------DATE--08/39/88
MESSAGE: NORITAKE PRICE INCREASE - PATTERN EDGEWATER
```

____DESCRIPTION____	CLASS	FRM	TO	_____VENDOR_____		STYLE __	
		SEA	SEA	NAME	NUM	NUM	NU
5PC.PLSETTING	50			NORITAKE CO	I	142	6207
DINNER III	50			NORITAKE CO	I	142	6201
CUP iII	50			NORITAKE CO	I	142	6202
SAUCER I	50			NORITAKE CO	I	142	6203
SALAD II	50			NORITAKE CO	I	142	6204
B&B II	50			NORITAKE CO	I	142	6205
14IN PLATTER	50			NORITAKE CO	I	142	6212
SUGAR	50			NORITAKE CO	I	142	6213
CREAMER	50			NORITAKE CO	I	142	6214
20 PC.SET	50			NORITAKE CO	I	142	6208
5PC.COMPLETER	50			NORITAKE CO	I	142	6209

```
W O R K S H E E T           DATE 08/23/88 PAGE    1 OF  1
                                 STORE:  19
PC TYPE     EFFECTIVE DATE     CANCEL DATE     REPRINT
            08/30/88                           N

    MARKED/APPROVED BY_____DATE __/__/__
```

__COLOR____	SIZE	UOM	OLD	NEW	C	__QUANTITY___			
M DESCRPTN	DESC		RETAIL	RETAIL	R	SEAS	TKT	MRKD	LN IT
		EA	77.50	81.50		---	----	0	01
		EA	24.50	25.50		---	----	3	02
		EA	23.50	24.50		---	----	3	03
		EA	11.50	12.00		---	----	1	04
		EA	16.00	17.00		---	----	2	05
		EA	12.00	12.50		---	----	2	06
		EA	95.00	100.00		---	----	0	07
		EA	54.00	55.00		---	----	(	08
		EA	35.50	37.00		---	----	)	09
		EA	310.00	326.00		---	----	(	10
		EA	249.50	257.00		---	----	(	11

```
                        QUANTITY TOTALS:        11
```

FIGURE H10   A price change worksheet.

PART TWO

DISCUSSION

Thalhimers is in no way responsible for the following views or presentation. They remain solely the responsibility of the author.

THE FLOW OF THE PROCESS AND OF INFORMATION

During the course of a day the sales associates at Thalhimers do many things. The two chief processes in which they get involved are stocking, which occurs in the morning, and the sales transaction itself, which occurs all day long. Figure H11 diagrams both of those key processes. For the most part, these processes are fairly well structured. While there is interaction between customer and sales associate during the transaction, particularly in the presentation of the merchandise and the closing of the sale, for the most part the process is a fairly

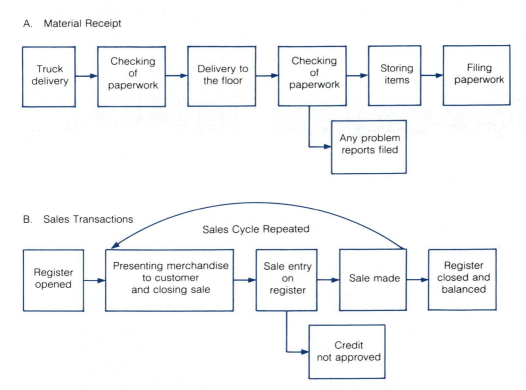

FIGURE H11   Rough process flows for material receipt and for sales transactions at the Cloverleaf Mall Store of Thalhimers.

A. Information flowing down from management
Merchandising shifts
- sales and promotions
- changes to merchandise presentations
- layout and space allocation changes

B. Information flowing up from the sales associates and support staff
Irregularities
- in transactions
- in inventory status
- in paperwork
- in cash balances
- other errors
Inventory counts

FIGURE H12   Examples of information flows at the Cloverleaf
Mall Store of Thalhimers.

standard one, well known to both parties. Similarly the stocking process is something that is a routine occurrence, day in and day out.

Information flows are also fairly standardized, although there are many different kinds of information that can be passed down from management to the sales associate and up from the sales associate to management. Figure H12 indicates some of the key information flows that go both down and up in the organization. For the most part, the information flowing downward relates to merchandising shifts, whereas the information flowing upward deals with irregularities in the routine of the inventory and sales transactions.

DEMANDS OF THE PROCESS ON THE WORKFORCE

Because Thalhimers is open so many hours, one key demand on the workforce relates to the scheduling of everybody's work hours. Evening and weekend work is sometimes required.

Another key demand relates to coping with the change that goes on around the employees all the time. Layouts are changing, inventory stock levels are changing, the character of the inventory is changing, and the workforce must cope with all of these changes. To help cope with these changes, there is considerable training. Workers are not only trained initially, but spend appreciable amounts of time week in and week out in training, both to improve their skills and to educate them about the merchandising changes in the store.

Another demand on the workforce is accuracy, both with respect to the transactions made and the inventory overseen. Such accuracy is crucial to the success of the store, and it is a routine to which they must apply themselves all the time.

DEMANDS OF THE PROCESS ON MANAGEMENT

Like the sales associates and others of the workforce, management must also adhere to and foster the importance of controls on transactions and inventory. The customer service department and the journal room are the store's nerve centers for control, and they must be supported.

Personnel functions are also extremely important, as indicated by the personnel department's status within the organization chart. Hiring—perhaps better termed "casting"—training, and advancement all consume a lot of management time and care. Sales associates' skills are critical to the sales volume that the store generates, and thus hiring and training are key functions of management.

The other key elements to sales increases are the layout itself and the presentation of merchandise. Good layout and good merchandise presentation depended not only on the analysis of sales per square foot figures, but also on intuition and feel for the psychology of the sales situation. The worth of powerful fashion "statements" throughout the store is a clear indication of the art involved in a store's design and operation.

Because fashion can be so fickle and people's tastes can change so abruptly, it is important for the store to monitor sales and costs on a continual basis. Thus not only are there controls on the transaction and inventory levels themselves, but also controls on sales and selling costs. Store management has to be ready to examine these costs and use them to make decisions about staffing levels and the responsibilities of sales associates and support personnel within the store.

QUESTIONS

1. Visit a department store near you. In what ways is its layout similar to that of Thalhimers? In what ways is it different?

2. One might suppose that theoretically, at least, departments ought to be given space in such proportions that the sales per square foot would be roughly the same anywhere in the store. Why is the point of view impractical?

3. Express some of the fashion statements you have observed at department stores. How does the store's layout, fixtures, and decor contribute to those statements?

4. What kinds of questions would you ask of a prospective employee to work in the Liz Claiborne shop? What characteristics would you look for? How would those characteristics and questions differ for someone working in the jewelry department?

5. What is the argument for paying sales associates on a commission basis? What is the argument for paying them on an hourly basis?

6. Outline the various controls that exist on the store's inventory. Why are there so many controls?

SITUATION FOR STUDY H-1

ADAMS CONVENIENCE STORE

The Adams Convenience Store, located on a major state artery, was open from 6 A.M. until midnight every day and sold grocery items, fast food, and gasoline. Gasoline, dispensed through self-service pumps, represented about 50 percent of total sales. Customers paid first and pumped afterward. All of the gasoline

pumps were multiproduct dispensers that handled both leaded and unleaded gasoline.

The store was laid out as in Figure H13. Seventy percent of the people who entered the store to do something other than to pay for gasoline, bought some sort of beverage. The fast food available at the rear of the store was

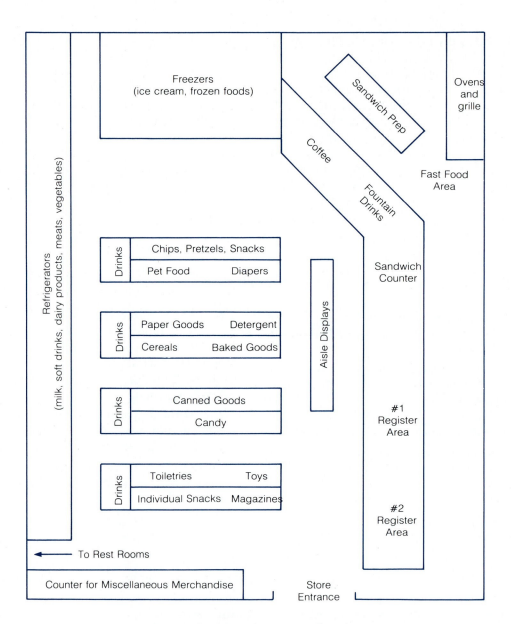

FIGURE H13   Adams Convenience Store layout.

the highest-margin item for sale; gasoline was the lowest-margin item. The Adams Convenience Store offered hot dogs, sandwiches, pastries, coffee, and other food items. There were two peaks for food item demand: breakfast and the four to six, after-work period. Sales slowed in mid-morning, early afternoon, and late at night.

The store operated two shifts. The store manager was there to open the store in the morning and stayed during the first shift; the store's assistant manager handled the second shift. During the busiest period of each shift there were a total of four working in the store: two to handle the fast food area and two to tend the registers. In addition to the manager and the assistant manager there were two full-time workers and the remaining were part-time employees. Pay averaged just above the minimum wage, and turnover rates often ran as high as 300 percent a year.

The manager and the assistant manager trained the others and determined which items met the company's definition for being short in supply and needed to be reordered. Orders were placed to a central Adams warehouse. The managers were also responsible for controls on cash and inventory so that everything was accounted for.

1. Why is the layout designed as it is? Give a rationale and explain what you think the typical traffic flow would be.

2. Why would the Adams Convenience Store invest in multiproduct gasoline pumps?

3. What do you see as the biggest challenges for the store's owners?

A PROFESSIONAL SERVICE
Arthur Andersen & Company
Accounting and Auditing Services
Charlotte, North Carolina

Arthur Andersen & Company was one of the world's leading accounting firms, with headquarters offices in Geneva, Switzerland, and in Chicago. As of the end of 1990, the firm employed 56,800 people worldwide and operated 299 offices in 66 countries. In the United States, Arthur Andersen was the largest of the so-called "Big Six" accounting firms. The firm was operated as a partnership; that is, the firm was owned and managed by a group of partners (in 1990 the partners totaled 2292) who had been elected by other partners in the firm.

The Charlotte office was the administrative office that coordinated the practice for the two Carolinas, including Columbia, South Carolina; Greensboro, North Carolina; and Raleigh, North Carolina. These four offices combined employed about 400 people, of whom 325 were professionals and 75 were support personnel. Of the 400, 290 worked in the Charlotte office. The office served over 450 clients in a variety of industries.

PART ONE

PROCESS DESCRIPTION

LINES OF BUSINESS

Although Arthur Andersen & Co. was known as a Big Six accounting firm, it did more than provide classic auditing attest services (described in detail later). Its practice also included tax, consulting, other accounting services, and a series of specialized services for smaller businesses. In fact, the auditing and entreprise groups accounted for a little less than half of revenues; the tax and consulting divisions accounted for the remainder. While this tour examines mainly the accounting and auditing practice of Arthur Andersen & Co.—

Charlotte, the tax, consulting, and enterprise practices merit brief separate attention.

The Tax Practice

The tax practice in Charlotte employed 29 professionals. It was an important component of the office's business, and was well established in the firm at large. There were two major components to the tax practice. One dealt with client compliance issues—preparing returns for clients, representing clients at Internal Revenue Service reviews, and providing defense for any clients in legal matters involving taxation. The other component involved advice on business transactions that had significant tax implications, such as mergers, acquisitions, and syndications. This kind of work typically complemented that of investment bankers and lawyers. Tax work consisted of many short-term jobs that often had to be done quickly but that typically did not involve substantial resources over extended periods of time; consulting or auditing services were longer term. Although there was considerable demand for tax services all through the year, the peak demands naturally occurred each February through April.

The Consulting Practice

The management information consulting practice was now formally known as Andersen Consulting. For the Carolinas, it was concentrated in Charlotte; of the 169 professionals employed in the consulting practice, 145 worked in the Charlotte office. The mission of the practice was to help clients obtain the information they needed to plan and manage their organizations. The practice was broad-ranging and included the development and installation of computer systems for financial and operations control of both manufacturing and service businesses. Much of this work was customized for the client and thus called for skill in drawing together the disparate elements of each project.

Consulting revenues were evenly divided among banking, manufacturing/textiles, health care, government work, and some miscellaneous businesses. The projects performed by the consulting division varied widely in their scope and duration, although many were accomplished for previous clients. Typical projects included the development of a new deposit system for bank customers and the installation of management information systems for a group of trucking companies.

Enterprise Practice

The enterprise practice was technically a part of the audit practice of the firm; however, attest services accounted for only about half of the entreprise practice's revenues. The remaining revenues were generated by a diverse array of services: assistance in preparing financial forecasts and cash-flow projections, development of long- and short-range business plans, consultation in approaches to minimize taxes and maximize after-tax cash flow, evaluation of lease vs. buy decisions, break-even analysis, capital budgeting, assistance with purchases, merger, or divestiture plans, and an assortment of other services. The entreprise practice had been created nearly 45 years ago and had grown in Charlotte since the office opened in 1958. By 1990 there were 70 clients, and some of the original clients' businesses had grown so much that they were no longer served out of the entreprise practice.

For the professionals in the entreprise practice, the demands were quite diverse. While each professional had fine auditing skills, they also had to foster other skills so that the wide-ranging demands of entreprises could be met: use of the microcomputer, preparation of busi-

The reception area, with Arthur Andersen's trademark doors.
(*Courtesy of Arthur Andersen & Co, Charlotte, North Carolina*)

ness plans, private placements for company stock, and so on. For these reasons, the entreprise practice was often difficult to schedule and manage—but it had been a significant source of growth over the years for all of Arthur Andersen & Co.

AUDITING ATTEST SERVICES

All publicly held companies (those regulated by the Securities and Exchange Commission) are required to have independent certified public accountants report whether their financial statements fairly represented their financial positions and results of operations. These reports were usually found in company annual reports (see Figure I1). Usually, these opinions were unqualified, but occasionally, accounting firms had to qualify them to alert shareholders to particular risks or problems in the financial statements of the company. Thus reports were important safeguards to company shareholders. The audit was the procedure by which Arthur Andersen & Co. developed and substantiated reports about the financial records of the client companies.

Arthur Andersen & Co.'s auditing methodology was designed to identify and concentrate on the risk areas of greatest exposure to a company's financial statements and the related key control elements put in place by management to mitigate the risks. It was a "top down" approach that addressed risks in two stages.

Report of Independent Public Accountants

To the Shareholders of International Paper Company:

We have audited the accompanying consolidated balance sheets of International Paper Company (a New York corporation) and subsidiaries as of December 31, 1990 and 1989, and the related consolidated statements of earnings, common shareholders' equity and cash flows for each of the three years in the period ended December 31, 1990. These financial statements are the responsibility of the Company's management. Our responsibility is to express an opinion on these financial statements based on our audits.

We conducted our audits in accordance with generally accepted auditing standards. Those standards require that we plan and perform the audit to obtain reasonable assurance about whether the financial statements are free of material misstatement. An audit includes examining, on a test basis, evidence supporting the amounts and disclosures in the financial statements. An audit also includes assessing the accounting principles used and significant estimates made by management, as well as evaluating the overall financial statement presentation. We believe that our audits provide a reasonable basis for our opinion.

In our opinion, the financial statements referred to above present fairly, in all material respects, the financial position of International Paper Company and subsidiaries as of December 31, 1990 and 1989, and the results of their operations and their cash flows for each of the three years in the period ended December 31, 1990 in conformity with generally accepted accounting principles.

Arthur Andersen + Co.

New York, N.Y.
February 8, 1991

FIGURE I1   An opinion.

The first stage focused on the principal external and internal factors influencing the client company's operations, such as the industry in which it operated, the nature and complexity of its businesses and products, the operational and financial planning and control activities of management, and management's attitudes toward risk control and financial reporting.

The second stage provided a systematic basis for evaluating individual internal controls over an organization's significant cycles of activity.

Much as a manufacturer is concerned about the integrity and capabilities of the manufacturing process, so, too, an Arthur Andersen & Co. auditor is concerned about the integrity and capability of the internal controls in the client company for capturing accurately all of the accounts billed and collected, the invoices to be paid, the expenses authorized, the inventory, and other data.

The audit attest process could be broken into three major phases: the planning phase, the specific risk analysis phase, and the final phase. These different phases required different amounts of time and attention from the various members of the "engagement team" working on the audit.

The planning phase, for example, accounted for about 10 percent of the typical audit's effort, although much more than 10 percent of the time of the senior members of the engagement team. (The senior members of the team were the partner or partners in charge and the manager—the professional with rank just below partner, who had anywhere from 5 to 12 years of service. The manager was actually in charge of the day-to-day progress of the audit.) The planning phase was concerned with defining the scope of work to be done and its timing. It identified those risks that seemed to be important and those changes in the character of the business that ought to be scrutinized. Once the planning phase was over, the partners returned periodically to review progress, to help work through particular problems, and to monitor the quality of the work in progress.

The specific risk analysis phase was concerned with fact finding. In this phase, the junior members of the engagement team (i.e., the staff accountants, and the "seniors") investigated the paperwork and controls of the client company. They checked to see that the controls actually worked. Sometimes, they identified substantive problems that had to be dealt with by the senior members of the engagement team. This phase could range from perhaps 30 percent of the time and effort in a small audit to 60 percent of the time and effort in a large audit.

The final audit phase led to the generation of the report. This phase updated the results of the specific risk analysis phase, involved substantiation of year-end balances, and included a review of the client company's financial statements and their accompanying footnotes. For large audits, this final phase might account for only 30 percent of Arthur Andersen & Co. time and effort, whereas for smaller audits it could account for fully 60 percent.

The total professional time devoted to an audit by the Charlotte office could vary dramatically, from 80 hours each year for the smallest audits to over 4000 hours each year for the largest. The median amount of time consumed for an audit was estimated at about 500 hours each year. The calendar for an audit varied somewhat. For the largest audits, Arthur Andersen & Co. professionals were in and out of the client company all the time; they were often part of quarterly reviews of the client's business. At more typical audits, however, the planning phase was done about 6 months into each fiscal year, the specific risk

A partner's office. (*Courtesy of Arthur Andersen & Co, Charlotte, North Carolina*)

analysis work was accomplished in months 7 through 11, and the final work was done in the first 3 months after the close of the fiscal year.

Although two-thirds of the Charlotte office's audit work was repeat business, the office was always eager to attract new business. It secured this business by drafting a proposal to the target client company. This proposal discussed the key aspects of Arthur Andersen & Co. and what differentiated it from other accounting firms. It introduced the firm's other major clients in Charlotte and the services the entire office could provide a client company. It discussed in some detail the audit approach that Arthur Andersen & Co. planned to take. It profiled the personnel making up the engagement team, and it discussed how that personnel would be managed over time to provide the kind of continuity that was valued by clients. The proposal also established the fee schedule.

MANAGING THE PRACTICE

The Pyramid

Arthur Andersen & Co.'s auditing practice in the Carolinas totaled 140 professionals. Of this number, there were 10 partners, 22 managers, 38 seniors, and 70 staff accountants. These different classifications could be depicted as a pyramid, with the staff as the base and the partners at the top. Each engagement had its own pyramid, as well, with one or two partners at the top, one or more managers, and various seniors and staff accountants.

Staff, seniors, and managers were all salaried positions. The partners were not salaried; their compensation depended on the profitability of the firm. If the partners were to make money, they had to use the salaried personnel of the firm effectively. This placed several demands on the partners: (1) effective scheduling of personnel so that everybody was working as much as possible but without excessive overtime (scheduling will be discussed later), and (2) fostering as much responsibility in the lower ranks as possible. Firm profitability was enhanced to the degree that effort and responsibility were thrust to lower levels of the pyramid (this was termed as having a broad-based pyramid). If the higher-paid senior members of an engagement team were free to perform other duties, such as bringing in additional business, everyone benefited and the firm as a whole would be profitable.

If a job could be run with a broad-based pyramid, it would likely be profitable. If, however, the pyramid were slender, it was likely not to be as profitable because the time of the senior members of the engagement team would not be as effectively levered as when the pyramid was broad.

Accounting firms like Arthur Andersen & Co. primarily operated on an "up-or-out" basis; professionals within the firm were either promoted to the next-higher rank or they left the firm. In a sense, the partners were the survivors, those who had proven themselves over the years by their performance and had demonstrated the qualities that made for effective partners.

Arthur Andersen & Co. was continually looking for innovative ways to keep highly trained individuals within the firm, even though they could not rise to partnership rank. In 1991, the firm created the "national partner," a senior level position just short of the equity partner rank, as a way to hang on to talented people.

There was considerable turnover at the lower levels of the pyramid. If one followed the path of new recruits in the Charlotte office, for example, one typically found that only 50 percent of each new cohort of college recruits were still with the firm after 3 years, and that only 25 percent of them were still with the firm after 6 years. After 10 years, the figure was 14 percent. Only about 9 percent reached partnership.

About three-quarters of the time, professionals left the firm of their own volition. Some left for more attractive, higher-paying positions in other companies. Others left because of personal incompatibilities with the degree of overtime or travel, or because of other elements of life on the job. Some returned to school. The remainder left at the suggestion of the firm itself; those were split between professionals who lacked the technical ability to do the job and those who lacked some other personal qualities that were required. While an up-or-out system might be viewed as harsh, Arthur Andersen & Co. was famed for its concern for the placement of its accountants in other jobs, often with valued clients.

The pyramid concept raised several issues. Broad pyramids meant lower costs, but because they encouraged the delegation of responsibilities to lower levels of the pyramid, there were quality control and cost-effectiveness issues associated with doing business that way. For example, staff might not have the capability or the training to do all that may be requested of them, or they might take a longer time than some more senior professionals in doing some job, thus raising the specter of cost-effectiveness.

Another issue involved client perceptions. The accountants at client companies were knowledgeable about firm operations, since they were frequently former Big Six professionals themselves. Often they would prefer experienced personnel and staff continuity. The Charlotte office was careful about making its assignments and had to consider each client's perceptions on staffing.

The Cycle of Business Planning

Given the labor intensity of auditing, business planning for the Charlotte office was very much an exercise in determining labor needs.

The business plan for the audit practice started with a forecast of chargeable hours for the Carolinas' four offices. The area had been growing and Arthur Andersen & Co. had been developing additional clients, so chargeable hours were growing at a healthy clip.

Once a defensible forecast of chargeable hours was developed, "productivity factors" (i.e., average chargeable hours per person per year) were applied to determine how many people would be needed. In general, the Charlotte office averaged between 1400 and 1500 chargeable hours per person per year. That number differed by level within the pyramid: Partners generally had the fewest and seniors the most. Nonchargeable hours were taken up in a variety of activities, including training, marketing and sales promotion, community service, administrative tasks, recruiting, and, of course, inefficiently used time. Given the application of the productivity factors to the forecasted chargeable hours, the office figured out how many people it needed. This, in turn, determined how many new recruits were needed to make up for any personnel shortfalls.

The business plan's forecast of profitability depended on the fee structure as well as the manpower plan. With the growth of business in the Carolinas, there was heavy competition for new business. The Charlotte office took this into account in developing its fee structure to match its chargeable hour plan and its staffing plan.

Scheduling

As mentioned previously, personnel scheduling was a key determinant of the office's profitability. The Charlotte office had responsibility for scheduling not only its own operation but coordinating those of Greensboro, Raleigh, and Columbia as well. One manager-level professional was assigned full time to the scheduling and other division administration functions.

The scheduling process began with the managers in charge of the office's engagements. For each engagement, the manager indicated how many hours of which levels of professional were required (see Figure I2). The manager was also permitted to request specific people to be part of the engagement. This planning could often be done far in advance, due to the recurring nature of much of the office's business. Each December and January, a rough-cut schedule for the following May through April period was devised.

The allocation of people to jobs was depicted on two different schedules: (1) the long-range schedule that planned people's assignments for an entire year, by week, and (2) the 20-week schedule, which showed the assignments of all staff persons, by week, for the next 20 weeks. The 20-week schedule used the same data base as the long-range schedule. Both of these schedules were known in the office as the "railroad," largely because the schedule itself looked like tracks on paper (see Figures I3 and I4).

The scheduling manager was responsible for pulling together the original schedule and then for adjusting it as time wore on and inevitable changes occurred. Naturally, the Charlotte office's profitability was greatest when everybody was fully scheduled and working effectively. The inexperienced staff accountants tended to have the most "open holes" in their schedules, and thus they were a constant concern for the scheduling manager. He reviewed the schedule continually to see whether all of the jobs being worked on were properly staffed. Was the pyramid broad enough for them? Were some projects in need of help? Were the Greensboro, Raleigh, and Columbia offices busy? Could professionals be swapped between offices? The Charlotte scheduler acted as the central clearing-

---

CLIENT NAME AND # COMPANY 555
DESCRIPTION OF WORK Audit
CLIENT YEAR-END 12-31
LOCATION OF WORK CLT
DATE SUBMITTED

MASTER JOB SCHEDULING SHEET

SUGGESTED STAFF PERSONS
IN CHARGE AA
STAFF BB

THIS JOB CAN BE STAFF WITH ONE-
MID-YEAR OR INTERN ☐   TAX ASSISTANT ☐   MIC ASSISTANT ☐

Staff Class	Total Hours	P	F	... Oct (7, 14, 21, 28)	Nov (4, 11, 18, 25)	Dec (16)	March (17, 24, 30)
PARTNER	20			2	2		16
MANAGER	68			4	8		8, 8, 40
STAFF SR	102			16, –, X, X	X, 16, X		16, 16, 40
EA	156			16, –, X, X	X, 40, X		40, 10, 40
IA	168				X, 40, X	8	40, 40, 40
TOTAL STAFF HRS	426						

Instructions

1. Total hours shown should agree with the hours shown in the fee estimate or reconciled thereto. "Cushion" should not be scheduled.
2. Requirements for recurring type audits of Foundations, Pension Plans, etc., may be submitted separately or included as part of the time submitted for recurring audit of the Company financial statements. However, such time should be clearly identified as part of "Description of Work." If submitted on a combined basis, there should still be a clear indication of the pension, quarterly review, recurring registration statement, etc., time requirements.
3. Requirements for nonrecurring work including registration statements and major one-time projects should be submitted on a separate job scheduling sheet.
4. Requirements should be shown based on the ideal scheduling, however, where the time is absolutely not flexible, please so indicate in the "Comments" section. This is extremely important!
5. Known overtime requirements should be shown by merely showing Total Hours as 45 or 55 or whatever. In general, we would prefer to minimize overtime in all cases. When required, we should, in particular, attempt to avoid overtime at preliminary dates and for extended periods of time. Our office policy on overtime requires Partner/Manager approval of overtime.
6. In determining time requirements for each job, please consider the office need to achieve a balance of various experience levels on each job. Approximately 50% of our staff has one year or less experience.
7. Minimize situations where staff are assigned to a job for periods of time exceeding 400–500 hours or for extended periods on one job, particularly if out of town. Consider expanding the number of staff assigned.

Comments
Final is not flexible

FIGURE I2   A sample master job scheduling sheet, as used at Arthur Andersen & Co.—Charlotte.

```
CAROLINAS                           PERSONNEL SCHEDULING            PAGE-  2        AS OF-20 NOV 85
DIVISION: CHARLOTTE AUDIT            PERSONNEL ASSIGNMENTS                          PREP-20 NOV 85
TO: 450561                                                                         RPT-EC01000
FOR: CC, ASR, 206440
HOME ADDRESS:

                        LOC         SCHED
JOB NUMBER/JOB YEAR END  OFF  PTR MGR   **  HRS TO 11    12           01       02       03          04          05
  JOB NAME/DESCRIPTION   DIV  SENIOR  STAT  DATE  18 25 02 09 16 23 30 06 13 20 27 03 10 17 24 03 10 17 24 31 07 14 21 28 05 12
------------------------ ---  ------- ---- ------ -- -- -- -- -- -- -- -- -- -- -- -- -- -- -- -- -- -- -- -- -- -- -- -- -- --
                              FGJ DLW  I   140:40    :  36:40 24:32  :     :50 50:50 50:50 50:    :     :     :     :     :
COMPANY 234              CC                        :     :     :     :     :     :     :     :     :     :     :     :     :
                                                  :     :     :     :     :     :     :     :     :     :     :     :     :
                              PAG RDG  I   240:    :     :     :     :     :     :     :     :10   :24  8:    :     :40 40>
COMPANY 345             CC                        :     :     :     :     :     :     :     :     :     :     :     :     :
                                                  :     :     :     :     :     :     :     :     :     :     :     :     :
                              FGJ JCH  I   260:    :     :     :     :     :     :     :     :     :     :40   :     :
COMPANY 456             CC                        :     :     :     :     :     :     :     :     :     :     :     :     :
                                                  :     :     :     :     :     :     :     :     :     :     :     :     :
4310000                       BRG                 :     :  3:  :     :     :     :     :     :     :     :     :     :
AUDIT DIV MEETING                                 :     :     :     :     :     :     :     :     :     :     :     :     :
                                                  :     :     :     :     :     :     :     :     :     :     :     :     :
555                                               : 2   :     :     :     :     :     :     :     :     :     :     :     :
P/M MEETING OR OFFICE MTG                         :     :     :     :     :     :     :     :     :     :     :     :     :
                                                  :     :     :     :     :     :     :     :     :     :     :     :     :
815                                               : 16: :     : 16: 8 :     :     :     :     :     :     :     :     :
HOLIDAY                                           :     :     :     :     :     :     :     :     :     :     :     :     :

•TOTAL ASSIGNED HOURS                             42 16    39 40 40 40       50 50 50 50 50 50 10    24  8       40    40 40
•TOTAL CHARGEABLE HOURS                           40       36 40 24 32       50 50 50 50 50 50 10    24  8       40    40 40
•TOTAL NON-CHARGEABLE HOURS                        2 16     3    16  8

•TOTAL OVERTIME HOURS                              2                         50 50 50 50 50 50 10    24  8       40    40 40
 TOTAL TENTATIVE HOURS
 TOTAL UNASSIGNED HOURS                           24 40  1     40 40 40             30 40 16 32 40 40    40

---------------------------------------------------------------------------------------------------
SCHEDULING CONSIDERATIONS:

---------------------------------------------------------------------------------------------------
•   INCLUDES TENTATIVE HOURS                                         ••••••••••••••••••••••••••••••
•• STATUS -  I = INCHARGE PERSON, R = REVISED SCHEDULE, T, X = TENTATIVE ASSIGNMENT,   •  CC        •
             C = STAFFING CONTINUITY, O = OUT OF TOWN                •  18 NOV 85    WEEKS 1 - 26  •
                                                                    ••••••••••••••••••••••••••••••
```

FIGURE I3   A long-range schedule, as used at Arthur Andersen & Co.—Charlotte.

```
CLT.RR RR-PGM                   AUDIT DIVISION PERSONNEL ASSIGNMENTS        DATE: 10/06/88
RAILROAD-PRINT                        TWENTY WEEKS REPORT                   PAGE: 1

DIVISION: CHARLOTTE AUDIT

EMPLOYEE  CLASS  10/10/88  10/17/88  10/24/88  10/31/88  11/07/88  11/14/88  11/21/88  11/28/88  12/05/88  12/12/88
AA        AESR   CO1   -40                                         HOLI  -16  CO1   -40 CO1   -40
                                                                                          CO37  -16
BB        AESR   CO2    -8 CO2   -40 CO2   -40 CO2   -40 CO14  -40 CO14  -40 VACAT -24 CO2   -40 CO14  -30 CO14  -50
                 CO3    -8                               CO2   -20           HOLI  -16 CO5   -40
CC        AESR   VACAT -40 VACAT -40                     CO20  -40           CO23  -24 CO23  -40           CO38  -24
                                                                             HOLI  -16
DD        AESR   CO4   -40 CO4   -40 CO4   -40 CO17   -8           CO17  -40 HOLI  -16 CO27  -40 CO27  -40 CO32  -40
EE        AESR                                                               CO24  -24
                                                                             HOLI  -16
FF        AESR                                 CO4   -40 CO4   -40 CO4   -40 HOLI  -16           CO31  -40
GG        ASR    CO5   -16 CO12  -50 CO12  -50 CO12  -50 CO6   -16 CO6   -40 CO6   -24 CO6   -40 CO6   -40
                 VACAT  -8                               CO12  -24           HOLI  -16
                 CO6   -16
HH        ASR    CO7   -40 CO7   -40 CO15  -40           CO21  -24 CO21  -40 CO21  -24           CO1   -40 CO1   -40
                                                                             HOLI  -16
II        ASR    VACAT -16                     CO18  -24 CO19  -40 CO19  -24 HOLI  -16                     CO33  -40
                 CO8   -24                     CO19  -16
JJ        ASR                                                               HOLI  -16 CO36  -32           CO34  -40
KK        ASR    CO9   -16 CO10  -32 CO10  -50 CO10  -50 CO10  -24           HOLI  -16                     CO11  -16
                 CO10   -8
                 CO11  -16
LL        ASR    CO13  -40 CO13  -40 CO13  -24 CO14  -40 CO14  -40           CO25  -24 CO29  -40 CO14  -30 CO14  -50
                                                                             HOLI  -16
MM        ASSR   VACAT -16 CO14  -40 VACAT -16 CO18  -24           CO22  -24 CO25  -40 CO30  -24 CO14  -30 CO14  -50
                           CO14   -8                                         HOLI  -16
NN        ASSR                       CO16  -40 CO16  -40 CO16  -40           HOLI  -16 CO5   -40
OO        AEST   CO1   -40 CO1    -8 CO10  -50 CO10  -50 CO19  -40 CO19  -16 CO23  -24 CO23  -40 CO1   -40 CO1   -40
                           CO10  -24                                         HOLI  -16
PP        AEST   CO35   -8 CO13  -40 CO13  -40 CO18  -16 CO14  -40 CO14  -40 CO26   -8           CO14  -30 CO14  -50
                 TEACH -16                                                   HOLI  -16
                 VACAT -16
```

FIGURE I4   A 20-week schedule, as used at Arthur Andersen & Co.—Charlotte.

```
CAROLINAS                           PERSONNEL SCHEDULING              PAGE-    1      AS OF-20 NOV 85
DIVISION: CHARLOTTE AUDIT                                                             PREP-20 NOV 85
TO: 450561                          PERSONNEL AVAILABILITY (CONDENSED)                RPT-EC03100

              PERS                  AVAIL 11      12                01        02        03        04        05
CLASS GROUP   NUMBER CLAS  PERSONNEL NAME  TENT 18 25 02 09 16 23 30 06 13 20 27 03 10 17 24 03 10 17 24 31 07 14 21 28 05 12
------------  ------ ----  --------------  ---- -- -- -- -- -- -- -- -- -- -- -- -- -- -- -- -- -- -- -- -- -- -- -- -- -- --
SENIORS       115312 ASR  AA              AVAIL:   24:   :   :   :   40:   :   :   40:40 40:40 40:40 16:   :40 40:40 40:
              206440 ASR  CC              AVAIL:   24:40 1:   :   40:40 40:   :   :   :30 40:16 32:40 40:   40:   :
              295868 ASR  DD              AVAIL:38 24:40 37:40 24:32 40:24  :   :40 40:40 40:   :24 32:40 40:40 40:40 40:
              374725 ASR  EE              AVAIL:38 24:   1:   24:32 40:   :   :40  :   :40 40:40 40:40 40:40 40:40 40:
              595772 ASR  HH              AVAIL:   :   1:   24:32 40:   :   :   :   40:40 40:   :40 40:40 40:40 40:
              657221 ASR  JJ              AVAIL:   24:40 37:40   :16 40:   :   :   :   :   40:   40:40 40:40 40:40 40:
              692981 ASR  KK              AVAIL:   :   37:40 24:32   :   :   :   :   40:40 40:40 40:40 40:40 40:
              743739 ASR  LL              AVAIL:   :   37:40 24:24   :   :   :   :40 40:40 40:40 40:40 40:40 32:
              778001 ASR  MM              AVAIL: 6  :   1:40   :   :   :   :   40:40 40:   40:40 40:40 40:40 40:
              941701 ASR  NN              AVAIL:38 24:40 37:40 24:32 40:40 40:40 40:40 40:40 40:40 40:40 40:40 40:40 40:

        STANDARD WORKLOAD  40 24 40 40 40 24 32 40 40 40 40 40 40 40 40 40 40 40 40 40 40 40 40 40 40 40
                          -- -- -- -- -- -- -- -- -- -- -- -- -- -- -- -- -- -- -- -- -- -- -- -- -- --
                                                                              •••••••••••••••••••••••••
                                                                              •  20 NOV 85  WEEKS 1-26   •
                                                                              •••••••••••••••••••••••••
```

FIGURE I5   A personnel availability chart, as used at Arthur Andersen & Co.—Charlotte.

house for the staffing needs of all of the Carolinas' offices. In trying to fill the open holes in the schedule, he relied most on the 20-week schedule, which was the one that was painstakingly updated with all the changes, and which was the office's controlling document for the next 20 weeks. That document was organized by individual and displayed the open holes for each professional in the Carolinas, as well as which engagements everyone was scheduled for. An associated document was generated automatically to show the converse—which professionals in the office were available in each week. This document identified candidate professionals who could help with a new or existing engagement (see Figure I5).

As might be expected, there were continual inconsistencies in the schedule that had to be resolved. These inconsistencies resulted from many things—new work, changes in personnel, or changes in the scope of an existing engagement. Consider the following situation. The Greensboro office not only had been very busy but was short of seniors as well. The existing seniors there were working too much overtime and needed to be relieved in some way. As it happened, a new senior had been transferred to the Charlotte office from Dallas and was due

soon. The scheduler's dilemma was how to help the Greensboro office without giving them the new senior for too long a time, because, after all, he had been transferred into Charlotte and not Greensboro. The scheduler knew that it would be toughest to adjust the schedule during the peak time of the year (February and March), so he concentrated on helping Greensboro during those two months. By consulting the schedule, he knew that the new senior could be used on the Company 792 engagement for the weeks of February 17, February 24, and March 3. That engagement also called for a senior's time during the week of December 2, which was fine, as the new senior was going to be in Charlotte at that time. In addition, Greensboro needed help on the Company 409 engagement for the weeks of February 3 and February 10. That also called for work in the week of December 23. This, too, fitted well into the new senior's schedule.

However, there were two other engagements, Company 642 and Company 322, that would need additional manpower and could not be assigned to the new senior. The scheduler looked to the 20-week schedule for holes and then also looked at the personnel availability sheet. No one senior had time available in all of the time periods required for the jobs under consideration: Thus there were some incompatibilities that the scheduler had to check into and resolve. Upon investigation, two seniors' schedules showed some promise. In evaluating the jobs assigned to each of them during this period, it looked like one would be the more available. However, he would not be free for all of the 3 weeks slated for those jobs. He was available during the weeks of December 9 and December 16, but he was not available during the week of January 20, as he was scheduled on another job in the Greensboro office. The scheduler then had to do some horse trading. In order for him to assign the senior to the Greensboro office for the 642 and 322 jobs, he needed to take the senior off his other assignment at Greensboro. By calling around to the interested parties, it was agreed that the senior could be taken off the Greensboro job for the week of January 20 and thus assigned to the 642 and 322 jobs that were coming up immediately. The hope was that the Greensboro office could delay work on that job until sometime later, or if that was not possible, perhaps use another senior for the week of January 20.

The scheduler continually made trade-offs in this way, for the most part following a hierarchy of preferences: (1) substitute a similar-level professional for the professional initially planned for (possible for preliminary audit work but not for final audit work), (2) substitute an available professional from a different level, if he or she were qualified, and (3) let the schedule slip so that the desired personnel could perform the job at a more convenient date. During the course of any week, there might be two or three problems that consumed up to 4 hours each to resolve. In addition, there were a host of smaller problems that might be resolved much more easily, say within an hour's time each.

The scheduler was in repeated contact with the managers who oversaw the office's engagements. Those managers informed the scheduler of changes in their needs, and they occasionally lobbied him for particular professionals to work their engagements. Sometimes, particularly with new clients, staff and seniors would also lobby the scheduler for those jobs. An important task for the scheduler was balancing the training and development needs of staff accountants and seniors against the practice's need for their services and the client company's desires for continuity in the personnel assigned to them.

Personnel Policy

While profitability was tied to the pyramid and to the efficient scheduling of people, the Charlotte office's managing partner believed that in the long run, Arthur Andersen & Co. would be successful only if it served its clients well. His major concern was with the development of the professionals in the office and the culture in which they worked. Culture, of course, is an elusive concept, but a variety of indications of the Arthur Andersen & Co. culture could be cited:

- The Arthur Andersen motto: think straight, talk straight.
- No secrets were kept around the office.
- Team work and attention to detail were highly valued.
- Also valued was client service and the urgency in that. There was a "code red" program that called for some member of the engagement team to return a client's phone call within 60 minutes, no matter where the engagement's lead partner or manager might find themselves.
- The pride that Arthur Andersen had in having the widely acknowledged premier training program of any of the Big Six.

- The desire that Charlotte's managing partner had for everyone to have fun doing their jobs. In support of this, the goal was to have every professional assigned to the industry of his preference at least half the time.
- All the office's professionals were reviewed each year. They filled out a form (Figure 16) and then met with a partner to discuss their performance and career development.

Training

One of the partners was responsible for monitoring the training of all the audit professionals. Training at Arthur Andersen & Co. was done either within the local office or at the firm-wide level. To this end, the firm operated a training center in St. Charles, Illinois, and brought professionals from all over the world to it on a regular basis. Continuing professional education was required of all CPAs by the national and various states' accounting societies (120 hours over 3 years with no less than 20 hours per year in any year), so even partners and managers spent time in training. For the most part, partners and managers averaged at least 40 hours per year, for example, most staff accumulated between 150 and 200 hours of training, with 100 to 120 hours spent locally, and the balance at either the regional level or at the St. Charles campus. Seniors did not spend quite that much time, but they too spent a considerable amount of time in training.

Training was considered as important as a client assignment for the professionals in the office. The training plan was usually developed well in advance, and put out "on the railroad." Good attendance was viewed as important for career development. The slow period from April through August was the best time of the year for training, although training programs were scheduled throughout the year.

The training program was considerably varied. Some of the programs were basic for the first- and second-year professionals, but other programs were termed either intermediate or advanced. Some of these courses dealt with interpersonal relationships, marketing, effective presentations, and other aspects of management development. Still other courses had industry orientations, so that professionals could be better steeped in the nature and problems of the specific industries they served.

Recruiting

Recruiting was another important function that was overseen by a partner and that demanded considerable time from the senior professionals in the office. Recruiting concentrated on local schools, although all the recruiting was done for the firm at large and not just for the Charlotte office. Recruiting was done at both the undergraduate and MBA levels.

The Manager's Life

Managers oversaw the day-to-day operations of each audit engagement. It was their job to see that the audit was done well and on time and that the fee level was appropriate. They were responsible for developing the staffing plan and budget for the engagement and for billing and collecting from the client. Managers wanted to avoid any surprises on an engagement, and thus it was in their interest to have seniors and staff that could be trusted and whose competence and capabilities would be unquestioned.

Managers spent a good deal of their time outside the office — perhaps 55 to 65 percent. Most of that time was spent at existing clients, attending to their needs and solving any problems that had cropped up. About 20 to 25 percent of the manager's time was spent with

TO: _____
                    Reviewing Partner

FROM: _____

DATE: _____

SUBJECT: ANNUAL REVIEW _____

1. Am I satisfied with the assignments I have had? What particular assignments (industry, technical specialization, research, compliance, etc.) would I like in the next year?

_____

_____

_____

2. What, if any, particular training would I like to receive during the next year?

_____

_____

_____

3. Are the demands made upon me as a professional (overtime, travel, work pace, etc.) acceptable?

_____

_____

_____

4. Am I progressing at a pace satisfactory to me?

_____

_____

_____

5. Is my performance being evaluated currently and adequately?

_____

_____

_____

6. My interests in professional and civic activities are:

_____

_____

_____

7. Ideas or suggestions for the Firm:

_____

_____

_____

8. Any concerns:

_____

_____

_____

FIGURE I6   An annual review form used at Arthur Andersen & Co.—Charlotte.

administrative chores. And because managers were partners-in-training to a large degree, they spent some of their time developing new clients and new business for the firm.

In the main, managers were pleased with their lives at Arthur Andersen & Co. Their jobs were viewed as challenging, motivating, and educational, and the partners gave them a good deal of autonomy. The partners were also regarded as fair, and the up-or-out nature of the business was not unduly confining because the managers felt that they could easily leave the firm for attractive jobs elsewhere.

The Partner's Life

Many duties fell on the partners in the Charlotte office. The typical partner incurred about 1000 hours each year that were charged to the engagements on which he was the senior member. Of that time, perhaps two-thirds was spent at the client, discussing the client's business and supervising the audit there. Other chargeable hours were spent in the planning phase and final report phases of the actual audit. As an accountant and auditor, the partner was responsible for solving problems, for analyzing risk, and for monitoring quality.

The other 1400 to 1500 hours of a partner's year were spent in many different activities: recruiting; training, including teaching the junior people; practice development, which was the marketing and sales function for generating new business; personnel matters, such as counseling junior professionals and reviewing their

progress; and providing counsel to other Arthur Andersen & Co. professionals on matters of the partner's own expertise (e.g., the Charlotte office was viewed as the firm's source of expertise for textiles).

The partners, as a group, are responsible for a multitude of functions. Not only did they have line responsibility for the audits being done, but they had to divide up the overhead functions necessary to further the practice: training, recruiting, expertise in special industry specializations (such as health care, manufacturing, closely held businesses), practice development, administration, and quality control.

Partners were well compensated. Their high incomes were a motivation for many of the junior people. Arthur Andersen & Co. partners were paid by splitting the worldwide profits of the company according to how many "units" they held. Each unit was stated in U.S. dollars. All partners started with a fixed quantity of units, and over time, these units were added onto, based upon seniority and merit. In keeping with the no-secrets aspect of the firm, files were kept on all partners, and all partners knew what everyone else in the firm made.

A manager was not promoted to partner based solely on the evaluations of the office in which he or she served. There were uniform standards for the promotion to partner that were overseen by a firm-wide committee. Upon becoming partners, managers were required to contribute some capital to the firm, but this was a rather modest amount relative to the income the partner made.

PART TWO

DISCUSSION

Arthur Andersen & Co. is in no way responsible for the following views and presentation. They remain solely the responsibility of the author.

THE FLOW OF THE PROCESS AND OF INFORMATION

Figure I7 is a very rough process flow diagram of the audit process. It shows the degree of involvement by the various levels comprising the engagement team. This process flow also includes the proposal stage and the selection and scheduling stage for the development of the audit team. The diagram depicts only the major phases of the audit process. One could, of course, develop a more detailed schedule of the work for any engagement, but that detailed schedule would be very particular to the client, and complex as well. It would include many of

the work elements of Arthur Andersen & Co.'s audit procedures; as such it is beyond the scope of this service tour.

Similarly, constructing a diagram of the information flow in a process like auditing is well-nigh impossible. The flows of information are so numerous and so idiosyncratic to the client and to the needs of the engagement team itself that it is not worth characterizing here. A Big Six accounting organization simply lives on information, and that information flow must be swift, it must involve all layers of the company, and it must carry differing quantities of information.

There are no real distinctions in either the process or information flows during peak versus nonpeak times. During peak times, of course, lots of overtime is put in, and people are perhaps more charged-up about work, but all of the steps must still be done, and all of the information must still flow as it does at nonpeak times.

	Proposal Writing	Engagement Team Selection and Scheduling	Planning Phase	Specific Risk Analysis Phase	Final Audit Phase
Senior Members of the Engagement Team (Partners and Managers)	High involvement with client and among themselves	High involvement, especially by managers. Scheduler is very much involved	High involvement	Little involvement by partner(s), except for periodic troubleshooting and for quality reviews Day-to-day involvement by manager	High involvement
Junior Members of the Engagement Team (Seniors and Staff)	Little or no involvement	Some preferences for work are stated	Little involvement by staff High involvement by seniors	High involvement. Much work done at client	High involvement

FIGURE I7   Rough process flow diagram for auditing services at Arthur Andersen & Co.—Charlotte.

DEMANDS OF THE PROCESS
ON THE WORKFORCE

The workforce at Arthur Andersen & Co. is composed of the salaried professionals (managers, seniors, staff) and the less numerous support people. The process demands on them are essentially a high degree of training and a tremendous amount of flexibility. The firm's accountants have to move from job to job, to put in long hours when called upon, and to be out in the field for, perhaps, long stretches of time. Some of the work is tedious, although much of the work can be challenging and rewarding.

The firm's accountants, at all levels, must make decisions all the time. Even in the preliminary phase of an audit, there are decisions to be made and many issues that need to be resolved. Thus the members of an engagement team have to be constantly on the lookout for problems or opportunities (e.g., add-on business) that they should surface to the senior members of the engagement team for resolution. This is one reason why so much continual training is required to keep everyone fresh and knowledgeable as times and clients change.

Accountants must also face the up-or-out nature of advancement within the firm. Happily, the alternatives to employment are generally good. Arthur Andersen & Co. accountants are typically in high demand by client companies and others. The care with which advancement decisions are made and the counsel given accountants through this process helps to ease any stress that this kind of advancement places on the accountants proceeding through the ranks.

THE PYRAMID[1]

Let us now depart from the organizational structure of Arthur Andersen & Co. to examine in more general terms the nature of the professional pyramid (Figure 18) as it applies in all sorts of professional service firms. For the sake of simplification, consider only three ranks of professionals: partner, manager, and junior. The partner is chiefly responsible for client relations and the running of the firm itself. The manager is the one responsible for the day-to-day activities of the project (engagement)—what there is to do, how it is to be done, and whether it is being done properly, on schedule, and within budget. The junior professional is assigned many of the tasks that constitute the "legwork" of the project. This dispersion of responsibility among partners, managers, and juniors has led some wags to term this hierarchy one of "finders, minders, and grinders."

What determines the shape of the pyramid—whether it is broad or narrow? There are two major determinants of the pyramid's shape:

1. The composition of work on the projects undertaken.
2. The utilization rates of the firm's professionals.

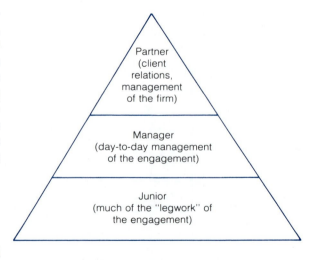

FIGURE 18   The professional pyramid.

Let's explore these factors in greater detail. Assume, for example, that a typical project of 600 hours required certain time commitments from the firm's professionals and that the professionals were used on projects to the degree shown in the following table.

PROFESSIONALS	TYPICAL TIME COMMITMENT[a] (hours)	UTILIZATION RATE[a] (percent)
Partner	60	50
Manager	140	70
Junior	400	85
	600	

[a]These are meant to be illustrative and do not reflect figures for Arthur Andersen & Co.

The utilization rates reflect the facts that other things take up professionals' time (training, recruiting, scheduling, counseling, soliciting new business) and that these other activities are relatively more demanding of the senior professionals in the firm. Given a planning figure of 2000 hours of work per person per year, one partner could sustain supervision of 16.67 average projects (calculated as 1000 hours of partner time available for projects divided by 60 hours of time per typical project, or 16.67 projects per year). A manager, on the other hand, could sustain direction of 10 projects (1400 hours available and 140 hours average for each project). Thus for the firm to be balanced, for every partner there have to be 1.67 managers. Similarly, a junior can work on 4.25 projects each year (1700 hours available and 400 hours for each project). In this way, the pyramid's shape is determined: Every partner supports 1.67 managers and 3.92 juniors.

The shape of the pyramid, in turn, largely determines the rate at which professionals can be advanced and how selective that advancement has to be. Assume, for example, that juniors are 6 years in rank and that managers are 4 years in rank. If there are 10 partners, the pyramid would look as in Figure I9. Suppose that every year a partner has to be added, either to sustain the growth of the firm or to replace a partner who retires or otherwise leaves the firm. Every year, then, a manager has to be

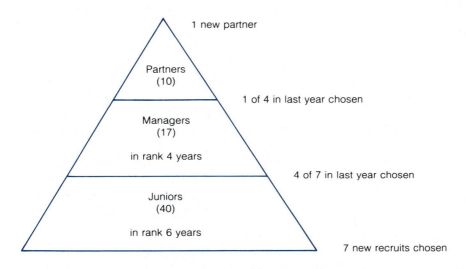

FIGURE I9   The pyramid and advancement.

made a partner in order for the pyramid to be in balance. If, on average each year, 4 of the 17 managers are in the fourth year, the advancement rate has to be 1 in 4. Similarly, if during any year, four new managers are required and there are seven juniors in their final sixth year, then roughly half of the juniors can be promoted to manager status. In this way, the pyramid sustains itself. Of the 11 juniors and managers in their last year, 1 becomes a partner, 4 become managers, and 6 leave the firm. Of the 7 new recruits, only 1 can expect to make partner after 10 years.

Demands of the Process on Management

The partners in a professional firm like Arthur Andersen & Co. have a number of responsibilities that they alone must shoulder. Many of these responsibilities relate to the workforce. Managing the pyramid well, as discussed earlier, is an absolute requirement. Partners must take the lead in recruiting new accountants, in training them, and in managing their advancement through the firm. These activities take up tremendous chunks of partner time.

Partners must also use that pyramid well in order to make money. Thus the assignment of accountants to engagements and the scheduling of those accountants are important areas of partner concern. Even though the actual schedule itself is accomplished by a manager level professional, the partners must develop the strategy underlying the schedules developed.

Partners are also primarily responsible for procuring new business. They are the ones who must contact the clients, develop proposals, and establish fees. And, of course, the partners must be, in themselves, excellent accountants. They must be intimately involved in the general risk analysis and the final phase of each audit. They are called on to troubleshoot and to review the quality of any audit through all its phases, particularly the preliminary phase. In addition to this line management authority, they are also called on by others in the firm as experts in certain areas (e.g., industries and certain accounting practices). Thus partners must wear many hats and are pulled in many different directions.

QUESTIONS

1. What advantages do you see to the hierarchical structure of an accounting firm like Arthur Andersen & Co.? Do you see any disadvantages?

2. What kinds of factors do you suppose would affect the fee schedule advanced in a proposal to a client?

3. In a partner-manager-junior type of organization, as described in the discussion to this service tour, suppose the time commitments were changed from a 60-140-400 breakdown to one of 100-200-300. Assuming the same utilization rates, how would the pyramid change, if it were to remain perfectly balanced?

4. What benefits and costs are involved in increasing the average chargeable hours in the office from its current level of 1400 to 1500 hours per year?

5. What kinds of trade-offs are the hardest for the office's scheduler? What kinds are the easiest?

6. What are the characteristics you would look for in the typical recruit for a staff accountant position?

SITUATION FOR STUDY I-1

JOHNSON AND TROTTER ADVERTISING

The Johnson and Trotter Advertising Agency was a large, New York based agency with a wide variety of clients. J&T was organized into six functional departments: account management, research, creativity, production, media, and legal. The account management department was charged with client relations and was responsible for coordinating the efforts of all of the other departments on the client's behalf. The research department was responsible for uncovering useful facts about the products and services advertised that may be of use in developing new ads, and they were also charged with substantiating the advertising claims made by the ads. The creativity department was the lead department in developing new ideas and the means by which the client's products and services could be advertised. The production department was responsible for making the print, radio, and TV ads that had been conceived by the creativity department. The media department interacted with all of the media in which the agency's clients advertised, while the legal department handled any legal issues raised by the agency's efforts.

The agency accomplished its work in teams. Members of the various departments generally worked on more than one account at the same time except for the account executive, who was charged with keeping all members of the product team informed about such things as the client's situation, research findings, creative ideas, production status, and any other information on the account. The account executive was also charged with keeping the entire effort on the established timetable and within budget. Members of each product team could expect to spend several years working for a client, before being rotated off. Any differences of opinion were generally dealt with by compromise within the product team. Account executives did not have the authority to overrule a specialist on a question involving that specialist's realm of expertise. If a difference of opinion persisted, the team could take its dispute to its superiors within each department, where it was usually resolved.

There were three quality control mechanisms at J&T: a strategy review board, a creative review board, and a media review board. At key stages of the firm's process, these quality control mechanisms could be invoked.

Promotion for the professionals of the agency came from within each department. For example, within account management, one typically started as an assistant account executive, moved up to account executive, then, on to account supervisor, management supervisor, and then executive vice-president for client services. A general manager oversaw all of the six functional groups.

1. What strengths do you see in the organization of Johnson and Trotter?

2. What potential disadvantages exist with this operation?

REFERENCE NOTE

1.   Much of the discussion is based upon David Maister, ''Balancing the Professional Service Firm,'' *Sloan Management Review* (Fall 1982): 15–29.

A PROJECT
Geupel DeMars, Inc.
Indianapolis, Indiana

Geupel DeMars, a subsidiary of the DeMars Corporation, was an Indianapolis-based construction management firm for industrial and commercial properties. The company was formed in 1927 and first worked on department store construction. Since that time it had gradually broadened its client base. In 1991 the firm employed 250 people. See the organization charts in Figure J1.

Geupel DeMars (GDI), as a construction management firm, acted as the agent for an Owner. It did no actual construction itself, but rather planned for the construction of the building, arranged for Owner-held contracts for the different aspects of the job, oversaw the work, and reported to the Owner. For its effort, the Owner paid Geupel DeMars a fee to cover the salaries and benefits of its employees on the job, plus a percentage markup.

As a construction management firm, Geupel DeMars was distinct from (1) an architectural/engineering (A/E) firm that designs buildings and does the engineering required to translate the design into documents that serve as the basis of contractor bids on the project, (2) a design/build firm that combines the design, engineering, and construction of a building into a single one-stop package for the Owner, or (3) a contractor that only builds.

The workings of a construction management firm are best seen by examining a particular project. For this tour, the project is the construction of Research Building No. 48 for Eli Lilly & Company. This building (see Figure J2) of 550,000 square feet, was slated for completion in early 1993 at a total cost of $135.2 million. The design envisioned a building of four stories, laid out in three wings (Biology, Chemistry, and Animal) tied to a central administrative section. The nature of the building called for features that were distinct from typical office buildings: special ventilation for the 162 labs, greater capacity HVAC (heating, ventilation, and air conditioning), purified water sources, and special drainage systems, among others.

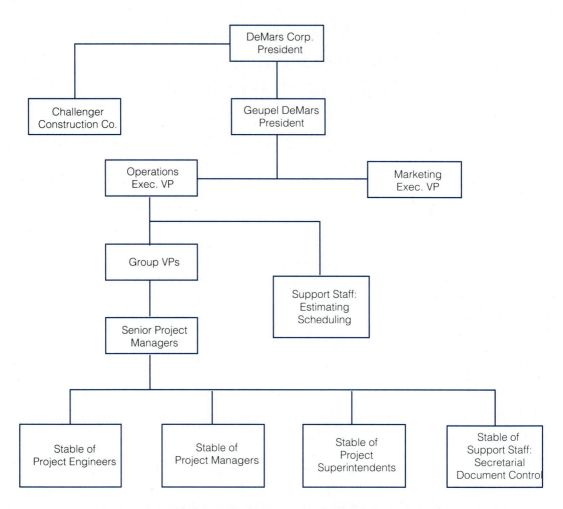

FIGURE J1   A. Simplified Organization Chart for Geupel DeMars

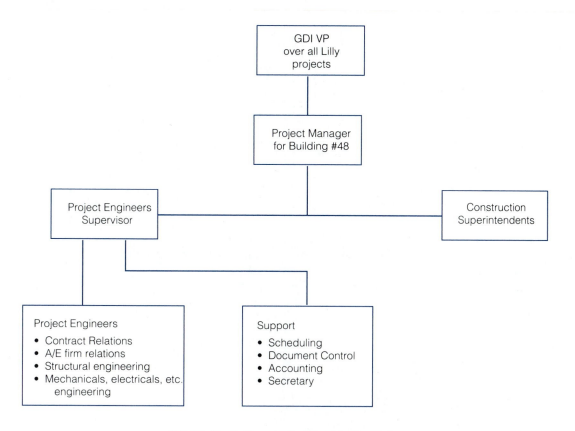

FIGURE J1   B. Organization Chart for the Project

PART ONE

PROCESS DESCRIPTION

PROJECT ORGANIZATION AND TIMETABLE

Research Building No. 48 was scheduled to take roughly three years to build from groundbreaking to completion. Prior to that time, considerable planning had to be done. Geupel De-Mars became involved with the project about two years before construction began. The na-

ture of its involvement in the project changed over time. To wit:

Year One, 1988

- *Personnel.* 0 in field; 2 in the office.
- *Tasks.* Gather data; estimate costs and constructability; develop overall schedule.

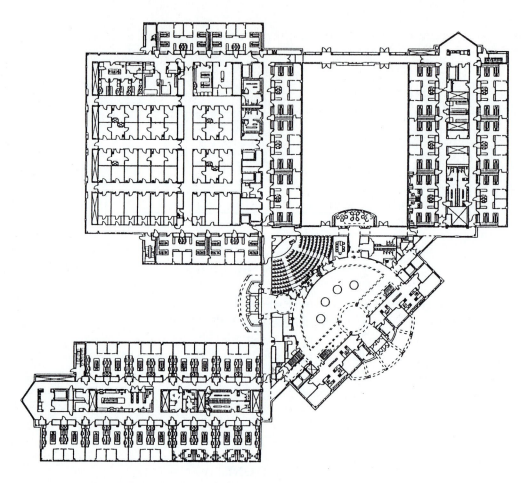

FIGURE J2   Floor plan for Research Building 48's first floor.

When Geupel DeMars entered the project, Lilly had already engaged the architectural/engineering firm (CUH2A of Princeton, New Jersey) and the building's design was proceeding. Although the location for the building was set, there was still considerable fluidity to the design: how many stories, how stretched out, how the various research wings would be connected. Geupel DeMars's role in this conceptual phase of the project involved the following tasks:

- Reviewing the plans and estimating the costs of various alternative designs.
- Reviewing the constructability of the building and identifying the cost-feature tradeoffs that the Owner (Lilly) would have to make, tasks known as value engineering.

• Identifying schedule parameters and inputs. Preparing and presenting alternative schedule strategies for delivery of the project.

In this conceptual phase, GDI provided cost estimates to the Owner with an accuracy of within 10–20 percent of actual costs for each of the building configurations seriously considered. These estimates were based on costs per square foot of interior space, costs per square foot for the face of the building (stone, glass, concrete), and costs for HVAC, plumbing, electrical requirements, and so on.

Year Two, 1989

• *Personnel.*   0 in the field; 2 in the office.
• *Tasks.*   Continue Year One tasks but with further refinement, establish budget.

The second year of the project continued the tasks begun in Year One. Over time, decisions were made that refined the project more and more. The project moved from "conceptual drawings" of the building to "schematic drawings," which were half to two-thirds complete in nature and on which materials began to be specified. These schematic drawings required renewed cost estimation and value engineering.

The character of Geupel DeMars's value engineering could include the following types of suggestions:

• *Selection of materials.*   The choice of materials can often affect the cost of the project by five to ten percent. Such choices can include the use of concrete versus structural steel, the type of roofing materials to use, and the choice of pipe materials for purified water systems, etc.
• *Design modifications.* The construction manager can suggest which design details are likely to be expensive to render and which

are not. Examples include roofing details such as flashings and eaves, structural concrete details on how the concrete is to be formed, and finish details such as door jambs and lighting fixture wiring systems.

The schematic drawings were followed by the even more specific "design development drawings" and the first of the "construction documents" upon which supplier and contractor bids could be made.

Year Three, 1990

• *Personnel.*   1 in the field; 4 in the office.
• *Tasks.*   Supervise excavation and initial construction; begin bidding procedures for contractors; establish procedures for scheduling, quality control and cost control.

Excavation of the site began in February 1990. During the rest of that year, the foundations were poured and the erection of the steel superstructure for the building was started. One superintendent in the field oversaw this work.

This year also saw the start of what was termed the "fast-track construction design." This process called for the identification of sequential "bid packages" of work, the scheduling of the design process to support this sequence, bidding, the award of initial contracts, and the subsequent commencement of work. The development and awarding of bid packages was done on a rolling basis and would continue for a year and a half. Major parts of the construction were treated in this way: excavation, foundation, concrete, structural steel, enclosure packages (skin, roof, doors); elevators, mechanicals (HVAC, fire protection, plumbing); electricals; and various interior finishes (painting, flooring, carpeting, ceiling, partitions, wall coverings, etc.). Likewise, as part of this process, came the purchase of equipment for the building by the owner.

This was also the year to establish the balance of the procedures that would govern the construction of the project as time went on. These procedures were essential to the control of the project (schedule, cost, quality) so that the Owner actually received what was designed and specified. These controls are explained in more detail later.

Year Four, 1991

- *Personnel.* 5 in the field; 9 in the office.
- *Tasks.* Continue construction supervision; continue the development and award of bid packages; monitor project schedule, costs, and quality and report to the Owner.

In this year, the building took shape and the need for field monitoring and supervision escalated dramatically. Bid packages continued to be assembled, bid, and awarded.

The year also saw more "administration and management" of the project as opposed to the earlier planning and estimating work that dominated the efforts of Geupel DeMars. This "management" essentially consisted of pursuing the control procedures that had been laid out in the previous year, reporting on progress to the Owner, and dealing with the myriad field questions and problems, both large and small, that inevitably accompanied the work of the contractors as they actually built the research building and as procurement proceeded.

Year Five, 1992

- *Personnel.* 8 in the field; 10 in the office.
- *Tasks.* Continue supervision of the construction; continue management of the project; start-up of major systems.

Year Six, 1993

- *Personnel.* 8 in the field; 10 in the office.
- *Tasks.* Close out the project for the Owner.

In this final year the construction was completed and the project closed out. Closing out a project meant several things:

- All contractors had completed their work, including their "punch lists" (i.e., the lists of repairs and inadvertent omissions that are identified prior to an Owner taking possession).
- The contractors had supplied the "as built" drawings, warranties, and guarantees.
- All paperwork had been finished, including all letters answered and items resolved.
- The project file was completed, including all copies of correspondence, all shop drawings (the detailed drawings from the contractors of which there were thousands of pages), all as-built drawings, all quality control documents, and all test reports.

THE MANUAL AND ITS CONTROLS

Prior to the start of construction, Geupel DeMars and Lilly prepared a procedures manual that outlined the specific duties of each party. This manual was the basic control document for the project. In it, procedures were described for such items as bidding, materials substitutions, submittals, quality control, requests for information (usually from a contractor to the A/E firm and the Owner), design changes, and progress payments to the contractors.

Submittals were a particularly important point of control. A submittal was the contractor's submission for review of any of several types of documents:

- Catalog and performance data for the materials to be used
- "Shop drawings"—the contractor's drawings detailing what actually was to be done
- Guarantees
- Job standards, consisting of certifications or approved samples that could be of use as field examples
- Maintenance data and operating instructions
- Installation instructions
- Physical samples of material and assemblies

Once the submittals were reviewed and approved by the A/E, the contractor could procure and install the material and equipment. Submittals thus led to the approval of materials, and materials were seen as driving both the schedule and the budget. Geupel DeMars was insistent that contractors follow a submittal schedule so that they performed on time with the proper information.

Substitutions were another important item to control. Substitutions of materials were usually made to reduce cost, to provide a better product (perhaps as a result of value engineering), or to speed up an aspect of the project that had fallen behind schedule. Substitutions required the approval of the Owner and the A/E firm.

There were a host of other controls on quality. For example, the superintendents completed reports each day on the work accomplished. There were reports on nonconforming work, which typically would necessitate repair. Independent tests were made to verify that items such as the soil, concrete, structural work, roofing, HVAC, and high voltage met design requirements. A periodic report was distributed to the Owner on (1) the construction progress, (2) the topics at morning meetings, and, (3) most importantly, a listing of "open issues."

Contractor Bidding

Geupel DeMars did no real construction on Building No. 48, but acted only as the agent for the Owner. A major task for the company was to assist the Owner in assembling the best available stable of contractors who (1) had the expertise, (2) met the Owner's financial requirement, and (3) were aware of the Owner's high quality standards. Working from the plans and engineering specifications of the architectural/engineering firm, Geupel DeMars assembled a total of about 30 bid packages for the diverse pieces of the construction. A bid package contained (1) a summary of work that spelled out all that the contractor was to do; (2) a manual detailing procedures used by Geupel DeMars and Lilly; and (3) the applicable construction drawings and technical specifications by the A/E firm. A bid package took about a week to assemble. Once assembled, the bid package was sent to between 4 and 6 contractors that had been invited to bid on the job. These contractors were generally well known to Geupel DeMars either from past work or from the formal approval process and were all considered to be capable of performing quality work of the scale required. (Often, the Owner would have its own preferred list). New or previously unknown contractors would be visited and their operations and financial conditions reviewed.

After the bidding documents were out for 2 weeks, Geupel DeMars held a pre-bid meeting with the invited contractors. At this meeting, GDI reviewed the manual and the summary of work and then, with the assistance of the A/E and the Owner, answered questions. Following the meeting, an addendum with meeting minutes and revisions was issued.

It took the contractors between 3 and 6 weeks to prepare their bids. After review of the bids, the apparent low bidder was invited to attend a pre-contract meeting between the contractor, the Owner, the A/E (if necessary), and GDI. This was a technical meeting that sometimes involved Geupel DeMars's field superintendents. If all issues were resolved, the Owner then signed a contract with the successful bidder. Construction then began on that contracted work.

DEALING WITH CONTRACTORS ON THE JOB

Once construction began, Geupel DeMars passed on information between contractors and the Owner and the A/E firm. (The Lilly team for this project numbered about 10 people. The A/E firm, at one point, had as many as 300 on the design effort, with about 10 on the continuing supervisory team.) Sometimes, the contractor would have questions about particular details of the construction, questions that were generally overlooked by all parties before then. These questions triggered a formal RFI (Request for Information). Geupel DeMars's role was (1) to follow up on the RFI, (2) to distribute the information to the appropriate people, and (3) to communicate any decided changes to the scope of work.

Geupel DeMars felt that it had failed if any major problems occurred. The company was always looking ahead to such things as the schedule of submittals, approved materials, and test results. Fortunately for all concerned, there were few problems of any magnitude with the Research Building #48 project.

FIELD SUPERVISION

As the building progressed, more and more attention was devoted to planning and supervising the daily construction activities. This was the responsibility of the field's construction superintendents and field engineers. Initially, there was only one to supervise the excavation and foundation work. As the superstructure was set in place, more superintendents joined the project and a greater division of labor ensued. For Research Building #48, there were different superintendents for each of the major trades represented by the contractors (e.g., structure, mechanicals, electricals).

The superintendents oversaw the quality of work being done, any testing of materials, and the coordination of the contractors' work. They reviewed requests for information. They also determined the percentage completion of various aspects of the job, which affected scheduling and the progress payments Lilly made each month.

SCHEDULING

After quality control in importance came the control of the project's schedule. The schedule affected both quality and cost. Although keeping on schedule was everybody's concern, there was a scheduler whose task was to document the schedule and the project's conformance to that schedule.

The schedule was derived in backwards fashion. The Owner typically had a completion date in mind. From that date the scheduler worked back to the relevant start dates.

The raw data for the schedule were the numerous activities that had to be accomplished. Some of these activities had to precede others, although many activities could be accomplished simultaneously. For the most part, the activities comprising the schedule followed the various bid packages. The contractors responsible for each bid package detailed their construction schedules, floor-by-floor, and this information served as a basis for the schedule. Geupel DeMars then applied its own experience and its knowledge of supplier timetables, especially for long leadtime items.

A computer program, Primavera Primavision, was used to document, monitor, and make changes to the schedule. Primavera kept track of all the designated activities, their expected times-to-completion, and their relationships to each other. The input to Primavera was built up bit-by-bit as GDI developed each bid package. The program's input began shortly after excavation was begun. By the end of the project, it was expected that 2000 activities would be captured. Of those 2000 activities, for example, 640 would pertain to mechanical and electrical installations. Only about 20 percent of the activities pertained directly to actual installation; the other 80 percent referred to various reviews, approvals, bidding, comments, documentation, and so on.

Primavera Primavision generated several documents that helped with the project's scheduling:

1. *Gantt Charts.* Figure J3 is a Gantt chart generated by Primavera. Gantt charts, discussed in Chapter 9, are simply bar charts that plot time for each activity. They show expected start and stop times, and the bars could be filled in to show the extent of actual progress at each point in time. Note that in Figure J3 the project is up-to-date. All of the activities that should have been accomplished by the time of the chart's date, April 1991, have indeed been accomplished.

The solid color bars represent activities that are designated as "critical." More formally, these are activities that lie on the so-called "critical path" (see Chapter 9). Activities on the critical path are those which, if delayed, will delay the entire project. For them, there is no spare catch-up time available to be used. They must be accomplished on time or the project gets delayed.

Sometimes, of course, an activity might be hurried up in order to put a delayed project back on track. Often, such hustling cost money in addition to the extra effort of those involved. This hustling was typically termed "crashing" an activity. For example, for Research Building 48, the erection of the curtain wall began 7 weeks late. The contractor, however, captured back some of the lost time by putting more people on the task than was originally planned.

2. *Time Logic Diagrams.* Another output of Primavera is a time logic diagram, such as depicted in Figure J4. This diagram depicts the precedence relationships among activities. In the diagram and the accompanying sheet of detail, the ties between activities become clear. For example, Figure J4 relates to Bid Group VII-2 (Fire protection), and among its first set of activities, there are these ties to other activities:

Activity 1110 — The bidding was due on December 12, 1990. Prior to the bidding, two things had to happen: Lilly had to sign the Phase II construction documents (Activity 1024), and GDI had to prepare the bidding documents themselves (Activity 1026). These two things were completed in October. The successor activity (1112) was the awarding of the contract. The expected duration of the activity, 37 days, is given in the ORIG DUR (Original Duration) column.

Activity 1112 — This is the successor activity to Activity 1110. It was accomplished by 1/11/91. We

VII-2 FIRE PROTECTION

1110 BIDDING DUE - FIRE PROTECTION 12/12
1112 AWARD CONTRACT - FIRE PROTECTION 1/11
1114 PREP PRELIMINARY DESIGN F.P. 3/29
1115 FIRE PROTECTION COORDINATION DRAWINGS 6/14
1116 OWNER REVIEW PRELIM DESIGN 5/10

VII-2 FIRE PROTECTION

1118 REVISE & RESUBMIT F.P. SHOPS 6/14
1120 OWNER REVIEW REVISED SHOPS 7/5
1122 FINALIZE DESIGN FOR INSURANCE REVIEW 8/9
1150 INSTALL F.P. PIPE SUPPORTS B-WING 9/13
1124 PROCURE & FAB PIPING B-WING 9/13
1160 PROCURE F.P. EQUIPMENT 12/27
1152 INSTALL F.P. PIPE SUPPORTS C-WING 10/18
1128 PROCURE & FAB PIPING C-WING 10/18
1154 INSTALL F.P. PIPE SUPPORTS A-WING 11/22
1132 PROCURE & FAB PIPING A-WING 11/22
1126 INSTALL F.P. MAINS & BRANCH PIPING B-WING 1/31
1156 INSTALL F.P. PIPE SUPPORTS H-WING 12/27
1136 PROCURE & FAB PIPING H-WING 12/27
1130 INSTALL F.P. MAINS & BRANCH PIPING C-WING 2/28
1162 INSTALL F.P. EQUIPMENT 5/15
1134 INSTALL F.P. MAINS & BRANCH PIPING A-WING 4/3
1135 B-WING MOCK-UP ROOM 01/15
1138 INSTALL F.P. MAINS & BRANCH PIPING H-WING 5/1
1137 C-WING MOCK-UP ROOM 02/12
1164 TEST DROPS & HEADS B-WING 7/24
1166 TEST DROPS & HEADS C-WING 9/25
1168 TEST DROPS & HEADS A-WING 10/23
1170 TEST DROPS & HEADS H-WING 11/27
1172 TEST F.P. SYSTEMS 1/1

ELI LILLY AND COMPANY
NEW RESEARCH BUILDING #48 - R3T
B.G. VII-2 PROJECT SCHEDULE

Sheet 1 of 2

Data Date: 22APR91
Plot Date: 14MAY91

Project Start: 1JAN90
Project Finish: 30MAR93

Primavera Systems, Inc.

ELI LILLY AND COMPANY PRIMAVERA PROJECT PLANNER NEW RESEARCH BUILDING #48 - R3T

REPORT DATE 14MAY91 RUN NO. 335 GEUPEL DeMARS INC. PROJECT #87480 (R3TA) START DATE 1JAN90 FIN DATE 26MAR93

CLASSIC SCHEDULE REPORT - SORTED BY ES,EF DATA DATE 22APR91 PAGE NO. 1

VII-2 FIRE PROTECTION

ACTIVITY ID	ORIG DUR	REM DUR	PCT	CODE	ACTIVITY DESCRIPTION	EARLY START	EARLY FINISH	LATE START	LATE FINISH	TOTAL FLOAT
1110	37	0	100	44	BIDDING DUE - FIRE PROTECTION 12/12	23OCT90A	12DEC90A			0
1112	22	0	100	44	AWARD CONTRACT - FIRE PROTECTION 1/11	13DEC90A	11JAN91A			0
1114	75	5	93	44B	PREP PRELIMINARY DESIGN F.P. 3/29	14JAN91A			26APR91	0
1115	60	40	33	44B	FIRE PROTECTION COORDINATION DRAWINGS 6/14	25MAR91A	14JUN91		14JUN91*	0
1116	10	10	0	44B	OWNER REVIEW PRELIM DESIGN 5/10	29APR91	10MAY91	29APR91	10MAY91	0
1118	25	25	0	44B	REVISE & RESUBMIT F.P. SHOPS 6/14	13MAY91	14JUN91	13MAY91	14JUN91	0
1120	15	15	0	44B	OWNER REVIEW REVISED SHOPS 7/5	17JUN91	5JUL91	17JUN91	5JUL91	0
1122	25	25	0	44B	FINALIZE DESIGN FOR INSURANCE REVIEW 8/9	8JUL91	9AUG91	8JUL91	9AUG91*	0
1150	25	25	0	44 BB	INSTALL F.P. PIPE SUPPORTS B-WING 9/13	12AUG91	13SEP91	12AUG91	13SEP91	0
1124	25	25	0	44B	PROCURE & FAB PIPING B-WING 9/13	12AUG91	13SEP91	16SEP91	18OCT91*	25
1160	100	100	0	44	PROCURE F.P. EQUIPMENT 12/27	12AUG91	27DEC91	26AUG91	10JAN92	10
1152	25	25	0	44 CC	INSTALL F.P. PIPE SUPPORTS C-WING 10/18	16SEP91	18OCT91	16SEP91	18OCT91	0
1128	25	25	0	44C	PROCURE & FAB PIPING C-WING 10/18	16SEP91	18OCT91	21OCT91	22NOV91*	25
1154	25	25	0	44 AA	INSTALL F.P. PIPE SUPPORTS A-WING 11/22	21OCT91	22NOV91	21OCT91	22NOV91	0
1132	25	25	0	44A	PROCURE & FAB PIPING A-WING 11/22 1/31	21OCT91	22NOV91	25NOV91	27DEC91*	25
1126	65	65	0	44 BB	INSTALL F.P. MAINS & BRANCH PIPING B-WING	4NOV91*	31JAN92	4NOV91	31JAN92*	0
1156	25	25	0	44 HH	INSTALL F.P. PIPE SUPPORTS H-WING 12/27	25NOV91	27DEC91	25NOV91	27DEC91*	0
1136	25	25	0	44H	PROCURE & FAB PIPING H-WING 12/27 2/28	25NOV91	27DEC91	30DEC91	31JAN92*	25
1130	65	65	0	44 CC	INSTALL F.P. MAINS & BRANCH PIPING C-WING	2DEC91*	28FEB92	2DEC91	28FEB92*	0
1162	100	100	0	44	INSTALL F.P. EQUIPMENT 5/15	30DEC91	15MAY92	13JAN92	29MAY92*	10
1134	65	65	0	44 AA	INSTALL F.P. MAINS & BRANCH PIPING A-WING 4/3	6JAN92*	3APR92	6JAN92	3APR92*	0
1135	0	0	0	44 BB	B-WING MOCK-UP ROOM 01/15	15JAN92*	15JAN92	15JAN92	15JAN92*	0
1138	65	65	0	44 HH	INSTALL F.P. MAINS & BRANCH PIPING H-WING 5/1	3FEB92*	1MAY92	3FEB92	1MAY92*	0
1137	0	0	0	44 CC	C-WING MOCK-UP ROOM 02/12	12FEB92*	12FEB92	12FEB92	12FEB92*	0
1164	40	40	0	44 BB	TEST DROPS & HEADS B-WING 7/24	1JUN92*	24JUL92	1JUN92	24JUL92	0
1166	45	45	0	44 CC	TEST DROPS & HEADS C-WING 9/25	27JUL92	25SEP92	27JUL92	25SEP92*	0
1168	45	45	0	44 AA	TEST DROPS & HEADS A-WING 10/23	24AUG92	23OCT92	24AUG92	23OCT92*	0
1170	50	50	0	44 HH	TEST DROPS & HEADS H-WING 11/27	21SEP92	27NOV92	21SEP92	27NOV92*	0
1172	25	25	0	44	TEST F.P. SYSTEMS 1/1	30NOV92	1JAN93	30NOV92	1JAN93*	0

FIGURE J3 (continued)

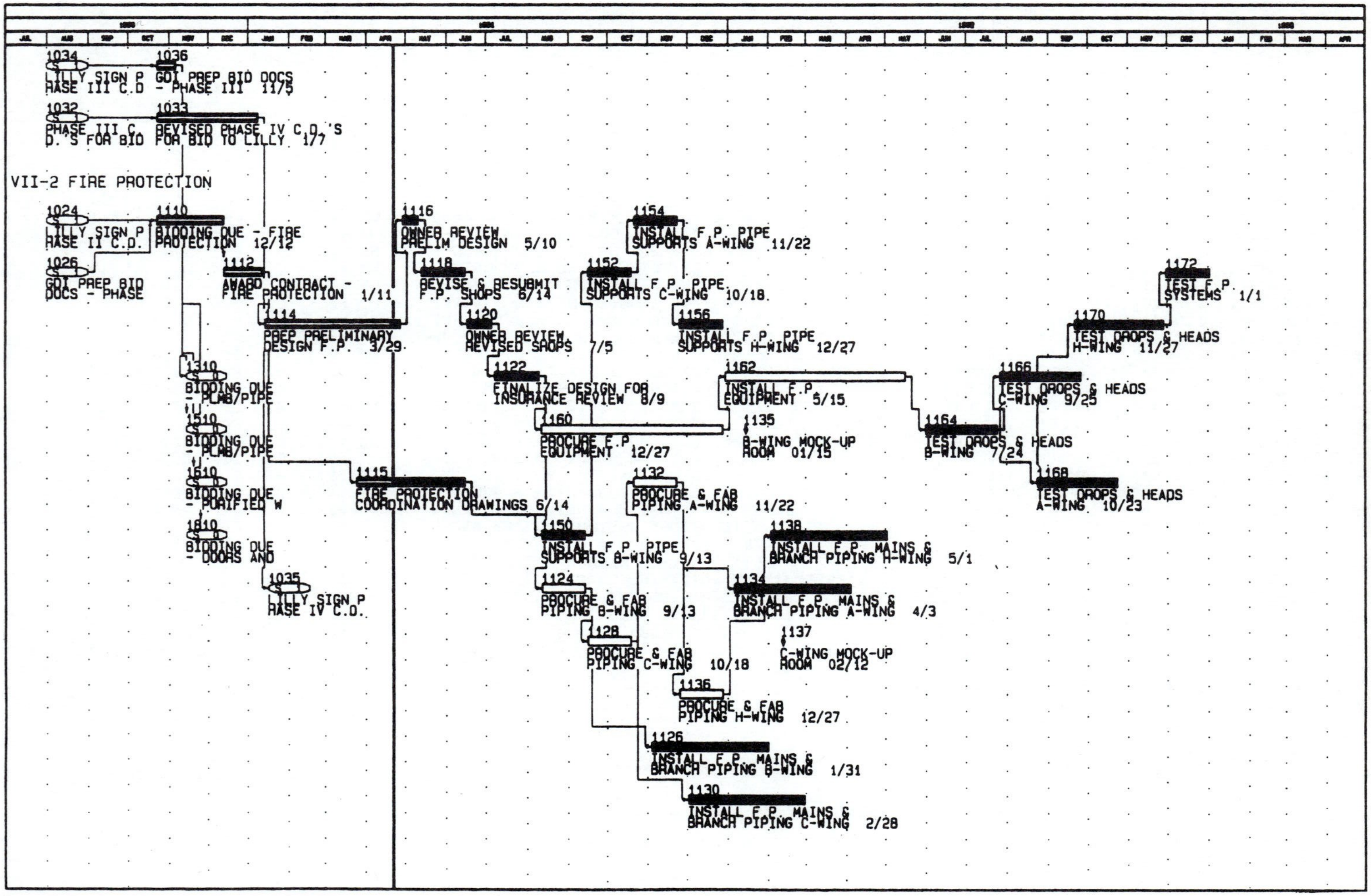

FIGURE J4   A portion of the project schedule for Research Building 48—Activity descriptions

VII-2 FIRE PROTECTION

ACTIVITY ID	ORIG DUR	REM DUR	PCT	CODE	ACTIVITY DESCRIPTION	EARLY START	EARLY FINISH	LATE START	LATE FINISH	TOTAL FLOAT
1110	37	0	100	44	BIDDING DUE - FIRE PROTECTION 12/12	23OCT90A	12DEC90A			
: 1024	4	0	100	PRED 6	LILLY SIGN PHASE II C.D.'S 10/12	9OCT90A	12OCT90A			
: 1026*	10	0	100	PRED C	GDI PREP BID DOCS - PHASE II 10/22	9OCT90A	22OCT90A			
: 1112*	22	0	100	SUCC	AWARD CONTRACT - FIRE PROTECTION 1/11	13DEC90A	11JAN91A			
1112	22	0	100	44	AWARD CONTRACT - FIRE PROTECTION 1/11	13DEC90A	11JAN91A			
: 1110*	37	0	100	PRED	BIDDING DUE - FIRE PROTECTION 12/12	23OCT90A	12DEC90A			
: 1114*	75	5	93	SUCC	PREP PRELIMINARY DESIGN F.P. 3/29	14JAN91A	26APR91		26APR91	0
: 1115	60	40	33	SUCC	FIRE PROTECTION COORDINATION DRAWINGS 6/14	25MAR91A	14JUN91		14JUN91*	0
1114	75	5	93	44	PREP PRELIMINARY DESIGN F.P. 3/29	14JAN91A	26APR91		26APR91	0
: 1112*	22	0	100	PRED	AWARD CONTRACT - FIRE PROTECTION 1/11	13DEC90A	11JAN91A			
: 1116*	10	10	0	SUCC	OWNER REVIEW PRELIM DESIGN 5/10	29APR91	10MAY91	29APR91	10MAY91	0
1115	60	40	33	44	FIRE PROTECTION COORDINATION DRAWINGS 6/14	25MAR91A	14JUN91		14JUN91*	0
: 1112	22	0	100	PRED C	AWARD CONTRACT - FIRE PROTECTION 1/11	13DEC90A	11JAN91A			
: 1150*	25	25	0	SUCC C	INSTALL F.P. PIPE SUPPORTS B-WING 9/13	12AUG91	13SEP91	12AUG91	13SEP91	0
1116	10	10	0	44	OWNER REVIEW PRELIM DESIGN 5/10	29APR91	10MAY91	29APR91	10MAY91	0
: 1114*	75	5	93	PRED	PREP PRELIMINARY DESIGN F.P. 3/29	14JAN91A	26APR91		26APR91	0
: 1118*	25	25	0	SUCC	REVISE & RESUBMIT F.P. SHOPS 6/14	13MAY91	14JUN91	13MAY91	14JUN91	0
1118	25	25	0	44	REVISE & RESUBMIT F.P. SHOPS 6/14	13MAY91	14JUN91	13MAY91	14JUN91	0
: 1116*	10	10	0	PRED	OWNER REVIEW PRELIM DESIGN 5/10	29APR91	10MAY91	29APR91	10MAY91	0
: 1120*	15	15	0	SUCC	OWNER REVIEW REVISED SHOPS 7/5	17JUN91	5JUL91	17JUN91	5JUL91	0
1120	15	15	0	44	OWNER REVIEW REVISED SHOPS 7/5	17JUN91	5JUL91	17JUN91	5JUL91	0
: 1118*	25	25	0	PRED	REVISE & RESUBMIT F.P. SHOPS 6/14	13MAY91	14JUN91	13MAY91	14JUN91	0
: 1122*	25	25	0	SUCC	FINALIZE DESIGN FOR INSURANCE REVIEW 8/9	8JUL91	9AUG91	8JUL91	9AUG91*	0
1122	25	25	0	44	FINALIZE DESIGN FOR INSURANCE REVIEW 8/9	8JUL91	9AUG91	8JUL91	9AUG91*	0
: 1120*	15	15	0	PRED	OWNER REVIEW REVISED SHOPS 7/5	17JUN91	5JUL91	17JUN91	5JUL91	0
: 1124*	25	25	0	SUCC	PROCURE & FAB PIPING B-WING 9/13	12AUG91	13SEP91	16SEP91	18OCT91*	25
: 1150*	25	25	0	SUCC	INSTALL F.P. PIPE SUPPORTS B-WING 9/13	12AUG91	13SEP91	12AUG91	13SEP91	0
: 1160*	100	100	0	SUCC	PROCURE F.P. EQUIPMENT 12/27	12AUG91	27DEC91	26AUG91	10JAN92	10
1150	25	25	0	44	INSTALL F.P. PIPE SUPPORTS B-WING 9/13	12AUG91	13SEP91	12AUG91	13SEP91	0
: 1115*	60	40	33	PRED C	FIRE PROTECTION COORDINATION DRAWINGS 6/14	25MAR91A	14JUN91		14JUN91*	0
: 1122*	25	25	0	PRED	FINALIZE DESIGN FOR INSURANCE REVIEW 8/9	8JUL91	9AUG91	8JUL91	9AUG91*	0
: 1152*	25	25	0	SUCC	INSTALL F.P. PIPE SUPPORTS C-WING 10/18	16SEP91	18OCT91	16SEP91	18OCT91	0
1124	25	25	0	44	PROCURE & FAB PIPING B-WING 9/13	12AUG91	13SEP91	16SEP91	18OCT91*	25
: 1122*	25	25	0	PRED	FINALIZE DESIGN FOR INSURANCE REVIEW 8/9	8JUL91	9AUG91	8JUL91	9AUG91*	0
: 1126	65	65	0	SUCC	INSTALL F.P. MAINS & BRANCH PIPING B-WING 1/31	4NOV91*	31JAN92	4NOV91	31JAN92*	0
: 1128*	25	25	0	SUCC	PROCURE & FAB PIPING C-WING 10/18	16SEP91	18OCT91	21OCT91	22NOV91*	25
1160	100	100	0	44	PROCURE F.P. EQUIPMENT 12/27	12AUG91	27DEC91	26AUG91	10JAN92	10
: 1122*	25	25	0	PRED	FINALIZE DESIGN FOR INSURANCE REVIEW 8/9	8JUL91	9AUG91	8JUL91	9AUG91*	0
: 1162*	100	100	0	SUCC	INSTALL F.P. EQUIPMENT 5/15	30DEC91	15MAY92	13JAN92	29MAY92*	10
1152	25	25	0	44	INSTALL F.P. PIPE SUPPORTS C-WING 10/18	16SEP91	18OCT91	16SEP91	18OCT91	0
: 1150*	25	25	0	PRED	INSTALL F.P. PIPE SUPPORTS B-WING 9/13	12AUG91	13SEP91	12AUG91	13SEP91	0
: 1154*	25	25	0	SUCC	INSTALL F.P. PIPE SUPPORTS A-WING 11/22	21OCT91	22NOV91	21OCT91	22NOV91	0

FIGURE J4 (continued)

know this is so for several reasons: the progress shown on the chart's bar, the 100% completion shown in the PCT column, the "0" in the REM DUR (Remaining Duration) column, and the "A", for Actual, after the early start and early finish dates. Activity 1112 has two successor activities: preparing a preliminary design and working up fire protection coordination drawings.

Activity 1115 — This activity is one of the successors to Activity 1112. It is on schedule, but it has not yet reached its conclusion. The percentage completion is 33 percent, with 40 of the expected 60 days' worth of work remaining. It has one successor activity, installing the fire protection pipe supports in the B-wing, slated to begin on August 12, 1991.

Observe that not all of the activities noted in the diagram have bars shown. The complexity of the relationships has forced Primavera to show them on a different sheet. This diagram is useful for depicting the relationships. Also observe that some of the forthcoming activities are colored solid, indicating that they are critical activities, but that some are not filled in. These latter activities are not on the critical path and thus have some slack associated with them.

Primavera was capable of generating other useful documents and to sort the activities in different ways. Sorts could be done by contractor or by floor of the building. By examining the scheduled activities in these ways, conflicts among contractors, and any subsequent rescheduling, could be held to a minimum.

Weekly meetings were held to track the schedule. Data for the schedule monitoring was provided by the superintendents on the site and by the GDI project engineers who followed the submittals and other paperwork. Every two weeks a rolling 4-week summary schedule was generated.

BUDGETING

The budget's major components included the following:

	Original Budget (in millions)
Construction (building materials, labor, Owner furnished equipment)	$ 99.4
Engineering (Owner's cost, A/E firm, GDI)	23.8
Contingency	12.0
Total	$135.2

Geupel DeMars monitored these costs and managed the construction costs, the contingency costs, and its own costs closely.

PART TWO

DISCUSSION

Geupel DeMars, Inc. is in no way responsible for the following views and presentation. They remain solely the responsibility of the author.

THE FLOW OF THE PROCESS AND OF INFORMATION

Figures J5 and J6 display process flow and information flow diagrams for a project like the construction of Building #48. The diagrams are fairly general and include numerous entries that can be repeated. For example, there is a whole sequence of the process flow diagram that repeats for each of the 30 bid packages. With the information flow diagram, the interactions of RFIs, submittals, and approvals are repeated almost a countless number of times as the project continues. Geupel De-Mars is really the "man in the middle" for a

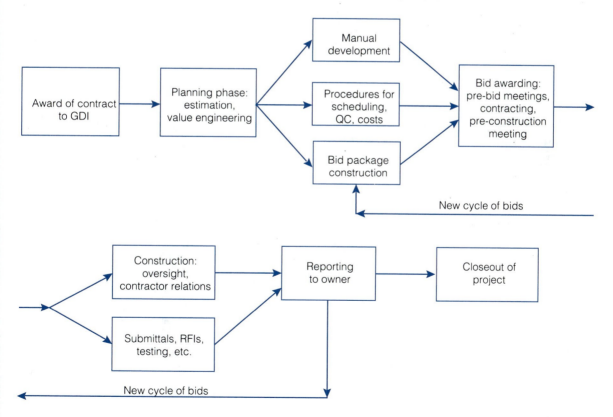

FIGURE J5   Process Flow Diagram for Geupel DeMars Project.

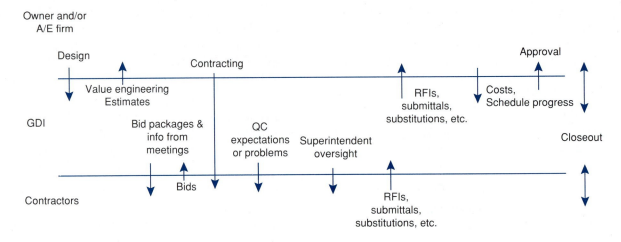

FIGURE J6   Information Flow Diagram for Geupel DeMars Project.

lot of these transactions, filtering information, monitoring progress and costs, making recommendations to the various parties, etc. Coordination and communication are essential to the smooth running of the project.

This is an example of so-called "fast track" construction that is completely analogous to concurrent engineering in a factory setting dealing with new product development. Fast track construction overlaps the phases of construction so that detailed design aspects of the building proceed even as the initial construction is being done. Such management of the process calls for a great deal of coordination among the players, and that is just what Geupel DeMars provides.

FEATURES OF THE PROCESS

There are a number of interesting and distinctive aspects of the project that differentiate it from the other processes investigated in this book:

1. The manning of this process is constantly changing. Not only are there varying num-

bers of construction workers on site, but there are variable numbers of architect/engineers, and importantly, varying numbers of GDI workers as well. There is a constant ebb and flow of people of various skills and in various quantities as the project progresses.

2. A variety of specialized talents are called for. Again, these are talents not only in the architecture/engineering and construction trades themselves, but also with GDI itself as it manages the project. GDI, for example, needs specialists for construction superintendents, cost estimation, scheduling, and contractor and A/E firm relations.

3. Projects take a significant degree of up-front planning in order to be carried out well. The budget for Building #48 reveals this degree of planning. So much of the project involves one-of-a-kind design that such planning cannot be avoided.

4. Constant coordination is required among the parties.

5. The means by which resources can be husbanded is generally by stretching out the timetable. The contractors do this to save costs, and only when forced by slips in the

schedule do they apply more labor or equipment to "crash" an activity. It is the same for GDI. Not all of the bid packages are prepared at the same time or bid on at the same time. Rather, because the job does not require it, and because it would tax GDI too much at the same time, the schedule of bid packages is spaced out. Such smoothing out of the work helps all concerned.

DEMANDS OF THE PROCESS ON MANAGEMENT AND THE WORKFORCE

At GDI the workforce and management are almost indistinguishable, as one could look at the project engineers as lower levels of management. For everybody, the demands of the process are quite similar. The process demands extraordinary planning skills of its workforce as well as tremendous attention to detail. The days of nearly everyone at GDI are filled with the follow-up and communication of details and, when called upon, the development of future needs and controls of all sorts. People live by their calendars, beepers, voice mail, faxes, and their ilk.

PLANNING AND CONTROL

The project lives and dies by the excellence of the planning that has gone into it and by the efficiency and thoroughness of the controls it has in place. All of these controls have to be planned for in advance so that all parties are clear about what is required of them. The chief controls are on:

- Quality (knowing in advance what the requirements of the job are and what constitutes satisfactory accomplishment)
- Schedule (knowing when the job has to be started and stopped)
- Cost (knowing what the flow of expenses is)
- Documentation (keeping a trail of paper about everything decided, everything accomplished, and everything changed).

The planning and control for the project outdoes that of the job shop and other kinds of processes. Similar kinds of documentation are kept: drawings, process and routing sheets (or their equivalents), tests of materials, change documents, quality documents, and schedules, but the quantities of them and care with which they are handled are typically extraordinary. After all, with a project you only get one shot at it, and it better be right the first time or other projects are not likely to be coming your way.

Drawings are an example. Consider the different kinds that are maintained: conceptual drawings, schematics, shop drawings, and as-built drawings. Everything about the building's construction is captured in these drawings. Everybody pours over them, communicates through them, and formally approves or changes them. And, they come by the hundreds and thousands.

QUESTIONS

1. Why does Geupel DeMars Inc.'s organization chart look the way its does?

2. What are the differences between Figures J3 and J4?

3. Describe your concept of a typical working day for a GDI project engineer.

4. Describe the relationship between project quality, cost, and schedule.

A COMPARISON OF PRODUCTION AND SERVICE PROCESSES

In the tours, ten different production and service processes were introduced and their key features described. There were threads in common among some of them as well as some sharp differences. The purpose of this chapter is to tie together the common threads and expose the sharp differences by comparing the processes described. Part One of this summary chapter deals with manufacturing and Part Two deals with services.

PART ONE

MANUFACTURING

TRENDS

First we should recognize that there are some clearly discernible trends among the six manufacturing processes introduced. The trends become evident when the processes are arrayed in the following order, a sort of "spectrum" of production processes:

- Job shop (example: Norcen Industries)
- Batch flow (example: Jos. A. Bank)
- Worker-paced line flow (example: Burger King Restaurant, Noblesville, Indiana)[a]
- Machine-paced line flow (example: GM C-P-C Group, Oklahoma City, Oklahoma)
- Continuous flow (example: International Paper Company, Androscoggin Mill)

The hybrid process represented by the Stroh brewery at Winston-Salem, which displayed aspects of both a batch flow and a continuous flow process, is somewhat more difficult to place since it is not as pure an example as the others.

Analyzing the Trends

To provide some cohesion and organization, this discussion of process trends is divided into six parts, each part devoted to a comparison and analysis of some specific features: (1) prod-

[a]The Burger King restaurant can be viewed usefully as both a manufacturing process (a burger factory) and a service process (a fast-food restaurant). For this reason, it is included in both parts of this chapter.

246

uct features, (2) general process features, (3) materials-oriented features, (4) information-oriented features, (5) labor-oriented features, and (6) management features. These six features will be addressed in turn.

Product Features

Arrayed as they have been here, the different processes introduced demonstrate some distinct trends involving the types of products manufactured and how those products compete against others. Specifically, the more one goes from a job shop toward a continuous flow process, the more it is generally the case that:

1. The number of different kinds of products made declines.
2. Product volumes increase to the point where t¹ continuous flow process is essentia producing a commodity for the mass market.
3. Product customization declines and product standardization increases.
4. New product introductions become less frequent and are more costly.
5. Competition is more likely to center on price.
6. Competition, at least in the middle ranges of the array, is more likely to emphasize aspects like workmanship, product performance, and product reliability; but as the process becomes more and more a continuous flow, these differences between rival products become narrower and narrower.

General Process Features

There are complementary trends in some general process features as well. For example, as one progesses down the array of processes from job shop to continuous flow, it is generally true that:

1. The pattern of the process becomes more rigid, and the routing of products through their various process steps becomes less individual, less unprescribed, and better defined.
2. Process segments become more tightly linked together.
3. Equipment becomes more specialized.
4. The operation becomes huge, and economies of scale are possible.
5. More, and generally larger, equipment is part of the process.
6. Equipment is less likely to be idle. Pieces of equipment become better balanced in size and speed to one another.
7. Equipment setups are fewer and run lengths are longer.
8. The pace of the process is determined largely by machine capabilities or regulated by machines or conveyors.
9. The pace of production keeps increasing.
10. The notion of capacity becomes less ambiguous and more measurable in physical, rather than dollar, units.
11. Additions to capacity come in large chunks, and incremental additions to capacity become less viable.
12. Bottlenecks become less and less movable and thus better understood.
13. Incremental change to the nature of the process itself becomes relatively more frequent and routine, but the impact of radical change to the process is likely to be more sweeping and thus scarier to contemplate.
14. Process layouts, with like machines grouped together, give way to line flow layouts.

Materials-Oriented Features

Again, keeping the array of different processes ordered from job shop through continuous flow process, some general trends in materials-oriented features can be observed. For example, as the process becomes more and more a continuous flow, it becomes more and more the case that:

1. The span of the process (vertical integration) becomes broader. A plant is more and more likely to start with "very raw" raw materials and transform them into products that may need little or no "finishing" before consumers purchase them.

2. Most processes take uniform materials and make differentiated products from them. Norcen Industries takes uniform blocks, bars, or rods of steel and machines a multitude of different parts from them. Jos. A. Bank uses the same materials to produce suits in different styles and sizes. The parts going into a Buick Century are much the same as go into a Pontiac 6000; moreover, General Motors goes to great lengths to make sure that cars that are supposed to be exactly alike contain exactly the same components. Such is not the case with many continuous flow processes. Often these processes take differentiated raw materials and make uniform products from them. One log of timber may not be the same as the next log, and so pulp and paper mills are constantly monitoring their raw materials and adjusting them so that the finished product, be it publication gloss or newsprint, looks exactly the same at the end of the roll as it does at the start. Similarly, steel plant blast furnaces make constant changes to their raw materials input mix.

3. As the time of actual production draws closer, materials requirements are generally known with more certainty.

4. Raw materials requirements are large, but their purchase and delivery can be made steady.

5. Supplier ties are long term, with frequent deliveries.

6. Because of large production volumes and steady purchases, control over suppliers for price, delivery, quality, design, and the like is great.

7. Control over the delivery time of the finished product becomes greater.

8. Work-in-process inventories, because of process design, become scant. Queues of work cease to exist.

9. Finished goods inventories are larger (relative to other inventories).

10. Finished goods are sold through formal distribution channels and can sometimes be forced down those channels for the sake of keeping production running smoothly.

Importantly, however, the batch/continuous flow hybrid process does not follow all of these trends. There is a definite work-in-process inventory situated between the batch flow portion of the process and the continuous flow portion. At least some of the raw materials are inventoried as a buffer stock to be drawn down in perhaps unexpected or haphazard fashion, while other raw materials are purchased to coincide with the production plan.

Information-Oriented Features

A number of trends are evident as well for many information-oriented features of the various production processes. As the process changes from job shop to continuous flow, generally it is more and more likely that:

1. Production has not been instigated by a bidding procedure.

2. Longer-term sales forecasts are used, and orders are "frozen" long before production is scheduled to start.

3. The corporation outside the plant is an integral part of the plant's scheduling and materials movement tracking.

4. Order scheduling is done on a very sophisticated basis.

5. A finished goods inventory is managed.

6. The flow of information and paperwork between management and workers is less.

7. Quality control measures become formal.

8. Inventory adjustments become important in responding to seasonal or business cycle changes in demand.

9. The process is less flexible in making swift adjustments to demand changes, and so production must be carefully planned in advance.

Labor-Oriented Features

Again, trends are evident across the spectrum of production processes explored, this time concerning labor issues. Progressing from job shop to continuous flow process, it is more likely that:

1. The labor content of the product becomes smaller and smaller, relative to the product's value.

2. Job contents diminish, although "art" is more likely to be found at either end of the process spectrum.

3. Labor is paid by the hour rather than by some incentive system. In fact, the progression of wage payment schemes tends to go from hourly or individual incentive rates for the job shop, through individual and then group incentive schemes, and then on to hourly rates.

4. The importance of setting standards for labor remains high. The mechanization of the continuous flow process, however, means that such standards are usefullness to define the process and its capacity than to assign the workforce to the equipment.

5. As production moves more and more to mechanical or technological pacing, the scramble to complete a lot of production to meet monthly goals or billings becomes less and less prevalent.

6. The path of worker advancement becomes better defined and even formal.

Management Features

Finally, some trends can be identified as well for several aspects of the management of these diverse production processes. Progressing from job shop to continuous flow process, it is more and more the case that:

1. Staff operations concerning such topics as materials movement, scheduling, capacity planning, new technology planning, and quality control become more important relative to line operations.

2. The size of the plant's management (line and staff) is often larger relative to the size of the workforce both because the capital intensity of the operation is greater and because staff operations are more important. Table TS1 uses statistics from the processes we have discussed to show the ratio of management staff to total employees.

3. Given that the plant involved is part of a multiplant company, the involvement of managers situated at the corporate offices (rather than at the plant itself) becomes greater. The corporation's influence may extend to operations as well as to capital planning and spending.

4. The operation is controlled more as a cost center, as opposed to a profit center.

5. The major challenges that management faces are significantly altered, largely shifting from day-to-day operational considerations to very long-term, high-expense items.

TABLE TS1	Ratio of management staff to total employment	
COMPANY	PROCESS	MANAGEMENT STAFF/ TOTAL EMPLOYMENT
Norcen Industries	Job shop	7/41 = 0.171
Jos. A. Bank	Batch flow	43/625 = 0.069
Burger King, Noblesville	Worker-paced line flow	7/67 = 0.104
C-P-C, Oklahoma City	Machine-paced line flow	430/5300 = 0.081
Stroh, Winston-Salem	Batch/continuous flow hybrid	80/670 = 0.119
International Paper, Androscoggin	Continuous flow	175/1200 = 0.146

THE PROCESS SPECTRUM

By comparing these trends it is fairly plain that entire lists of characteristics hang together to describe particular processes. Table TS2 is an effort to compile just such lists for the range of production processes that have been introduced. Note that the batch/continuous flow hybrid, exemplified by the Stroh brewery, has been segregated from the others so that the process spectrum stretching from job shop through to continuous flow process remains as pure as we can reasonably expect.

Table TS2 offers some generalizations about particular types of production processes, drawing mainly from the processes discussed in the plant tours. Not all of the generalizations may ring true for all of the production processes one may conceivably classify in each category from job shop to continuous flow process. Most of the generalizations, however, are representative of a typical production process in each category. For completeness, one could also place the project in the spectrum, to the left of the job shop and sharing a number of its characteristics.

PART TWO

SERVICE OPERATIONS

COMPARISON OF SERVICES

The characterization of services as service factories, service shops, mass service, and professional service can be used as well for comparing service processes in much the same way that Table TS2 compared manufacturing processes. This is accomplished in Table TS3. The various features compared there are placed in to various groups: service, process, customer-orientation, labor, and management. These features undergird the challenges for management that were introduced earlier.

TABLE TS2 Comparing processes of different types

FEATURES	(1) JOB SHOP (Example: Norcen Industries)	(2) BATCH FLOW (Example: Jos. A. Bank)	(3) WORKER-PACED ASSEMBLY LINE (Example: Burger King Restaurant, Noblesville)	(4) MACHINE-PACED ASSEMBLY LINE (Example: C-P-C Group, Oklahoma City)	(5) CONTINUOUS FLOW (Example: International Paper, Androscoggin Mill)	(6) BATCH/CONTINUOUS FLOW HYBRID (Example: Stroh Brewery, Winston-Salem)
Product Features						
Product mix	Generally custom products	Lots of generally own-designed products	Mostly standard products; some opportunities for selected options	Same as for 3	Standard products with little or no customization possible; not produced in discrete units, so has to be measured in tons, barrels, and so on	Same as for 3 and 4
Products compete largely on:	Speed of delivery, product customization, new product introduction	Product performance, product reliability and workmanship, delivery reliability, new product introduction, flexibility to produce either low or high volumes	Product performance, price, product reliability and workmanship, delivery reliability	Product performance, price, product reliability and workmanship, delivery reliability	Price	Product reliability and workmanship, price
Products unlikely to compete on:	Price				New product introduction, product customization	
New product introduction	All the time; easy	Frequent; routine	Sometimes	Sometimes; generally expensive	Hardly at all; very costly	Infrequent; expensive

continued

251

TABLE TS2 Comparing processes of different types (continued)

FEATURES	(1) JOB SHOP (Example: Norcen Industries)	(2) BATCH FLOW (Example: Jos. A. Bank)	(3) WORKER-PACED ASSEMBLY LINE (Example: Burger King Restaurant, Noblesville)	(4) MACHINE-PACED ASSEMBLY LINE (Example: C-P-C Group, Oklahoma City)	(5) CONTINUOUS FLOW (Example: International Paper, Androscoggin Mill)	(6) BATCH/CONTINUOUS FLOW HYBRID (Example: Stroh Brewery, Winston-Salem)
Process Features						
Process pattern	No rigid pattern; product can be routed anywhere; sometimes a dominant flow	Not all procedures performed on all products; product can be routed many ways; often a dominant flow	Clear pattern, though special treatment of some products sometimes permitted	Clear, rigid pattern, though some off-line work possible	Clear, very rigid pattern	Same as for 5
Linking of process segments	Very loose	Loose, but "cells" can be created	Between tight and loose; tighter if JIT followed	Tight, especially if JIT followed	Very tight	Loose link between different process types
Type of equipment	General purpose	Mostly general purpose	Specialized	Same as for 3	Same as for 3	Same as for 3, 4, and 5
Balance of equipment	Balance of speed and time done in only the grossest, long-run terms. At any one time, an imbalance is likely to exist	Balance likely to be imperfect between segments of process but better coordinated than typical job shop	Machinery speed and size in good balance with peak needs	Speed and size of equipment very well balanced. Capable of being adjusted together over small changes in line speed	Good balance of speed and size. Any excess capacity often placed in latter portion of process to provide insurance against breakdowns or unusual order requests	Same as for 5
Type of layout	Process layout; similar machines grouped together	Process layout; similar tasks and equipment grouped together	Line flow layout; distinct for product produced	Same as for 3	Same as for 3	Two distinct layouts, one for batch and one for the continuous flow
Capital use	Labor intensive; machines frequently idle	Labor intensive, although less machine idleness	Although equipment is specialized, it is fairly cheap; labor still a big item	Capital intensive	Very capital intensive; machines nearly always used	Same as for 5

Typical size of operation	Generally small	Generally medium-sized	Variable	Large	Mammoth	Same as for 4
Economies of scale	None	Few, if any	Same as for 2	Some, perhaps	Yes	Same as for 5
Yields	Often dependent on setup and product complexity	Often dependent on workers; yields usually high	Same as for 2	Often dependent on both workers and equipment function; yields usually high	Often dependent on raw materials; yields can be variable	Can vary depending on type of hybrid
Notion of capacity	Very fuzzy; definable vaguely in dollar terms; useful only in long run	Fuzzy; product mix implies a dollar definition only	Increasingly clear; some physical unit measures possible	Clear; physical unit measures	Same as for 4	Same as for 4 and 5
Additions to capacity	Incremental over full range of possible capacity	Larger increments possible, but over full range of possible capacity	Same as for 2	Changes can be made, but costly to do so because capacity comes in large chunks; otherwise, mild fluctuations possible within relatively narrow limits (such as line rebalance)	Only modest range for incremental change; otherwise, huge chunks of capacity required	Comparatively modest range for incremental change; then huge chunks of capacity required
Speed of process (dollars of output/unit of time or dollars of output/dollars of input/unit of time)	Slow	Reasonably slow	Increasingly fast	Fast	Fast, sometimes astounding	Same as for 5
Pacing	Worker discretion key	Worker-paced	Worker-paced but set within some bounds by management action (such as line balance)	Machine-paced but can be a management goal as well (such as line balance)	Determined technologically; built into equipment	Generally determined technologically but some leeway available
Bottlenecks	Movable; frequent	Movable, but often predictable	Occasionally movable, but often predictable	Generally known and stationary	Known, stationary	Same as for 5

continued

TABLE TS2 Comparing Processes of different types *(continued)*

FEATURES	(1) JOB SHOP (Example: Norcen Industries)	(2) BATCH FLOW (Example: Jos. A. Bank)	(3) WORKER-PACED ASSEMBLY LINE (Example: Burger King Restaurant, Noblesville)	(4) MACHINE-PACED ASSEMBLY LINE (Example: C-P-C Group, Oklahoma City)	(5) CONTINUOUS FLOW (Example: International Paper, Androscoggin Mill)	(6) BATCH/ CONTINUOUS FLOW HYBRID (Example: Stroh Brewery, Winston-Salem)
Nature of process change	Incremental	Mostly incremental; some significant radical changes possible	Mostly routine (rebalance); sometimes radical (equipment)	Same as for 3	Most change increment but radical change possible; means big bucks and sweeping conversions	Sometimes radical; sometimes incremental
Place of technological change in process itself	Little impact; unlikely to be revolutionary	Important once in a while; usually incremental	Increasingly important; embodied in equipment	Important; embodied in equipment	Far-reaching surprisingly regular	Same as for 4
Setups	Many; varied expense	Some setups needed, but generally easy to do	Same as for 2	No setup required; line already set up	Few and expensive, if any; process organized to simplify most kinds of setups	Little or no setup required; process simplifies need for most kinds of setups
Run lengths	Short	Medium	Some long, some short	Long	Very long	Same as for 5
Materials-Oriented Features						
Materials requirements	Uncertain	Can often be placed statistically within reasonably narrow bounds	Known statistically within fairly close limits	Certain once production plan established	Same as for 4	Some aspects certain, others known statistically
Character of materials	Set bill of materials; uniform quality; can adapt to nonstandard types	Set bill of materials; uniform quality; often many types possible	Set bill of materials; uniform quality; can adapt to nonstandard types	Same as for 3	Sometimes variable bill of materials: variable quality, since often processes are agricultural/mining extracts	Sometimes variable quality, sometimes uniform quality

Vertical integration	None	Sometimes backward, sometimes forward	Same as for 2	Sometimes backward, often forward	Often backward and forward	Same as for 2 and 3
Inventories; raw materials	Small; most raw materials purchased to coincide with orders	Moderate; some purchased to coincide with orders and some purchased to provide buffer stock	Varies; often steadily purchased since material needs are generally known within reasonably narrow bounds	Varies; often steadily purchased to coincide with production plan	Often large, but can vary and be steadily purchased to coincide with production plan	Varies; some purchased for buffer stock and some purchased to coincide with production plan
Work-in-process	Large	Moderate	Little	Same as for 3	Very little	Inventory placed between batch and continuous flow segments of process; moderate batch WIP, little continuous flow WIP
Finished goods	Low, if any	Varies	Same as for 2	Can vary; often thrust down distribution channels	Varies; often thrust down distribution channels; safety stocks often required	Same as for 5
Control over suppliers	Low	Moderate	Great	Same as for 3	Same as for 3	Same as for 3, 4, and 5
Control over customers	Little or none	Same as for 1	Same as for 1	Same, as to delivery	Same as for 4	Same as for 4 and 5
Supplier ties	Informal; spot buys	Some spot buys, some longer term contracts	Contracts increasingly long term	Formal; long term	Formal; generally long term	Same as for 5
Customer ties	Informal; repeat business encouraged, however	Some informal, some formal distribution	Can be informal or formal	Formal distribution channels	Same as for 4	Same as for 4 and 5

continued

255

TABLE TS2 Comparing Processes of different types (continued)

FEATURES	(1) JOB SHOP (Example: Norcen Industries)	(2) BATCH FLOW (Example: Jos. A. Bank)	(3) WORKER-PACED ASSEMBLY LINE (Example: Burger King Restaurant, Noblesville)	(4) MACHINE-PACED ASSEMBLY LINE (Example: C-P-C Group, Oklahoma City)	(5) CONTINUOUS FLOW (Example: International Paper, Androscoggin Mill)	(6) BATCH/CONTINUOUS FLOW HYBRID (Example: Stroh Brewery, Winston-Salem)
Information-Oriented Features						
Order handling and sales	Often bid for; sales are to order	Varies; some to order, and some from stock with lagged adjustments to that stock	Same as for 2	Sales well established ahead of time or from finished goods inventory; lagged adjustments to stock	Sales well established ahead of time or from finished goods inventory	Same as for 5
Degree of information coordination outside factory	Needed only for bids, receipt of any supplied materials, and to initiate supplies	Needed only to monitor sales and to initiate supplies	Needed to monitor sales and to place orders for supplies; sometimes for order scheduling	Elaborate order scheduling, materials tracking; various levels of forecasts; great deal of corporate communication	Elaborate order scheduling, materials tracking, forecasting; great deal of corporate communication	Monitoring sales, placing supply order; little corporate communication on day-to-day operations
Information systems within factory	Elaborate, viewed as central; lots of flow between factory workers and management; lots of paperwork	Less elaborate, but still considerable; less feedback required; considerable paperwork	Little information needed, basically just to communicate order; flow from management to workers. Opposite flow used primarily to signal breakdowns; generally more informal little paperwork	Same as for 3	Little information needed, basically just to communicate product change; flow from management to workers. Opposite flow used primarily to signal breakdowns; generally more informal	Same as for 5

Trigger for production	Order itself; expediting common	Could be order or level of finished goods inventory; some expediting	Level of finished goods inventory, longer term forecasts, or "frozen" orders; little expediting	Level of finished goods inventory, longer term forecasts, or "frozen" orders; no expediting possible	Same as for 4	First portion of process triggered by forecasts; second portion triggered by "frozen" orders
Scheduling	Uncertain, flexible; always subject to change	Flexible, but not as uncertain; less subject to change	Process designed around fixed schedule	Same as for 3	Easy to group similar jobs or orders; fixed schedule often set technologically and well in advance	Similar jobs or orders grouped together; fixed schedule set in advance, at least for second portion of process
Quality control	Informal, by each worker; spot checks; machine capabilities can be determined	Can be more formal, though often is not	Some on-line checks, some postassembly checks; process capability can be monitored	Same as for 3	Essentially done by process control people; designed into process; periodic sampling often done and process capability monitored	Much of quality designed into process; periodic sampling often done and process capability monitored
Response to cyclicality in demand	Overtime, shift work, some subcontract, hire/fire	Overtime; adjustments can be made by building and depleting inventory, shift work, and hire/fire	Overtime work or closing line early; some adjustments can be made by building and depleting inventory, rebalance, and close down shift or plant	Same as for 3	Inventory adjustments; otherwise, shift or plant is shut down	Same as for 5
Worker payment	Hourly; piece rate or other incentive wage	Often piece rate or other incentive wage	Hourly base; sometimes also tied to percentage of standard that crew achieves	Hourly	Same as for 4	Same as for 4 and 5

continued

257

TABLE TS2 Comparing Processes of different types (*continued*)

FEATURES	(1) JOB SHOP (Example: Norcen Industries)	(2) BATCH FLOW (Example: Jos. A. Bank)	(3) WORKER-PACED ASSEMBLY LINE (Example: Burger King Restaurant, Noblesville)	(4) MACHINE-PACED ASSEMBLY LINE (Example: C-P-C Group, Oklahoma City)	(5) CONTINUOUS FLOW (Example: International Paper, Androscoggin Mill)	(6) BATCH/ CONTINUOUS FLOW HYBRID (Example: Stroh Brewery, Winston-Salem)
End-of-month syndrome (more produced at end of month for billing than at beginning)	Inevitable	Often happens	Close to nonexistent	Same as for 3	Nonexistent	Same as for 5
Labor-Oriented Features						
Advancement for worker	Knowledge of more and more machinery and machine capabilities. With more skills and/or seniority acquired, greater pay and responsibilities given, such as "lead worker." Seniority can lead to change in shift assignment	Knowledge of more and more machinery and machine capabilities. With more skills and/or seniority acquired, greater responsibilities given, such as "lead worker." Seniority can lead to change in shift assignment or department	With more skills and/or seniority acquired, greater responsibilities given, such as "lead worker" or "group leader." Seniority can lead to change in department or shift assignment	Seniority can lead to change in department or shift assignment	Seniority can lead to change in shift or, sometimes, department assignment	Same as for 5
Labor content per $1 of product value	Very high	High	Medium	Low	Very low	Same as for 4
Job content	Large	Medium	Small	Same as for 3	Often small "push button" stuff; but can be "art" as well	Same as for 5

Management Features

	1	2	3	4	5	6
Importance and development of standards for labor	Key for scheduling planning growth; big purpose of information system; sometimes key for wage payment	Often key for wage payment; needed also for scheduling product mix	Crucial for process design	Same as for 3	Important largely for assigning workforce to equipment	Same as for 5
Staff-line needs	Small staff (information, quotes, and new product development). Much line supervision needed	Small staff (generally methods related). Line supervision more critical	Large staff for process redesign, methods, forecasting, capacity planning, and scheduling. Line supervision and troubleshooting still critical	Same as for 1	Large staff for technology and capacity planning, and scheduling. Line supervision less crucial; maintenance key	Same as for 5
Degree of corporate influence on operations, if plant within a multiplant company	Modest	Same as for 1	Same as for 1	Great, for both operations and capital expenditures	Same as for 4	Variable; more likely that corporate influence is with capital expenditures than with day-to-day operations
Means of control	Usually a profit center	Can be either a profit center or a cost center	Same as for 2	Usually a cost center	Same as for 4	Same as for 4 and 5
Challenges to management	Scheduling, bidding, information flows, expediting product innovation, shifting bottlenecks	Order processing, labor issues and pay, handling cyclicality	Balance (process design), product design, managing workforce, technological advances, capacity planning, materials management	Same as for 3	Capital needs, maintenance, site, technological change, vertical integration, raw materials sourcing	Same as for 5

continued

TABLE TS3 A service comparison

	SERVICE FACTORY (Example: Burger King Restaurant)	SERVICE SHOP (Example: Ogle-Tucker Buick)	MASS SERVICE (Example: Thalhimers-Cloverleaf)	PROFESSIONAL SERVICE (Example: Arthur Andersen & Co.)
Service Features				
Mix of services	Limited.	Diverse.	Limited.	Diverse.
Products compete largely on:	Price, speed, perceived "warmth" or "excitement."	Wide choice, competence.	Price, choice, perceived "warmth" or "excitement."	Competence, range of expertise.
New or unique services introduced or performed	Infrequent.	Routine.	Limited experimentation.	Routine.
Process Features				
Capital intensity	High.	High.	Low.	Low.
Pattern of process	Rigid.	Adaptable.	Rigid.	Very loose.
Ties to equipment	Integral part of process, little choice applies.	Equipment important to process, but usually several options exist for its use.	Limited ties to equipment, more tied to plant and layout.	No close ties to plant or equipment.
Importance of balance of tasks and any equipment to smooth process functioning	Balance critical.	Balance often not critical.	Balance not critical.	Balance can be critical.
Tolerance for excess capacity	Excess capacity abhorred.	Excess capacity often not a problem.	Excess capacity implies workforce adjustment that is fairly easily made.	Excess capacity abhorred.
Ease of scheduling	Sometimes tough to schedule, peak demand can be difficult.	Scheduling more easily done.	Scheduling easily done.	Sometimes tough to schedule, peak demand can be difficult.
Economies of scale	Some.	Some—permits better equipment use and thus justification.	Few, if any, except those related to any inventories.	Few, if any, although some specialization can occur.
Notion of capacity	Fairly clearcut, sometimes definable in physical terms.	Fuzzy, very dependent on mix of demands. Only definable in dollar terms.	Not as fuzzy as with service shop. Limits are often due to plant, not processing time.	Fuzzy.
Layout	Line flow-like preferred.	Job-shop or fixed position.	Typically fixed position although layout may change frequently, customers move through layout.	Job-shop frequently.

260

Additions to capacity	Can be in variable increments, requires balance of capital and labor.	Can be in variable increments, aspects of balance more murky.	Often takes big changes to plant to enact. Processing can sometimes be sped up by adding some labor.	Means adding primarily to labor in incremental fashion.
Bottlenecks	Occasionally movable, but often predictable.	Movable, frequent.	Typically well known, predictable.	Can sometimes be forecast, but otherwise are uncertain.
Nature of process change	Sometimes routine (rebalance), sometimes radical (new equipment).	Occasionally radical (new equipment and procedures).	Process change seldom occurs, although it can be radical (such as big change to plant).	Mostly incremental.
Importance of material flow to service provision	Both inventories and flow are important.	Inventories important but not so much the flow.	Inventories are often important and must be controlled.	Incidental to most services.

Customer-Oriented Features

Importance of attractive physical surroundings to marketing of service	Can be critical.	Often insignificant.	Critical.	Often insignificant.
Interaction of customer with process	Little, brief.	Can be great.	Some.	Typically, very great.
Customization of service	Scant.	Significant.	Scant.	Significant.
Ease of managing demand for peaks and nonpeaks	Can be done through price.	Some promotion of off-peak times can be done, but often difficult.	Same as for service shop.	Often very difficult to manage demand, may not be responsive to price.
Process quality control	Can be formal, amenable to standard methods (such as control charts).	Can be formal. Checkpoints can easily be established. Training can be critical to quality.	Mainly informal. Training critical to quality.	Mainly informal. Training critical to quality.

continued

	SERVICE FACTORY (Example: Burger King Restaurant)	SERVICE SHOP (Example: Ogle-Tucker Buick)	MASS SERVICE (Example: Thalhimers-Cloverleaf)	PROFESSIONAL SERVICE (Example: Arthur Andersen & Co.)
Labor-Related Features				
Pay	Typically hourly.	Varies, could include individual incentive or commission schemes.	Same as for service shop.	Salary, often with bonus of some type.
Skill levels	Generally lower skills	High skills.	Variable, but most often lower skill.	Very high skills.
Job content	Small.	Large.	Often medium, but variable.	Very large.
Advancement	With more skills and/or seniority acquired, greater responsibility given. Seniority can lead to change in department or shift assignment.	Often, worker is an independent operator of sorts and can exert some control on what he gives and gets from job; limited hierarchical progression.	Often a hierarchy to progress upward through.	Often a pyramid, up or out. Top of pyramid exerts leverage over bottom of pyramid.
Management Features				
Staff-line needs	Large staff for process redesign, methods, forecasting, capacity planning, and scheduling. Line supervision and troubleshooting still critical.	Limited staff, mostly line operation.	Some staff, often focused on personal issues.	Limited staff, many line managers wear multiple hats.
Means of control	Variable. Can be cost or profit	Usually a profit center.	Usually a profit center.	Usually a profit center.

INDEX

Accounting and auditing services, 209
Adams Convenience Store, 205
Apparel manufacturing, 57
Arthur Andersen and Co., 209
Assembly lines, 89, 139. *See also* Line
  balance
Auto service and repair, 163
Automobile assembly, 91

Backward integration. *See* Vertical
  integration
Batch flow process, 57
Beacon Glass Works, 24
Bidding, 29, 235
Big City Hospital Emergency Room, 179
Bottlenecks, 147
Brewing, 115
Brown, Smith and Jones, 82
Buchanan Tobacco Co., 134
Burger King, 139

Capacity, 9
Capacity management, 20, 22, 109, 130
  in batch flow process, 80
  in job shop, 46
Capacity utilization, 37
Construction management, 229
Continuous flow process, 1
Contractor bidding, 235
Country Gelatin Co., 133
Critical path, 237

Dispatching, 164

Environmental management, 7

Forward integration. *See* Vertical integration

Gantt chart, 237
General Motors Corp., Oklahoma City
  plant, 89
Geupel DeMars, Inc., 229
Grievance procedures, 69, 107

Hybrid process, 115

Industrial engineering, 67, 102
Information flow diagram, 19, 46, 78, 109,
  130, 151, 176, 203, 223, 243
International Paper, Androscoggin Mill, 1
Inventories, 13
Inventory control, 95, 195

Japanese management. *See* Just-in-time
  manufacturing
JIT. *See* Just-in-time manufacturing
Job shop, 29
  control within, 29
  record keeping and, 44
Johnson and Trotter Advertising, 227
Jos. A. Bank Clothiers, 57
Just-in-time manufacturing, 96

Layout
  assembly line, 92
  job shop, 36
  line flow, 142
  retail, 183
Legacy Homes, 155
Line balance, 102
Line flow process, 89, 139
Location decisions, 10

Manufacturing choices, 246
Mass service, 183

Norcen Industries, 29

Ogle-Tucker Buick, 163
On-site expansion. *See* Capacity management
Organization chart, 108, 190, 230
Owens, Inc., 50

Paper making, 2
Peak versus nonpeak operation, 144
Performance measurement, 17, 126, 197
Piece rate wage system, 61

Plant engineering, 106
Plant layout. *See* Layout
Precedence diagram, 237
Process flow diagram, 18, 45, 78, 109, 116, 129, 151, 176, 203, 223, 243
Process mapping. *See* Process flow diagram
Process spectrum, 250
Production control, 70, 193
Production planning, 10, 72, 94, 119, 245
Professional service, 209
Project, 229
Project management, 229
Purchasing, 13, 72, 95, 124, 149, 171
Pyramid
  in professional services, 214, 224

Quality control, 43, 70, 101, 126, 149, 169
Queuing, 140

Scheduling, 236
  personnel, 215
Service factory, 139
Service operations, 251

Service shop, 163
Shift schedule, 15
Small City Newspaper, 157
Standards and incentives, 49, 81, 130
Streeter Die and Stamping Co., 52
Stroh Brewery Company, 115
Sunmeadow Dairy, 25
Supervision, 72, 107, 150, 175, 220, 236

Technological change, 77, 150
  in job shop, 42
Technology, 21
Thalhimers, 183

Vertical integration, 8

Waiting lines. *See* Queuing
Warehouse operations, 71
Welch's Ice Cream, 85
Work force management, 14, 21, 32, 61, 69, 81, 106, 110, 125, 131, 148, 152, 166, 177, 189, 204, 219, 224, 245